D1569487

*Critical Essays on*

# SEAMUS HEANEY

# CRITICAL ESSAYS
## ON
# BRITISH LITERATURE

Zack Bowen, General Editor
*University of Miami*

# Critical Essays on
# SEAMUS HEANEY

*edited by*

ROBERT F. GARRATT

*G. K. Hall & Co.*
*An Imprint of Simon & Schuster Macmillan*
*New York*

*Prentice Hall International*
*London   Mexico City   New Delhi   Singapore   Sydney   Toronto*

G. K. Hall & Co.
An Imprint of Simon & Schuster Macmillan
866 Third Avenue
New York, New York 10022

**Library of Congress Cataloging-in-Publication Data**

H 434

Critical essays on Seamus Heaney / edited by Robert F. Garratt.
    p.    cm. —(Critical essays on British literature)
    Includes bibliographical references and index.
    ISBN 0-7838-0004-5
    1. Heaney, Seamus—Criticism and interpretation.    2. Northern Ireland—In literature.    I. Garratt, Robert F.    II. Series.
PR6058.E2Z63    1995
821'.914—dc20                                                    94-48144
                                                                 CIP

H 434
        6-23?c

10    9    8    7    6    5    4    3    2    1

Printed in the United States of America

# *Contents*

◆

# General Editor's Note

◆

The Critical Essays on British Literature series provides a variety of approaches to both classical and contemporary writers of Britain and Ireland. The formats of the volumes in the series vary with the thematic designs of individual editors, and with the amount and nature of existing reviews and criticism, augmented, where appropriate, by original essays by recognized authorities. It is hoped that each volume will be unique in developing a new overall perspective on its particular subject. Robert Garratt begins his introduction by seeking to establish Heaney's place in contemporary poetry, and then tracing the evolution of Heaney's subject matter and philosophy over the last two or three decades, linking his production to corresponding critical emphases and debate regarding Heaney's political, nationalistic, and aesthetic concerns, as well as an increasing influence of both ancient and modern writers on his work. The selected essays include three originally written for this volume, by Hazard Adams, Lucy McDiarmid, and Carla de Petris.

ZACK BOWEN
*University of Miami*

# *Publisher's Note*

◆

Producing a volume that contains both newly commissioned and reprinted material presents the publisher with the challenge of balancing the desire to achieve stylistic consistency with the need to preserve the integrity of works first published elsewhere. In the Critical Essays series, essays commissioned especially for a particular volume are edited to be consistent with G. K. Hall's house style; reprinted essays appear in the style in which they were first published, with only typographical errors corrected. Consequently, shifts in style from one essay to another are the result of our efforts to be faithful to each text as it was originally published.

# Introduction

ROBERT F. GARRATT

It is no longer necessary to introduce Seamus Heaney when discussing his poetry or his critical essays, nor is it essential, as it once was, to place his work in an Irish context for readers to appreciate or understand it. Over the thirty years since he has first appeared in print his reputation has grown to include his recognition, on both sides of the Atlantic, as a leading poet and critic. Given the reception his work has received over the past decade alone, it seems certain that future literary historians will regard Heaney as, if not the most important poet of the late twentieth century, then among the top three or four. Most critics agree with Robert Lowell's assessment that in twentieth-century Irish poetry only the great Yeats ranks ahead of Heaney in talent and achievement. In the introduction to their 1982 poetry anthology, Blake Morrison and Andrew Motion proclaim Heaney the most important contemporary British poet.[1] Bolder voices place him at the head of the prominent English-language poets of his day, in the company of Ted Hughes, John Ashbery, Geoffrey Hill, and Derek Walcott.[2] Those who make such lists may quibble over Heaney's position and rank, but they concur that he is one of those rare poets who can both please the general reader and engage the academic specialist and literary critic.

Gauging the rank of a contemporary writer is always difficult, but in Heaney's case these assessments seem obvious enough. From the publication of his first book of poems in the mid-1960s, Heaney enjoyed an enthusiastic reception among readers. His ability to portray with vivid exactitude the details of his childhood in rural Ireland made him accessible to the general reading public, while his use of the modern poetic tradition and his facility with language impressed the more specialized audience of scholars and critics. Some of the poet's popularity no doubt derives from his appearances as a lecturer and reader on college and university campuses and at public literary events throughout Ireland, Europe, and North America, prompting one recent reviewer to judge Heaney's stature the result of a managed career "with particular attention to the fact that we live . . . in an age of public relations and mass communications."[3] This view overlooks the obvious fact that people read Heaney's poetry because they enjoy it; they attend his public lectures on literary topics because they are familiar with his critical writing and know he will have something to say. Moreover, Heaney has evolved as a writer and his readers have responded well to that. His latest books reveal a literary consciousness that recognizes both the fragility and the strength of poetry in a world of politics and pressing social issues. In recent essays, the poet's explanation and treatment of the role of poetry in the modern world gives his readers a sense of his intellectual and aesthetic range.

Heaney's ability to evolve a complex and erudite aesthetic while maintaining a basic simplicity and integrity at the heart of his work is the foundation for his greatness as a poet and his appeal to both the general reader and the specialist. The balance he achieves demonstrates a writer's power to draw strength from the parochial and at the same time enrich that sense of the known place (what Heaney has termed the "given life") with the greater perspective of other political and literary cultures and traditions. Thus in Heaney's poetry the importance of the Northern Irish landscape, rural life, Irish history, and contemporary Northern Irish politics becomes, paradoxically, more intensified as it is mediated by an imagination that has cultivated worldly, cosmopolitan views. As Heaney's poetry develops, we understand the importance of the Irish literary tradition, the heritage of Yeats, Joyce, Patrick Kavanagh, and William Carleton, but not in isolation as a thing unto itself. Instead, the sense of tradition has expanded with an awareness of a cultural vantage point that includes Dante's medieval Florence, Robert Lowell's New England, T. S. Eliot's 1940s London, or the Eastern Europe of Osip Mandelstam and Czeslaw Milosz. Thus Heaney's Irish experience is ratified by a larger tradition to which the poet insists it belongs.

This expansive aesthetic results from the poet's understanding of the importance of growth to artistic achievement. He was called to writing by his love of reading and his acute sense of the language spoken in his part of Northern Ireland. This was a complex and volatile brew for a young writer caught between two cultures: "I speak and write in English, but do not altogether share the preoccupations and perspectives of an Englishman. I teach English literature, I publish in London, but the English tradition is not ultimately home. I live off another hump as well."[4] That other hump, the matter of Ireland, provided Heaney with his early voice and has sustained him throughout his career as both a poet and a critic. Once embarked on a poetic career, however, the writer-as-reader began to reach out beyond the familiar boundaries. In an early essay, Heaney remarked on the resilience of Yeats's poetics in seeking new ground, finding new ways, developing new voices, and avoiding the repetition of old material. In this model the young poet saw great significance and began in the early 1970s to embark on a rigorous reading program that included Yeats, Dante, Mandelstam, and contemporary American poetry. As Heaney remarks in an essay on the Irish literary tradition, his evolving and changing poetic stems as much from the study of poetry as it does from the labor of writing: "Long before he puts pen to paper, the writer has been a reader."[5] Beginning with *Field Work* (1979) and *Preoccupations* (1980), his first collection of prose pieces, Heaney's writing has been enriched with the fruits of his study. This is apparent in the change of style in the later poetry, but also in the appropriation of the narrative strategies and techniques of other writers, notably Dante, Yeats, and Joyce. But more important, as is clear from Heaney's recent prose collection *The Government of the Tongue* (1988), the shift in his poetics parallels his widening interest as a reader in world literature, which in turn determines his growth as a poet.

In general the history of Heaney criticism follows the patterns of the poet's evolving aesthetic. The early reactions came primarily in Irish and British, reviews that introduced the young poet as a new voice from Northern Ireland, part of the rich poetic activity in and around Queens University, Belfast, in the 1960s. These early critical remarks on Heaney followed the appearance of the first two books, *Death of a Naturalist* (1966) and *Door into the Dark* (1969). They were essentially appreciations of the poet's ability to capture the details of a rural world that was gradually being changed by the pace of modern life. American readers were slower to recognize this new talent, with only limited reviews of the early poetry. Indeed, the first significant critical assessment of Heaney's work in North America was written by Heaney's friend and fellow Irish poet Derek Mahon in an introductory essay on the new poetry from Ulster.[6] The early commentary praised the young poet's eye for the everyday routine of life on a Northern Irish farm, the work of thatching, eel fishing, potato digging, gathering berries, or simply observing wildlife. These early reviews also expressed the sense of a connection between the experience of nature and the writing of poems, something that would remain consistent throughout Heaney's work. Descriptions of digging, thatching, beating shape into iron, and other features of labor that figure prominently in these early poems were read as self-conscious metaphorical treatments of the act of writing. In almost all the writing about the early Heaney readers were struck by the poet's extraordinary way with language in the rich and heavy expression of his poetry, especially his use of the sound of words and of colorful phrases. Most of this commentary suggested the promise of the young writer.

Perhaps remembering the brilliant success and excitement of Heaney's first two books, reviewers were on the whole lukewarm in their reaction to the publication of *Wintering Out* (1972). Those who were new to Heaney found in this third book the same qualities that shaped the early reviews, especially the vivid imagery and the powerful and energetic diction. For most of those familiar with Heaney's work, however, *Wintering Out* was a disappointment. Some felt that the poet should be more sensitive to unrest in Belfast and Derry. Stephen Spender, reviewing *Wintering Out*, remarked that too much concentration on language prevented a wider focus on real events, and the anonymous *Times Literary Supplement* reviewer wanted more political and social awareness from Heaney.[7] Others complained on aesthetic grounds that the poet repeated rather than developed the early successes, that his third book demonstrated a kind of hesitancy or insecurity in the poetic voice, as if he were stuck in some in-between stage, looking forward and backward. On the whole the commentary itself hesitated between warm praise and cool rebuke.

There was nothing tepid about the critical reaction to Heaney's fourth book, *North* (1975). The collection startled the reading public and dazzled the reviewers who proclaimed it a breakthrough for Heaney. The reaction to *North* ushered in a new phase of Heaney criticism, a move toward political aesthetics rather than a repetition of the general introductions and appreciations of early reviews. Most remarked upon the way in which *North* framed contemporary events within a larger historical narrative of ancient Celtic and Norse lore, metaphorically connecting the sectarian killings in Northern Ireland to the ritualized human sacrifice of pre-Christian Jutland. Here was the book that reviewers felt was long overdue: an Irish writer confronting and interpreting the social and political issues of his day. Those, especially in Britain, who had criticized Heaney for not speaking out on "the troubles" commended him for his voice in *North*. It demonstrated a great poetic leap for Heaney, especially in the complexity of the book's conception, which struck some as a powerful act of aesthetic distancing and victory of the imagination over terror.[8] The reception was also favorable among North American readers, who saw *North* as a powerful poetic blend of myth and contemporary politics. It was *North*, more than any other book of Heaney's, that had the greatest impact on readers outside of Britain and Ireland. The enthusiasm surrounding the reception of *North* propelled Heaney's literary reputation.

The response to *North* established Heaney as the foremost contemporary Irish poet, but it was by no means uniform. For all of its admirers, the book also had detractors, especially among Irish readers. For these, some of whom lived in Belfast, *North* struck a sensitive nerve and provoked the first great controversy in Heaney studies, one that continues to this day. What many Irish readers found objectional can generally be described as an aestheticization of violence, although the responses were quite varied. In a well-known attack on *North*, Ciaran Carson argued that the mythic comparisons in *North* actually obscure the atrocities they intend to illuminate. The result is a kind of fictionalizing in which religion, myth, and history overpower the real social issues they are meant to clarify.[9] Another version of this argument seized upon Heaney's reluctance to speak out clearly for his position, faulting him for a strategy that encases political beliefs and convictions in metaphor or opaque poetic language.[10] Others criticized Heaney for being too partisan in his politics and found in *North* a retreat into tribal loyalties that asserts a nationalist position.[11] In Ireland, at least, it appears that poetry does make something happen.

*North* stands as a pivotal book in Heaney's development, one that takes leave of early preoccupations and anticipates the complexities of later books. Heaney himself sees the book in this way,[12] and for the most part his critics tend to agree with him. With the publication of *Field Work* and *Preoccupations*, Heaney's reviewers and critics took notice of a new direction in the poet's work, one that began to situate the given life within a wider perspective. For one thing, the poetry after *North* becomes haunted by other writers, some in allusory form, others invited in by name as subjects in their own right. Wordsworth, Dante, Yeats, Lowell, Kavanagh, and Joyce are among the literary ghosts invoked throughout the later poetry, often in direct comparison with Heaney's own life or work. Other ghosts, many of them literary, are encountered directly in the purgatorial journey described in *Station Island* (1984). The remarkable encounter with the shade of Joyce at the book's close has been the subject of many critical interpretations.[13]

The shifts in Heaney's later poetry involve more than poetic echoes or literary subject matter, however; they are also apparent in the conception and narrative strategy in *Field Work* and the books that follow, all of which seem more self-contained and deliberately unified than the early volumes. The coherence of *Station Island*, to take an obvious example, has been noted by a number of readers, but the same coherence is also present in *The Haw Lantern* (1987). One reader argues that a thematic pattern runs throughout the later volumes, from *North* through *The Haw Lantern*.[14] Another remarkable feature of the recent work is the sustained interest in translation, both in the traditional sense, such as in *Sweeney Astray* (1984) or in the Ugolino story from *Inferno*, cantos 32 and 33, which ends *Field Work*, and more philosophically as a means of interpreting and transferring material from the past to make it available to the present. It is the second sense of translation that informs Heaney's work with the Field Day Theater Company and his interest in the Eastern European poets, which he discussed in his second prose collection, *The Government of the Tongue*.

The recognition of this change in Heaney's poetry constitutes the third stage of Heaney criticism, an attempt to place Heaney's Irish qualities in the wider context of world culture. In general, reviewers and critics read the expanding horizons of the later poetry as a conscious attempt on Heaney's part to break free from the various limitations placed on any artist. The use of other traditions and other writers can offer new insights and afford familiar matter a fresh hearing. Moreover, as a poet who has so closely identified with an Irish poetic tradition and who has been read within the political perimeters of the that tradition, Heaney has seen the wisdom of extending the frontiers of his own writing. In remarks on Thomas Kinsella's translation of Irish poetry, Heaney notes, "He [Kinsella] too has been concerned to widen the lens, to make Irish poetry in English get out from under the twilight shades of the specifically English tradition."[15]

Keeping in mind that what one poet says about another is often self-revealing, we can note the interest Heaney has taken over the past fifteen years in writers from other cultures and traditions. Following the lead of two of the modern writers he most admires, T. S. Eliot and Osip Mandelstam, Heaney turns to Dante as an important example of the poetic imagination under pressure. First and foremost, Heaney reads Dante as a poet who was defined by the politics of his age and who struggled in his poetry to understand and even to resolve that conflict. Also, Dante is for Heaney, as he was for Eliot and Mandelstam, the quintessential poet of middle age, who takes stock of himself in life's journey and turns a crisis into a poetic achievement. Important as Dante is in the poetry from *Field Work* to the present, however, he is only one of a number of non-Irish and non-English poets who loom large in Heaney's mature imagination. American poets Robert Lowell, Elizabeth Bishop, and Sylvia Plath; the Polish poets Zbigniew Herbert and Czeslaw Milosz; and Eliot and Mandelstam have all in different ways served Heaney in his effort to see the familiar and the local as part of a larger poetic horizon.

Critical work on the later Heaney has responded in kind. A good deal of the work on the later poetry involves the identification of these wider traditions as well as discussion of influences and uses of sources. A number of critical essays on *Station Island*, to take an obvious example, have explored the facets of the Dantean presence in the book from thematic as well as structural vantage points. Other critics have responded to the practice of "translation" in the later Heaney, not only in the obvious examples of the Sweeney poems and *The Cure at Troy: A Version of Sophocles' Philoctetes* (1990), but also in the philosophical hold of the concept on the poet's imagination as revealed in his essays in *The Government of the Tongue*. As recent critics have pointed out, "translation" for Heaney becomes a complex activity of fidelity to a text, identification with an author, and the application of historical narrative to contemporary experience.[16] It has also been energized and nurtured by Heaney's association with the Field Day Theater Company, one of whose successes has been Brian Friel's play *Translations*. Some of the recent commentary has been concerned with the sense of continuity in Heaney's work, the way in which the later poetry seeks identification with a tradition but also strives to reshape and redefine it.[17]

Whether they address a specific topic such as influence or treat a wider spectrum such as tradition, all of these studies progress comparatively, measuring Heaney's work in the context of other literary works or cultural issues. In this particular critical praxis, the later commentary is unlike the response of what I have called the first stage of Heaney reception, which tended to focus primarily on the work as a single unit, or in the context of other works by Heaney. Recent studies have located Heaney's work within larger debates about culture. Some critics have applied the specific concerns of contemporary literary theory to expand the discussion of Heaney's work. Politics and political aesthetics are thus subsumed within cultural criticism and include the exploration of related ideas such as identity, ethnicity, gender, religion, and concepts of community. Heaney's poetry has also been read as part of a discourse of decolonization in which Irishness opposes the cultural values of British hegemony. Similarly, critics have attempted to situate Heaney's poetics in a broader, non-English tradition that includes European and American influences. The effort in all of these studies is to consider Heaney's work in the broadest possible context in order to give the poetry a wider hearing, to read the familiar subjects, called "the given life" of the parish, as part of the conditions of a more cosmopolitan culture.

One related and crucial theme that emerges clearly in the history of Heaney reception evolves around the problematics of poetic identity. The poet himself explores the issue in the autobiographical sections of *Preoccupations* when he gives his version of Northern Irish education and society. Critics have followed suit. In early introductory essays by Benedict Kiely and John Wilson Foster, the connection between writer and locale provides the key to reading the poems.[18] Political, social, and religious identity become important topics for those critics who discuss Heaney's treatment of Northern Irish unrest and sectarian violence, especially the poetry from *Wintering Out* through *North* and *Field Work*.[19] Similarly, the question of poetic identity has become a central concern in the wider discussions of culture as it is reflected in Heaney's work. In one of the first examples of cultural criticism on Heaney, Anthony Bradley argues that Heaney's rewriting of the English pastoral tradition allows him to establish a sense of Irishness.[20] Recent work on cultural aesthetics, sexuality, gender, and poetics has considered Heaney's interrogation of identity in matters of religion, nationality, and literary tradition as shaping his work.[21] For all of these critics, identity—from the early poems, which negotiate Heaney's ties with the earth, to the work of the 1980s, where literature and writing become frequent subjects—provides a crucial tension for the poet, which occasions and energizes the poetry. Heaney's own explanation of this phenomenon comes by way of Yeats: out of the quarrel with others we get rhetoric; out of the quarrel with ourselves we get poetry.

A brief word remains to be said about the chronological development of Heaney criticism. As in any significant accumulation of critical reception on a single writer, the work on Heaney over the past thirty years shows an historical pattern in which certain readings build upon those that precede them. With the exception of the early monograph by Robert Buttel, most of the work done on Heaney's poetry through the mid-1980s appeared in articles scattered through literary and scholarly journals. The commentary tended to follow the issues in the poetry and accumulated as Heaney continued to publish, with the great push in Heaney criticism coming after the appearance of *North*. Over the past ten years, however, there has been an explosion of critical commentary on Heaney, both full-length critical studies and collections of essays. In the 1980s, the criticism gained considerable momentum in order to account both for Heaney's continual productivity (seven books from 1975 through 1988) and for certain critical controversies, most notably the question of Heaney's political commitment as a writer. The 1990s promise even more critical attention. If recent activity is any measure, we are in the midst of a flurry of Heaney criticism. In the past five years alone, five books, a number of essays, and regular reviews have appeared.[22]

In this collection I have tried to present critical perspectives on Heaney's writing that reflect the pattern and important issues of that reception. No collection can hope to completely capture the history of reception. Nonetheless, the essays here are representative. They cohere around the principle that Heaney's own poetic development determines the pattern of that criticism. In some cases the essays have the advantage of recent perspective; they respond or clarify the issues introduced by earlier critics. Others are important because they offer an unique perspective on the poetry. Three essays, those by Hazard Adams, Lucy McDiarmid, and Carla de Petris, are original to this collection and address areas of Heaney scholarship that have received little or no attention. All of the essays have been selected not only because of their merit, but also because they give shape to the general discussion of Heaney's development as a poet, building and extending other studies that are not included.[23]

The design of this collection reflects the three essential phases of Heaney criticism that I have described. Section 1 concentrates on separate volumes and tends to identify subjects, themes, and linguistic features of the poetry. Although the second section emphasizes discussion of Heaney as a political writer, the essays are not exclusively devoted to politics, nor do they confine their discussion of the political to the sectarian issues that emerged in Irish reaction to the publication of *North*. Many of the essays, including those by David Lloyd and Nathalie Anderson, treat the political in the wider context of cultural criticism. The last section of this collection reflects the more recent stage of Heaney criticism, which places his work in a comparative context. While the earlier selections attempted to show Heaney's Irishness as not a limitation to the poetry but rather a part of a greater literary tradition, the essays in Section 3 focus primarily on an aesthetic in which Heaney's later writing deliberately engages the work of other writers. A short bibliography of primary and secondary works follows the essays.

In preparing this book, I wish to acknowledge a number of individuals who provided assistance of different kinds along the way: the University of Puget Sound for a summer research grant and a released unit of teaching at the early stages of my work; Zack Bowen and Melissa Solomon for their encouragement and patience; Holly Jones, Lori Ricigliano, and Camille Riggs for help in the preparation of materials. I am indebted to many critics and reviewers whose work I have read in preparation for this collection and to those with whom I have had conversations on the topic of Heaney criticism, especially Declan Kiberd, Seamus Deane, Liz Cullingford, Bill McCormack, and Tony Bradley. Finally, to my wife, Barbara, and son, Christopher, for their understanding and support throughout this project.

## Notes

1.  See their introduction to the *Penguin Book of Contemporary British Poetry* (London: Penguin, 1982).
2.  Chief among these voices are Helen Vendler in various *New Yorker* pieces, some of which are collected in *The Music of What Happens* (Cambridge, Mass.: Harvard University Press, 1988), and John Carey, who proclaimed Heaney the major poet of the English-speaking world in the *Sunday Times*, 18 November 1979.
3.  Desmond Fennell, *Heresy* (Belfast: The Blackstaff Press, 1993), 155.
4.  "Belfast," *Preoccupations* (London: Faber, 1979), 34.
5.  "The Interesting Case of John Alphonsus Mulrennan," *Planet*, January 1978, 34.
6.  "Poetry in Northern Ireland," *Twentieth Century Studies* 4 (November 1970): 39–43.
7.  Stephen Spender, "Can Poetry Be Reviewed?" *New York Review of Books*, 20 September 1973, 8–14; "Semaphores of Hurt," *TLS*, 15 December 1972, 1524.
8.  The majority of commentary on *North* supports this position. See Richard Murphy's "Poetry and Terror," *New York Review of Books*, 30 September 1975, 38–40, as characteristic.
9.  "Escaped from the Massacre?" *The Honest Ulsterman* 50 (Winter 1975): 183–86.
10.  See D. Fennell's "Whatever You Say, Say Nothing," in *Heresy*, 130–70, and M. P. Hederman, "Seamus Heaney: The Reluctant Poet," *Crane Bag* 3, no. 2 (1979): 61–70, as examples.
11.  The most vociferous critic of this persuasion is Edna Longley, who has dogged Heaney for over a decade, chastising him for his Catholic and nationalist art. See her " 'Inner Emigre' or 'Artful Voyeur'?" in Tony Curtis, ed., *The Art of Seamus Heaney* (Brigend, Mid Glamorgen: Poetry Wales Press, 1985), 65–95.
12.  See the interview with John Haffenden in J. Haffenden, ed., *Viewpoints: Poets in Conversation* (London: Faber and Faber, 1981), 57–75.
13.  See, for example, Blake Morrison, "Encounters with Familiar Ghosts," *TLS*, 19 October 1984, 1191–92; Helen Vendler, "Echo Soundings, Searches, Probes," *New Yorker*, 23 September 1985, 108–16; Robert F. Garratt, *Modern Irish Poetry: Tradition and Continuity From Yeats to Heaney* (Berkeley: University of California Press, 1986; rev. ed. 1989); 277–85.
14.  John Hildebidle, "A Decade of Seamus Heaney's Poetry," *Massachusetts Review* 28:3 (Autumn 1987): 393–409.
15.  "The Poems of the Dispossessed Repossessed," *The Government of the Tongue* (London: Faber and Faber, 1988), 32.
16.  See Henry Hart, *Seamus Heaney: Poet of Contrary Progressions* (Syracuse, N.Y.: Syracuse University Press, 1992), 138–53; Alan Peacock, "Meditations: Poet as Translator, Poet as Seer," in Elmer Andrews, ed., *Seamus Heaney: A Collection of Critical Essays* (New York: St. Martin's Press, 1992), 233–55.
17.  See Dillon Johnston, *Irish Poetry after Joyce* (Notre Dame, Ind.: Notre Dame University Press, 1985), and Robert F. Garratt, *Modern Irish Poetry: Tradition and Continuity From Yeats to Heaney*, the first studies to gauge Heaney's use of tradition.
18.  Benedict Kiely, "A Raid into Dark Corners: The Poems of Seamus Heaney," *The*

*Hollins Critic* 4 (4 October 1970): 1–12; John Wilson Foster, "The Poetry of Seamus Heaney," *Critical Quarterly* 16 (Spring 1974): 35–48.

19.   In addition to those articles previously mentioned, see D. E. S. Maxwell, "Imagining the North: Violence and the Writers," *Eire-Ireland* 8:2 (Summer 1973): 91–107.

20.   "Landscape as Culture: The Poetry of Seamus Heaney," J. D. Brophy and R. J. Porter, eds., *Contemporary Irish Writing* (Boston: Twayne Publishers, 1983), 1–14.

21.   A number of the essays in this collection concentrate on this problem. See also Elizabeth Cullingford, "Thinking of Her . . . as . . . Ireland: Yeats, Pearse, and Heaney," *Textual Practice* 4:1 (Spring 1990): 1–21.

22.   Five full-length critical studies and two collections of critical essays have appeared since 1988 (see Selected Bibliography). There has been a significant increase in the number of articles published annually on aspects of Heaney's work.

23.   My choices were restricted occasionally by exorbitant fees or refusal to gain permission to republish.

# GENERAL STUDIES

◆

# Crossed Pieties [On the Early Poetry]

ALAN SHAPIRO*

There's an old Gaelic poem which goes, "Who ever heard / Such a sight unsung / As a severed head / With a grafted tongue." This image—of a culture severed from the body of its own traditions and forced to speak another language—indicates the profound dilemma facing every Anglo-Irish poet fated to discover and express in English, the oppressor's tongue, his personal and national identity. One might even say that this identity resides, if anywhere, in the hyphen separating the Anglo from the Irish. Pulled in one direction by the English literary tradition, pulled in another by a social and political tradition which continues its centuries-old antagonism to all things English, the Irish poet finds himself inescapably involved in a bleak and unromantic triangle: if Irish culture is his wife, English is his mistress, and to satisfy one is necessarily to betray the other. And yet it is precisely in the Irish poet's response to this dilemma, in the thematic and stylistic strategies he devises to maintain his own identity in the oppressor's language, that one can find in Anglo-Irish poetry what seems distinctly Irish.

No contemporary Irish poet has struggled with this problem more self-consciously, or more successfully, than Seamus Heaney. In both *Preoccupations*, his recently collected essays and reviews, and in his first four books of poetry now published together under the title, *Poems: 1965–1975*, these tensions and crossed pieties inherent in Irish poetry are what preoccupy him most. In one essay he defines the role of poetry "as divination . . . as revelation of the self to the self, as restoration of the culture to itself." He desires a poetry of place and origins, of connection to the Irish past, and of almost sacramental fidelity to the physical contours of the Irish present. In his first two books, *Death Of A Naturalist* and *Door Into The Dark*, Heaney attempts to satisfy this desire by writing almost exclusively of regional life and work, of hunting, blackberry picking, turf gathering, and of the various ways "living displaces false sentiments" in the rural world. The characters he's drawn to—thatchers, diviners, farmwives, and fishermen—embody continuity with the past, seem to bear or affirm the past in what they do. In one poem, he sees in laborers gathering potatoes ("Heads bow, trunks bend,

*Reprinted from *Parnassus: Poetry in Review* (Fall/Winter 1983 and Spring/Summer 1984): 336–48.

hands fumble toward the black / Mother") "centuries of fear and homage to the famine God." In another, he calls the door into a blacksmith's shop "a door into the dark"; and though the dark is actual, it also becomes a figure for an older way of life, as later in the poem the blacksmith, standing in the doorway, "recalls / A clatter of hoofs where traffic is flashing in rows / Then, grunts and goes in," turning his back on the present.

Unlike the blacksmith, however, Heaney moves in two ways in these poems, turning, as he says in one essay, outward to the present, "to a clarification of life," as well as inward, "to a ramification of roots and associations." Yet in neither movement does he succeed in articulating an indigenous poetic idiom. And I think we can find the reasons for this failure in "Digging," the opening poem of *Death Of A Naturalist*, and the first poem in which Heaney claims to have gotten his feelings into words, "or, to put it more accurately, where I thought my feeling got into words." "Digging" defines the kind of poetry the beginning Irish poet wants to write. Sitting by a window, he hears his father digging turf outside in the same way his grandfather dug turf twenty years earlier, and the two figures, one real, the other recollected, merge into an image of continuity:

> Nicking and slicing neatly, heaving sods
> Over his shoulder, going down and down
> For the good turf. Digging.
>
> The cold smell of potato mould, the squelch and slap
> Of soggy peat, the curt cuts of an edge
> Through living roots awaken in my head.

Yet realizing he has "no spade to follow men like that," he says, "Between my finger and thumb / The squat pen rests. / I'll dig with it." "Digging" bears all the earmarks of a Heaney poem, the qualities for which he's justly admired: an intense regard for metaphor, a dense specificity of detail, and a rich evocation of place. Descriptive language, here and throughout his work, is his most effective way of preserving his own identity and at the same time asserting his regional allegiance.

Yet one feels that Heaney protests too much in "Digging," as though the bold, untroubled confidence—"I'll dig with it"—belies an underlying fear that in writing poetry he'll be departing, rather than continuing, the family (and cultural) tradition. He evades this fear, I think, refraining from making it part of the subject, by the very qualities we admire. Description enables Heaney to sidestep the difficulties inherent in this enterprise. For despite his desire to restore "the culture to itself," the principal influences on his early work are American and English as much as Irish. Along with the Irish poet Patrick Kavanagh, poets such as Wordsworth, Hopkins, Frost, and Ted Hughes (some of whom he writes about at length in *Preoccupations*) stand behind his first two books. Kavanagh may influence what he chooses to articulate, that is, a close, unromantic attention to rural life, but it is the American and English poets who influence the manner of articulation. It is difficult, for instance, not to hear Wyatt's "My Galley Charged With Forgetfulness" in these lines from "Valediction," a poem from *Death Of A Naturalist*:

> . . . In your presence
> Time rode easy, anchored
> On a smile; but absence
> Rocked love's balance, unmoored
> The days . . .
> > Need breaks on my strand;
> You've gone, I am at sea.
> Until you resume command
> Self is in mutiny.

Or Frost's "For Once, Then, Something" in these lines from the personal "Helicon":

> As a child, they could not keep me from wells
> And old pumps with buckets and windlasses.
> I loved the dark drop, the trapped sky, the smells
> Of waterweed, fungus and dank moss. . . .
>
> Now, to pry into roots, to finger slime
> To stare, big-eyed Narcissus, into some spring
> Is beneath all adult dignity. I rhyme
> To see myself, to set the darkness echoing.

More than the darkness echoes in this poem. Considering that many poets learn to write by imitating the best poems in the language, and that the best poems in English are not all by Irishmen, it's no wonder that Heaney's early poems, impressive as they are, are mostly apprentice pieces.

In one essay, Heaney distinguishes between craft and technique. "Craft," he says, "is what you can learn from other verse. Craft is the skill of making. . . . Technique," on the other hand, "involves not only a poet's way with words, his management of meter, rhythm and verbal texture, it involves also a definition of his stance toward life, a definition of his own reality." If we associate technique with Heaney's Irish loyalties, his passionate regionalism, and craft with his English literary training, we can say that what characterizes these early poems is a craft at odds with and insufficient for the full expression of a burgeoning technique. This tension between craft and technique accounts for the formal awkwardness of many of these poems, for Heaney's compulsion to swim too hard against the iambic current.

Two blank verse poems, "For The Commander Of The Eliza" and "Death Of A Naturalist," illustrate my point. Set in the mid-nineteenth century during the Irish potato famine, "For The Commander Of The Eliza" is a dramatic monologue spoken by an English sea captain who comes upon a boatload of starving Irish peasants and refuses to give them aid. Because the speaker is English, Heaney can let him speak a clean blank verse line with little rhythmical variation. Even when the variations do occur, the iambic cadence still rings clear:

> We'd known about the shortage but on board
> They always kept us right with flour and beef
> So understand my feelings, and the men's
> Who had mandate to relieve distress
> Since relief was then available in Westport—
> Though clearly these poor brutes would never make it . . .
>
> Next day, like six bad smells, those living skulls
> Drifted through the dark of bunks and hatches
> And once in port I exorcised my ship
> Reporting all to the Inspector General . . .

In addition to the emphatic meter, the almost complete absence of grammatical pauses within the line increases the sense of regularity and restraint appropriate to the speaker's strained attempt to keep his guilt in check as he clumsily rationalizes his refusal to help the poor.

If "For The Commander Of The Eliza" is hyper-metrical, "Death Of A Naturalist" isn't metrical enough. The verse is heavily varied because Heaney himself is speaking, not an English persona:

> All year the flax-dam festered in the heart
> Of the townland; green and heavy headed
> Flax had rotted there, weighted down by huge sods.
> Daily it sweltered in the punishing sun.
> Bubbles gargled delicately, bluebottles
> Wove a strong gauze of sound around the smell.
> There were dragon-flies, spotted butterflies,
> But best of all was the warm thick slobber
> Of frogspawn that grew like clotted water
> In the shade of the banks. Here, every spring
> I would fill jampotfuls of the jellied
> Specks to range on window-sills at home,
> On shelves at school, and wait and watch until
> The fattening dots burst into nimble-
> Swimming tadpoles . . .

This is a poem about the loss of innocence and the realization of the presence of evil in the natural world and, by implication, in the self. One day the speaker finds that "the angry frogs" had "invaded" the flax dam:

> I ducked through hedges
> To a coarse croaking that I had not heard
> Before. The air was thick with a bass chorus.
> Right down the dam gross bellied frogs were cocked
> On sods; their loose necks pulsed like sails. Some hopped.
> The slap and plop were obscene threats. Some sat
> Poised like mud grenades, their blunt heads farting,
> I sickened, turned and ran. The great slime kings
> Were gathered there for vengeance and I knew
> That if I dipped my hand the spawn would clutch it.

In overall design and tone this incident recalls the boat-stealing episode in "The Prelude." "The great slime kings" are Heaney's version of Wordsworth's "huge peak, black and huge." Like Wordsworth, out of a troubled conscience Heaney attributes a sense of retribution to the natural scene. But the blank verse is anything but Wordsworthian. Heaney thickens the pentameter line with heavy syllables to the point of clotting ("Flax had rotted there, weighted down by huge sods"), and dense, figurative language ("Poised like mud grenades, their blunt heads farting"). He remains close enough to the iambic norm to keep it as constant expectation, but one he continually disappoints. He reminds us, in other words, that he's writing blank verse only to dramatize his independence from the tradition that blank verse implicates. The result is that his subject has to fight against the form; that is, the formal properties seldom issue from or respond to what he's trying to say. And this flaw applies, I think, to much of Heaney's accentual-syllabic verse, early and late. It's not that he's incapable of writing a passage of regular blank verse, as the passage from "For The Commander Of The Eliza" demonstrates. Rather, Heaney feels compelled by his Irish pieties to break or maim the formal elements, even if it means writing awkwardly, in order to assert his own identity.

In the essay "Belfast," Heaney discusses this divided consciousness; in his terms, poetry emerges from a quarrel with the self, a quarrel that's both national and sexual: "The feminine element for me involves the matter of Ireland, and the masculine strain is drawn from the involvement with English literature. . . . I was symbolically placed between the marks of English influence and the lure of the native experience, between 'the demesne' and 'the bogs.' " With this quotation in mind, it is possible to read two related poems, "Antaeus" and "Hercules and Antaeus" (from his fourth book, *North*), as acting out this quarrel in his work between the Irish and the English influences, which is to say, between his Irish technique and his English craft. In "Antaeus," written actually in 1966, the year *Death Of A Naturalist* was published, Antaeus describes himself as nursed by "earth's long contour / her river-veins," "cradled in the dark that wombed me / and nurtured me in every artery / like a small hillock." Antaeus represents the native culture, the indigenous experience, whose power depends entirely on contact with the earth or region that nurtured him:

> Let each new hero come
> Seeking the golden apples and Atlas.
> He must wrestle with me before he pass
> Into the realm of fame
>
> Among sky-born and royal:
> He may well throw me and renew my birth
> But let him not plan, lifting me off the earth,
> My elevation, my fall.

The tone here is as innocently confident as the tone of "Digging," but it's qualified, as the tone of "Digging" isn't, by what we know will happen to the giant. If Antaeus is the spirit of native culture, Hercules in "Hercules and Antaeus" is a figure for "the masculine strain" within the poet "drawn from involvement with English literature":

> Antaeus, the mould-hugger,
>
> is weaned at last:
> a fall was a renewal
> but now he is raised up—
> the challenger's intelligence
>
> is a spur of light,
> a blue prong grasping him
> out of his element
> into a dream of loss
>
> and origins—the cradling dark,
> the river-veins, the secret gullies
> of his strength,
> the hatching grounds
>
> of cave and souterrain,
> he has bequeathed it all
> to elegists. Balor will die
> and Byrthnoth and Sitting Bull.

Just as the English once subdued the Irish, the Herculean poet vanquishes his own experience in writing about it, destroying its terrestrial power "into a dream of loss . . . pap for the dispossessed."

"Antaeus" is not as full a treatment of this quarrel as "Hercules and Antaeus." For one thing, the hero does not figure in the poem, and so the giant's faith in his native strength is as yet untested. For another, the poem suffers, as most of Heaney's early work does, from being the product of a literary tradition at odds with his passion for locale and place. In terms of craft, "Antaeus" is already vanquished by his anticipated adversary, despite the boast that he can beat all challengers. The enforced variety of rhymes (some hardly rhymes at all) betray how hard the poet has to strain to find them. And the antithesis which closes the poem, "My elevation, my fall," makes Antaeus sound more like an Augustan poet than a regional spirit.

On the other hand, though the giant is defeated in "Hercules and Antaeus," in terms of form and phrasing the poem is itself a kind of triumph. Part of the reason is that Heaney by this time has moved to a short free verse line which allows him more freedom in drawing the syntax through the poem. In "Antaeus," the line breaks are dictated by the form and meter, not by the meaning. Here they dramatize the action and emotion of the poem. And in so doing they realize the two senses of the word "verse," which Heaney cites in his essay on Wordsworth's music: " 'Verse' comes from the Latin *versus* which could mean a line of poetry but could also mean the turn that a ploughman made at the head of the field as he finished one furrow and faced back into another." In "Hercules and Antaeus" the syntax turns expressively from line to line. This is especially true in the break between the third and fourth stanzas ("into a dream of loss / and origins") which not only emphasizes Hercules' triumph as he lifts Antaeus off the ground, "out of his element," but also acts out the severing from origins that the lines describe.

In "Belfast" (quoted earlier), Heaney says that he thinks of "the personal and Irish pieties as vowels, and the literary awareness nourished on English as consonants." One can hear and see this distinction effectively yet unobstrusively at work in the two names, Hercules and Antaeus, as well as in the way Heaney associates the hard consonants with Hercules ("Snake-chocker, dung heaver"), and the softer vowels and assonances with Antaeus ("the secret gullies / of his strength, / the hatching grounds / of cave and souterrain"). This is further reason for reading "Hercules and Antaeus" as an oblique comment on Heaney's practice as a poet, on the English and Irish tensions in his work, as much as a political allegory.

I have gone on at length about these two poems because they illustrate what happens when Heaney changes from traditional form to free verse, a change which first takes place in *Door Into The Dark*, his second book. It is by no means an exclusive change or a conversion, for Heaney continues to write in form; but his best poems, the ones that come closest to perfecting a personal and Irish idiom, are written in the short, dense free verse line. Free verse seems to liberate Heaney from the stylistic self-consciousness that burdens his formal work; it enables him to get free of the compulsion to smudge or crack the English lens, instead of seeing through it. And the reason is, obviously, that free verse does not bear as much traditional connotation and influence as the accentual syllablic line; it becomes, for him, a more pliable instrument, more responsive to his temperament and to his desire to articulate the lore of native life. It's not surprising then that his first fully achieved free verse poem, the last poem in *Door Into The Dark*, "Bogland," is about the bog as a distinctly Irish symbol of geographical memory, bearing and preserving within itself the Irish past:

> We have no prairies
> To slice a big sun at evening—
> Everywhere the eye concedes to
> Encroaching horizon,
>
> Is wooed into the cyclops' eye
> Of a tarn. Our unfenced country
> Is bog that keeps crusting
> Between the sights of the sun.
>
> They've taken the skeleton
> Of the Great Irish Elk
> Out of the peat, set it up
> An astounding crate of air.
>
> Butter sunk under
> More than a hundred years
> Was recovered salty and white.
> The ground itself is kind, black butter
>
> Melting and opening underfoot,
> Missing its last definition
> By millions of years.
> They'll never dig coal here,
>
> Only the waterlogged trunks
> Of great firs, soft as pulp.
> Our pioneers keep striking
> Inwards and downwards,
>
> Every layer they strip
> Seems camped on before.
> The bogholes might be Atlantic seepage.
> The wet centre is bottomless.

In addition to the usual evocative detail, there's much to praise here: the way the rhythm quickens and slows in response to what's described, as light syllables give way to heavy ones ("Melting and opening underfoot" "The waterlogged trunks / Of great firs, soft as pulp"); the way the line breaks here and there quietly dramatize the sense ("Our pioneers keep striking / Inwards and downwards / Every layer they strip / Seems camped on before"); or the way the last line ends on such lightly stressed syllables that the line produces the very sensation of bottomlessness that it presents.

"Bogland" is, I would argue, the decisive poem in Heaney's collection, for the best poems in *Wintering Out* and *North*, his next two books, grow naturally, without awkwardness, out of its implied equation between landscape and mind. In *Wintering Out* especially, place and language seem almost interchangeable, as language is seen as shaped and nurtured by the soil and weather, inflected by the contours of the land itself. If the river Moyola in "Gifts of Rain" is a metaphorical statement about language ("an old chanter / breathing its mists / through vowels and history / . . . hoarder of common ground"), the act of speaking in "Toome" becomes the penetration of a landscape ("My mouth / holds round / the soft blastings / *Toome, Toome,* / as under the dislodged slab of the tongue / I push into souterrain"), just as in "Anahorish," Heaney's "place of clear water" turns into a "soft gradient / of consonant, vowel-meadow." In almost imagist fashion, language and landscape interanimate each other, so much so that to explore one is inevitably to discover something about the other. It is as if despite a history of dispossession and political oppression, as in Hardy's "In Time of 'The Breaking Of Nations' " the land provides a source of enduring value, is itself the figurative and literal origin of culture (in all senses of the word), transcending yet authenticating the language of the tribe.

Not surprisingly, in "The Tollund Man," Heaney's most compelling exploration into the Irish past and its relation to the Irish present, what symbolizes the Celtic past, its legacy of violence, and its tradition of political martydom still painfully alive today, is the severed head of a man killed and dumped in a Jutland bog as a sacrificial offering to the Mother Goddess. And perhaps it's not too far-fetched to see "The Tollund Man" as also symbolizing the plight of the Irish poet. Heaney would pray to this severed head, as to a Saint,

> To make germinate
> The scattered, ambushed
> Flesh of labourers,
> Stockinged corpses
> Laid out in the farmyards. . . .

> Something of his sad freedom
> As he rode the tumbril

> Should come to me, driving,
> Saying the names
>
> Tollund, Grauballe, Nebelgard,
> Watching the pointing hands
> Of country people,
> Not knowing their tongues.
>
> Out there in Jutland
> In the old man-killing parishes
> I will feel lost,
> Unhappy and at home.

"The Tollund Man" does for Irish culture what in one essay Heaney claims for Patrick Kavanagh's "Great Hunger": it satisfies "the hunger of the culture for its own image and expression." The image, however, is by no means a consoling one; though Heaney would feel at home standing before it, he would, in essence, feel at home in loss, in "the old man-killing parishes." Yet despite the unflinching acknowledgement of violence and dispossession, there is something genuinely consoling in the articulation itself, in the ability of the intelligence to face up to and define the barbarism that persists within the psyche and the culture, just as it was once preserved within the bog.

In *North*, Heaney continues his free verse investigation into the stratified layers of the Irish past, "Striking inwards and downwards." As in "The Tollund Man," the memories he unearths are never comforting, nor is his relationship or kinship with the past a simple one. If poetry involves the restoration of the culture to itself, what he restores are images of atrocity and sectarian violence predating the English invasion. "The Grauballe Man," for instance, now perfected in Heaney's memory (which like the bog transforms and preserves what it contains)

> is hung in the scales
> with beauty and atrocity
> . . . with the actual weight
> of each hooded victim
> slashed and dumped.

Though he still regards the bog with an almost sexual love, "the Goddess Mother" is also implicated in the violence she preserves, mingling the erotic and the violent, "the love seat" and "the grave," as though human sexuality and violence were merely the animation of principles at work within the physical world. In one line Heaney can declare, "I love the spring / off the ground," and in next, "Each bank a gallows drop." In "Kinship," the bog is "insatiable bride. / Sword swallower, / casket, midden." "Our mother ground," he tells us in another section of the poem,

> is sour with the blood
> of her faithful,
> they lie gargling
> in her sacred heart.

Here as in many of the poems in *North*, it is difficult to distinguish the tone of bitter disgust from that of reverence.

This ambivalence accounts for the undeniable power of the best poems in the book ("Punishment," "Hercules and Antaeus," and "Funeral Rites"—perhaps the best political poem since Yeats's "Easter 1916"). It also accounts for why *North* seems less successful as a whole than *Wintering Out*. Many of these poems are damaged by qualities we might be at first inclined to praise: a dazzling metaphoric ingenuity, a profoundly sensuous regard for language, and a fastidious attention to the physical world. I suggested earlier that this richness of descriptive language is one strategy by which Heaney can assert his personal identity and at the same time remain faithful to his national one. Description, in other words, functions as a kind of safeguard against the English elements of his literary heritage. In *North*, however, description takes on the aura of theatricality, a stage-Irish flaunting of his powers, not a legitimate use of them. It no longer serves to keep in check the English influence; it protects him, rather, from the legacy of violence he finds within his national past (and present). It is almost as if Heaney attempts to resolve his complicated attitude, his fascination and repulsion, stylistically through the dazzle of descriptive language; but the language only sanitizes the violence it appears to articulate so unflinchingly.

Consider, for instance, how the phrase "the mild pods of the eye-lids," from "The Tollund Man," does more than just describe or beautify the subject. Once we recall that the Tollund Man was sacrificed to the Mother Goddess in order to insure the renewal and fertility of spring, we realize that the simile sets up and justifies Heaney's later prayer to him "to make germinate" (within Heaney's imagination) "the scattered, ambushed / Flesh of labourers." In contrast, these lines from "The Grauballe Man"—

> As if he had been poured
> in tar, he lies on a pillow of turf
> and seems to weep
> the black river of himself

—or these lines from "The Bog Queen"—"My body was braille for the creeping influences"—seem like a mere display, demonstrating what W. S. Di Piero has called "a too exclusive attention to the sheen and noise of language, such that flamboyance and inventiveness, however sincere and in service to however serious a theme, come to displace clarity and integrity of feeling." Even the language / landscape trope begins to sound a little overdone ("I push back, / through dictions, / Elizabethan Canopies. / Norman devices, / the erotic mayflowers / of Provence." "This is the vowel of earth / dreaming its root"). What once had the freshness and excitement of discovery in *Wintering Out* takes on in *North* the stale predictability of mannerism, whose function is to shield Heaney from, by prettifying, the realities it once enabled him to explore.

A harsh judgment. But having made it, I now want to add that only a poet of major talent can err so skillfully. Even when he is not at his best, Heaney remains an engaging and serious poet, capable of working the language with an intensity we would be quick to praise in a lesser poet's work. Part of this capability derives from sheer talent; but perhaps a more important part derives from native talent responding to the pressures of social and political circumstances, to the crossed pieties inherent in the very language Heaney speaks and writes with. If these pressures sometimes cause Heaney to work the language too intensely until, in the words of the neo-Augustan critic, Archibald Alison, he deserts "the end of the art, for the display of the art itself," they also give his best work an intelligent urgency (and I stress both words here) that no other poet writing in English today can equal. In *Poems: 1965–1975* and *Preoccupations*, as well as in his fifth collection of poetry, *Field Work*, Heaney struggles honestly and often brilliantly to satisfy "the hunger of the culture for its own image and expression." His best poems—"Bogland," "The Tollund Man," "Funeral Rites," "Punishment" and "Casualty" (from *Field Work*)—satisfy that hunger. And not just for the Irish, but for all of us who look to poetry for a clarification of life.

# The Poetry of Seamus Heaney
## [On *Wintering Out*]

JOHN WILSON FOSTER*

With three full-blown volumes and several pamphlets to his credit, Seamus Heaney has already assembled a body of work of extraordinary distinctiveness and distinction.[1] At the age of thirty-four he has been proclaimed an exciting talent by many and a possibly major poet by several. Single-mindedness of purpose, a fertile continuity of theme, high competence in execution, a growing unmistakability of voice: these are Heaney's strengths and they place him in seriousness and maturity beyond hailing distance of most younger British poets.

These make him sound dull, whereas Heaney writes a verse that achieves, but does not depend upon, immediate impact. The most eye-catching feature is a use of rawly physical metaphors for things in and out of the physical world: frogs are "mud grenades, their blunt heads farting"; granary sacks are "great blind rats"; a quiet river wears "a transfer of gables and sky"; a pregnant cow looks as though "she has swallowed a barrel." Heaney's metaphors are so right, so conclusive that they generate within the poem and across the canon an axiomatic quality that is perilously close to being self-defeating; they can even in cumulation constitute their own kind of preciosity. In consequence, the poet occasionally gives the impression of a man hastening to patent a style. Craft, with which unlike most poets today Heaney is preoccupied, is not merely honest skill but also Daedalean cunning. He will seemingly not be deflected from working his enviably rich vein as he strikes deeper and deeper towards some unseen mother lode. The metaphor is apt, for Heaney's theme thus far has been "working the earth," and his exploitation of this coincides with the "whole earth" movement in Britain and the United States. Just as important, it coincides with the attempts of several writers in Northern Ireland to delve beneath the violent surface of life in the province into lore, history and myth, on the principle that the poisonous plant can best be understood by its roots. Heaney may have been engaged upon this before terror struck in 1969, but the "Troubles" have surely lent his poetry urgency and authenticity.

*Reprinted from *Critical Quarterly* 16 (Spring 1974): 35–48.

Troubles or no, digging deep has always been a hazardous business in Ulster, for it is to resume the dark, in Heaney's phrase, and the dark is fearful. It is arguable whether or not the fear with which Heaney's poetry is soaked is justified by the trove he has brought back from the Ulster heart of darkness. The impersonal insights are undeniable and remarkable, but the poet's degree of emotional involvement is more problematic. And has the poet up to now worked deep, in conceit and extended metaphor, at the expense of modal variety? These are questions not to be answered until the tangy and peculiarly seasoned quality of Heaney's poetry has been savoured. Should he reach perfection in his present mode, he will have become a notable minor poet. Should he instead widen his themes, break into new modes, and learn to trust his feeling, Seamus Heaney might well become the best Irish poet since Yeats.

I

Early Heaney poetry startled with its physicality. What a pleasure it was to come upon for the first time imagery so bluff, masculine and dead-on:

> All year the flax-dam festered in the heart
> Of the townland; green and heavy headed
> Flax had rotted there, weighted down by huge sods.
> Daily it sweltered in the punishing sun.
> Bubbles gargled delicately, bluebottles
> Wove a strong gauze of sound around the smell.

Heaney's first volume, *Death of a Naturalist*, whose titular poem I have just quoted, is as heavily laden with assonance, alliteration, imagery of touch, taste and smell, and with synesthesia (the buzz of bluebottles visualised as gauze) as the flax is with sods. Extensive description of a static scene can, as we shall see later, lead Heaney into confusion, despite a Ted Hughes–like vividness. Heaney is on firmer ground when recreating the *processes* of the earth and how man interacts with nature through ritual, custom and work. Not only are Heaney's poems about manual work on the farm—ploughing, planting, harvesting, horse-shoeing etc.—but they are themselves manuals on how the work is actually done. It is amusing, for instance, to set "Churning Day" beside E. Estyn Evans's account of churning in *Irish Heritage* (1942) and *Irish Folk Ways* (1957). Heaney in such a poem is folklorist, recalling old customs that survived into his native Londonderry of the nineteen-forties. Of course, by dint of education, travel and rural changes, Heaney is no longer at one with his rural origins and so his rehearsal of the customs he witnessed or participated in as a child assumes the quality of incantation and commemoration. The poems, he would have us believe, are substitutes for the farmwork he was once close to. In "Digging," the first poem of his first volume, and one that functions as a crude but effective manifesto, the poet recalls his father, like *his* father before him, expertly cutting turf on Toner's bog, and says: "But I've no spade to follow men like them." The ex-peasant, newly urbanised, newly middle-class poet proclaims his alternative: "Between my finger and my thumb / The squat pen rests. / I'll dig with it."

In one respect, Heaney has been fairly literally true to his word. If the early poems are about the use of tools—the churn-staff, the bill-hook, the spade, the hammer—they themselves are verbal mimicries of tool-using. From his evident reading and the intimacy of his recall, one senses Heaney's preparation before each poem, like that of the thatcher (in the poem of that name) of whom the poet writes: "It seemed he spent the morning warming up." Heaney plainly likes to execute each poem, once preparations are com-plete, with "the unfussy ease of a good tradesman" ("The Outlaw"). The poem's rhythm can imitate the rhythm of the body and lungs during the work—the curt clauses echoing the blows of a riveter's hammer in "Docker," chopped lines and caesurae imitating turf-cutting in "Digging," variable line length contrasting the actions of setting and lifting fishing-lines in "A Lough Neagh Sequence." But though craft is manual, there is scope in its circumspection for delicacy, pride and even, as "Thatcher" demonstrates, magic:

> Couchant for days on sods above the rafters
> He shaved and flushed the butts, stitched all together
> Into a sloped honeycomb, a stubble patch,
> And left them gaping at his Midas touch.

No less than "Digging," "Thatcher" is a poem about writing poetry, and Heaney admires not merely the craftsman's cautious preparation and paced execution but also his sense of participating in a long tradition. Heaney's own traditions would seem loosely to be those of English (or Welsh) rural intimacy (John Clare, Thomas Hardy, R. S. Thomas), Ulster rural regional-ism (John Hewitt, John Montague), and the post-Movement at its best (Larkin's expert verse-turning—learned from poets as diverse as Donne and Owen—spiced with Ted Hughes' menace).

Heaney has taken Yeats's advice to heart and striven to learn his trade. *Death of a Naturalist*, fine book though it is, is very much an apprentice's book, shot through with extravagances and infelicities. In "Trout" we are asked in the space of a few words to envisage the fish as a "fat gun-barrel" (a curious cartoon image) and at the same time as a tracer-bullet, a volley and a ramrod, images vivid in themselves but odd in combination. In "Docker," something more important is being said and garbled in the saying.

> There, in the corner, staring at his drink.
> The cap juts like a gantry's crossbeam,
> Cowling plated forehead and sledgehead jaw.
> Speech is clamped in the lips' vice.

This is a startling caricature not just of any docker but of a laconic Belfast docker and therefore a Protestant, as Heaney makes clear in a second stanza that proved prophetic:

> That fist would drop a hammer on a Catholic—
> Oh yes, that kind of thing could start again;
> The only Roman collar he tolerates
> Smiles all round his sleek pint of porter.

Belfast's fundamentalism is clinched to the city's industrial lifestyle:

> Mosaic imperatives bang home like rivets;
> God is a foreman with certain definite views
> Who orders life in shifts of work and leisure.
> A factory horn will blare the Resurrection.

So far, so excellent, but then Heaney images the docker as a Celtic cross, an unwitting incongruity or misguided stroke of ethnic ecumenism. The sharp vision of the Belfast Protestant docker is further blurred with concluding lines that could be used of working-class family men other than dockers and which are therefore anti-climactic: "Tonight the wife and children will be quiet / At slammed door and smoker's cough in the hall."

## II

It might be said that in *Death of a Naturalist*, with its prolific use of elementary poetic devices and overplus of image-making, Heaney was merely learning how to handle the turf-spade. It is likely, however, that the spade, wielded with whatever expertise, is too restricted a tool for Heaney's intellect and sensibility. At any rate, his second and third volumes evidence the pen metamorphosing from spade back again to pen.

Yet digging in one form or another remains the archetypal act in Heaney's poetry. What is found when the earth is overturned is sometimes good, such as the cream-white healthy tubers in "At a Potato Digging," though in the same poem we are reminded that this was not always so and that "wild higgledy skeletons / scoured the land in 'forty-five, / wolfed the blighted root and died." Deeper down, finds are liable to be more interesting. Because of the strange power in bog water which prevents decay, much of Ireland's past has been preserved within the three million acres of bog— utensils, jewellery and most characteristically the wood from Ireland's vanished oak forests:

> A carter's trophy
> split for rafters,
> a cobwebbed, black,
> long-seasoned rib
> under the first thatch.
> ("Bog Oak")

The laid open turf-bank is also a memory-bank, permitting us to read "an approximate chronological sequence of landscapes and human cultures in Ireland going back several thousand years."[2] Digging turf can often be interrupted—or continued—to become excavation. Since the investigation of Irish bogs was conducted under Danish leadership,[3] it is fitting that Heaney's imagination should be fired by P. V. Glob's illustrated account in *The Bog People* (1969) of the preserved bodies of Iron Age men found in Danish and European fens. The first documented bog body came, with reciprocal appropriateness, from the North of Ireland in the eighteenth century, but no body yet found compares in state of preservation with the man from the Tollund fen in Denmark, now on exhibition, and about whom Heaney has pledged:

> Some day I will go to Aarhus
> To see his peat-brown head,
> The mild pods of his eye-lids,
> His pointed skin cap.

It is a rhetorical vow fulfilled in its making. There is no reason for Heaney to leave Ireland. As he has concluded in "Bogland," dedicated to an Irish-American scholar and which begins by noting that Ireland has "no prairies / To slice a big sun at evening," "Our pioneers keep striking / Inwards and downwards." These two lines look like a recipe for provincialism, but the objective correlatives for striking downwards are manifold in Heaney's poetry—digging, ploughing, drawing well-water, taking soundings, fishing, divining. Analogies too are fertile. If "going down" is in one sense going, pioneer-fashion, into the unknown, it is also "going home," an equation punningly contained in the word "gravitate" indirectly exploited in "Gravities" from Heaney's first volume and "The Salmon Fisher to the Salmon" from his second. In Heaney's poetry things tend to revert, to resume by descent their dark primal condition.

*Death of a Naturalist* was Heaney's preliminary and noisy spadework, the clearing of brush and scrub. Gradually there is a movement towards the spare and vertical shapes of *Wintering Out*, serious attempts to sink shafts narrowly and deep. Between the surface clatter of *Death of a Naturalist* and the striking downwards in *Wintering Out* comes the intermediate task in *Door into the Dark* of striking inwards, recognising the inner fears to be overcome before the real digging is begun. To go home and to go down are both finally to confront the dark. Darkness resides in the crevices and recesses around the farm, in stable, forge and barn. It was childhood fear of this dark, as much as subsequent education and urbanisation, that contributed to the poet's "death" not only as a "naturalist" but also as the kind of unthinking accomplice of the earth we regard the peasant farmer as being. Less literally, the dark conceals the subterranean violence of Irish life which through history has erupted into warfare ("Requiem for the Croppies"). And it is close to the centre of religious faith—the darkness of confessional and monastery, both projections in space of the dark recesses of the soul. When he steps into the early Christian stone oratory of Gallarus on the Dingle peninsula, Heaney is possessed by compulsions to descend and return:

> You can still feel the community pack
> This place: it's like going into a turfstack,
> A core of old dark walled up with stone
> A yard thick. When you're in it alone
> You might have dropped, a reduced creature
> To the heart of the globe. No worshipper
> Would leap up to his God off this floor.

Excessive respect for the dark is shared not only by children and religious adults, but by primitives. The dark blurs the distinction between pagan and Christian. Raised a Catholic, an upbringing that has shaped "In Gallarus Oratory," Heaney has nonetheless kept intimate traffic with the elder faiths of the Irish countryside which lie, bog-like, beneath the visible Roman Catholicism that has often coopted them. Such traffic arises from the poet's actual experience in youth: "Personal Helicon" recounts the same fascination with wells that presumably lay at the heart of ancient Irish well-worship.[4] Then there were the hearth stories about the supernatural, celebrated in "Fireside." And also, one suspects, wide reading in the literature. "The Blinker" is a so far uncollected poem admonishing us to take traditional steps to ward off malign people or spirits who could " 'blink' a cow so that its milk would yield no butter" (Evans) or who can, as Heaney has it, "steer venom from his rimmed eye / / Until the milk is bile and gall."[5] Heaney's precautions are identical to Evans's: the use of a holed flint, smearing a ball of butter on the wall once the butter breaks, driving a coffin nail into the churn, twisting a rowan twig around the churn.[6] Heaney appropriates Evans's material and shapes it into the likeness of fear, not merely of bog-sprites and evil people but also—through the reader's ability to make the imaginative leap—of the evil that stalks Northern Ireland today, usually under cover of darkness as befits dastardliness.

*Door into the Dark* is not a sustained assault upon the dark but a series of forays. Poetry as sortie (and therefore usually short) is suggested in Heaney's remark that poetry is a kind of raid into dark corners, a remark Benedict Kiely used as the title of his spirited essay on Heaney's first two volumes.[7] "All I know is a door into the dark," proclaims Heaney in "The Forge," but at sonnet's end he has yet to open that door, and stands transfixed upon the threshold, dumbly witnessing the blacksmith go back into his grotto-like forge. Likewise he recalls watching Kelly's unlicensed bull in "The Outlaw" who, after the businesslike conception, "resumed the dark, the straw." No one would expect the child to brave the dark, but few of the poems in *Door into the Dark* are childhood recollections and yet the dark remains unchallenged by the end of the book. Heaney has a marked reluctance to strike inwards, to cross the threshold, to explore the emotional and psychological sources of his fear; and fear therefore outweighs understanding in his work, as darkness outweighs illumination. We might choose to see his Roman Catholic upbringing coming into play here. Heaney's feeling in Gallarus oratory is indistinguishable from the penitent's desire to confess inside the dark confessional or pray inside the monastic sanctum. (The suggestion of defiance in "No worshipper / Would leap up to his God off this floor" surely stems from Heaney's being native to a fundamentalist corner of Ireland whose majority abhors kneeling and the monastic tradition.) But Heaney is no readier to confess his personal feelings to his readers than the penitent is to discuss his confession with anyone other than his priest. The privacy of religious belief becomes the privacy of poetic feeling. Furthermore, the rites of confession and absolution, like the need for orders and retreats, assume man's severely limited direct access to his God. Much must be taken on trust. By an unavoidable analogy, Heaney's description of the oratory as "a core of old dark walled up with stone / A yard thick" is an apt image for the tabernacular resistance Heaney's poetic mystery puts up in the face of comprehension and analysis, both his and the reader's.

In the meantime, the poet remains masterly at composing the signals and symptoms of fear into verse as compactly layered as good turf. At the poetic centre of *Door into the Dark* is a fine group of poems called "A Lough Neagh Sequence." Accounts of how the lough fishermen catch eels, interwoven with accounts of the life-cycle of the fish, are brilliant public metaphors for that psychic disturbance in Heaney's poetry whose precise meaning remains as intractable as bog oak. The sequence also interweaves the key Heaney motifs of descent, homing and darkness in the fashion of a metaphysical conceit. The eels travelling overland at night form a "horrid cable" that encircles the poet's world of experience, threatening it with mysterious and malign power yet defining its shape and continuity. The completed circle of eels is also an "orbit" of fears, and this implies a gravitational tendency to descend as well as to circumscribe.

The conceit lies at the heart of *Door into the Dark*. The volume is a marked improvement over *Death of a Naturalist* in terms of surer control and more effective conservation of energy. But the tautness of the conceit and the dramatic distancing it involves can obscure psychic and emotional issues as readily as immature and uncontrolled fertility. Moreover, the particular conceit of Heaney's choice—that of the circle or orbit—threatens to make his poetic philosophy a closed system, a state of affairs which is not helped by what I earlier called the axiomatic rightness of his images.

## III

Thus far, Heaney has sought not to understand but to propitiate the fearful dark. Commemoration of the experiences of a rural childhood is also an attempt to exorcise. In *Death of a Naturalist*, fear was generated and exorcised inexpensively. The trouble began with the first couplet of the first poem: "Between my finger and my thumb / The squat pen rests; snug as a gun." Since the poem is about digging, the image of the gun introduces a piece of gratuitous menace. Often with equal gratuity, images of ballistics and detonation pepper the volume. Frogs are "mud grenades" in the titular poem; crocks are "pottery bombs" in "Churning Day"; "Dawn Shoot" is about shotgunning foxes; when the poet slaps the animal in "Cow in Calf" the blows "plump like a depth-charge"; the fish in "Trout" is a gun-barrel and a bullet; sea explodes, wind strafes, and space is a salvo in "Storm on the Island"; the spectrum of colour on the canvas bursts, "a bright grenade," when the painter "unlocks the safety catch / On morning dew" in "In Small Townlands." The menace of the book, however vindicated in the gunlaw of Ulster society since, is unearned. So too are the exorcisms. The poet is a trifle arrogant and facile in "Follower." "An Advancement of Learning," about the poet's face-off with an embankment rat, is a piece of Wild Western-ese. In "The Early Purges," the poet remembers as a six-year-old seeing kittens drowned in a bucket, but has since, despite the nostalgic irony, overcome the trauma: "living displaces false sentiments / And now, when shrill pups are prodded to drown / I just shrug, 'Bloody pups.' " Why?— "on well-run farms pests have to be kept down." The child's feelings were impractical, yes, but surely not false either in the sense of being counterfeited or of being superficial. Throughout Heaney's poetry one senses beneath the hardboiled exterior a certain shyness or shame about deep feelings which are dramatised away from the poet when not disavowed altogether.

The reader might reasonably expect at least to find the poet humanly vulnerable and open-hearted in matters of love. Until *Wintering Out*—and there only fleetingly—he would be disappointed. The love poems in *Death of a Naturalist* are placed coyly at the end of the book and they are, moreover, removed in a metaphysical style from immediacy of feeling. "Valediction," "Scaffolding," "Poem for Marie" and "Honeymoon Flight" are all conceits and while clever and even beautiful (for example, "Scaffolding") keep the reader outside the taut, stave-like lines of their stanzaic compounds. There are no first-person love poems in *Door into the Dark* (sex in this volume is associated with the seasons and with rural rites) but Part Two of *Wintering Out* contains several marital love poems in which for the first time Heaney seems emotionally unsure of himself and therefore capable of poetic *moods*. The beautiful but brittle assurance of "Scaffolding" is now, in "Summer Home," an entire curve of emotion from premonition through revulsion, placation, passion and recrimination to the final chastened assertion: "Yesterday rocks sang when we tapped / Stalactites in the cave's old, dripping dark—/ Our love calls tiny as a tuning fork."

This poem may be the signpost to Heaney's future poetry, but for most of *Wintering Out* he is still content to impersonalise his feelings. If, for instance, natural and preternatural fears are more honestly evoked and allayed than in either of the two previous books, it is by dint not of greater emotional investment but of sounder analogies. Glob concludes that the bog people were participants in fertility rites and then sacrificed to a fertility goddess, and Heaney seizes on this. The encouragement of fertility through violent death is an ancient irony and one senses in "The Tollund Man" its appropriateness for contemporary Ulster. Heaney's fear of the dark becomes in *Wintering Out* a fear of the violence in what Evans calls "the immemorial peasant tradition which dominates the heart of Ireland" and of the way this violent and sacrificial past fingers out through analogy and recurrence to the present. A group of other poems in *Wintering Out* is concerned not with depth-readings of the Irish earth but with topography. Above as well as below the ground are the signatures of the past inscribed for us to see. In these "topographical poems" which are also "language poems," parts of speech and parts of landscape are identified as a Catholic Ulsterman looks and listens around and considers what he has gained and lost by living in the planted North. It is a kind of respite on the side-lines of conflict; it is interesting to note that Heaney has given up his post at Queen's University, Belfast and become a full-time writer in the South of Ireland, far from the war zone. But as the titular phrase from "Servant Boy" implies, there is also in the book a notion of endurance, for everyone from Northern Ireland is at the moment "wintering out / the back-end of a bad year."

Poems such as "Fodder" and "Oracle" furnish locality and custom with the tongues and ears of dialect. The "soft blastings" (ex-plosives, we might say) of the words *Toome, Toome* summon up for the poet

> a hundred centuries
>
> loam, flints, musket-balls.
> fragmented ware,
> torcs and fish-bones.

Things are equally interesting above the ground. "Anahorish" posits a phono-logical as well as physical topography: "*Anahorish*, soft gradient / of conso-nant, vowel-meadow." "Gifts of Rain" likens the modulation of the rich vowels in *Moyola* to the Derry river itself. Heaney's use of a slow-moving river to image the Anglo-Irish dialect is endorsed when we read elsewhere that "for both plosives and fricatives [in Anglo-Irish dialect] affricate conso-nants with slow separation of the organs of speech, are often heard."[8] The river in flood threatens livelihoods but it has for the poet female allure as it breathes its mists, like an old chanter, "through vowels and history." "Broagh" is another small hymn to a Londonderry place-name which also rehearses in sound the landscape it labels. Rain in the poem ends suddenly "like that last / *gh* the strangers found / difficult to manage." Strangers are those outside Ireland who have trouble, unlike the Irish, (Protestant *and* Catholic), with the guttural spirant.[9] Irish names and pronunciations are survivals, for since Spenser's day the native Irish have had to come to terms with the Anglo-Saxon culture. Heaney is realist enough to know that to talk of the Irish language as a living thing is to take "the backward look." The poem of that name images the failure of the Irish language as the staggering flight of the snipe. The snipe's trajectory is simulated in the poem's slender, irregular form, from the bird's startling explosion when flushed through its feinting flight until it disappears into available cover some distance away. The snipe flees "its nesting ground" as the Irish language and culture fled from their sure origins "into dialect, / into variants." The linguist in the "nature reserves" of controlled field-work who transliterates Irish and English (such as the variant Irish names for the snipe, *"little goat of the air, / of the evening, / / little goat of the frost"*) is reenacting the actual, unconscious and continuing linguistic process among the people. The snipe drums an elegy for the Irish language and culture as it slipstreams behind the vanished bittern and wild goose.[10] At poem's end, the snipe disappears among "gleanings and leavings / in the combs / of a fieldworker's archive."

Heaney's feelings about all this are typically enigmatic. "Traditions" begins with a flat assertion:

> Our guttural muse
> was bulled long ago

by the alliterative tradition,
her uvula grows

vestigial

For Heaney then the Irish language and culture are, after Joyce, not merely a river but female—vowel-vaginal, we might say, unlike the Anglo-Saxon tradition which is male, terrestrial, phallic-consonantal. The imputation of rape is reinforced by the suggestion of coercion in the first line of the second part of the poem:

We are to be proud
of our Elizabethan English:
"varsity," for example,
is grass-roots stuff with us

Is the poet resentful? Is he bridling at the pride of Ulster Protestants in the Elizabethan cast of Ulster dialect? Seemingly, and yet feeling in the poem fizzles out. In the third part of the poem Heaney will have no truck with the passion-rousing problem of identity. The "whingeing" Macmorris in *Henry the Fifth*, identified by Thomas Flanagan (to whom "Traditions," like "Bogland," is dedicated) as the first stage-Irishman,[11] who asks "what ish my nation?" is answered, "sensibly," according to Heaney, by Leopold Bloom who said, "Ireland, I was born in Ireland." Neither in emotion nor logic are we prepared by the first two premiss-parts of the poem for this flat conclusion. "Traditions" is a broken-backed syllogism and poem.

Heaney's conceit (landscape = body = sex = language) and the way it sabotages emotion leads him into such difficulties throughout these language-poems. In "A New Song," the poet meets a girl from Derrygarve, which place-name recalls for him the Moyola's "long swerve, / / And stepping stones like black molars / Sunk in the ford." At first the girl is merely a "chance vestal daughter" evoking a "vanished music" and pouring "a smooth libation of the past." This realistic acceptance of irrecoverable history is where "Traditions" and "The Backward Look" conclude. "But now," claims the poet

our river tongues must rise
From licking deep in native haunts
To flood, with vowelling embrace,
Demesnes staked out in consonants.

Does "must" mean "shall inexorably" or "ought to"? Is the stanza blueprint or prophecy? Instead of acceptance there is the promise of resurgence, and the military metaphors of the last stanza are ominous:

> And Castledawson we'll enlist
> And Upperlands, each planted bawn—
> Like bleaching-greens resumed by grass—
> A vocable, as rath and bullaun.

This is a difficult stanza to paraphrase, elliptical to the point of being cryptic. It seems to say this: Castledawson, Upperlands and other bawns (or fortifications) established by the seventeenth-century Scots planters will be enlisted in the cause of resurgence. The planted bawns, whose names were originally foreign and "furled" consonants in the Irish "language-scape," have been rendered obsolète (like bleaching-greens—used by the planters in their linen-trade—resumed by grass), for the planters have in the course of time become Irishmen. The "furled consonants of the lowlanders" have become merely Irish sounds (vocables) similar to "rath" and "bullaun," equally obsolete native Irish objects (rath a fortification, bullaun a ritual basin-stone). For Heaney, obsolescence can be a primal state and, insofar as the obsolete is preserved in custom, speech or bog, can exert an influence on the present. It is this obsolescence-primality-nativeness of the Irish that will resurge.

When we have figured this out, we have yet to decide if Heaney is referring to a linguistic or cultural resurgence (or both) and what form it is to take. Is the poem a veiled reference to the possibility of Protestant and Catholic Ulstermen solving their political problems on the heels of the possibly departing English (whose "demesnes" are to be flooded)? It is impossible to tell. Unfortunately these resourceful poems are so cerebral that when they fail as arguments (not necessarily by being false but by being unclear), they fail ultimately as poems.

## IV

The ambiguity of the language-poems does, however, reflect Heaney's dilemma as a poet, suspended between the English and (Anglo-) Irish traditions and cultures. Correlatives of ambivalence proliferate in his verse: the archetypal sound in his work (and to be savoured in the reading) is the guttural spirant, half-consonant, half-vowel; the archetypal locale is the bog, half-water, half-land; the archetypal animal is the eel which can fancifully be regarded (in its overland forays) as half-mammal, half-fish.

There is good reason for Heaney to be Janus-faced. He was reared in the countryside of Northern Ireland and was steeped in its lore, yet he served his poetic apprenticeship in a Belfast chapter of The Group, a subsidiary of that most English of holding companies, The Movement. Philip Hobsbaum, unofficial head of the chapter, has since tried to appropriate Heaney's work in the name of an essentially English tradition. In a recent article,[12] Hobsbaum claims the wedding sequence from *Wintering Out* as the best of Heaney so far, and places it firmly within that mainstream of contemporary English verse that he describes elsewhere as relating back to Owen, master of the half-rhyme, and through him back to the Keats of "The Fall of Hyperion" and back to Shakespeare. Another line through the same tradition could, he says, be traced "through Redgrove and Hughes through [Edward] Thomas and Rosenberg to the blank verse fictions of the Romantics, Shakespeare and even back to the medieval poets. Either way, it's the central line of English poetry."[13] I have no quarrel here with Hobsbaum's concept of the English mainstream but rather with the way he seems in his general criticism to permit considerations of membership to this historic club to stifle the individuality and in some cases un-Englishness of contemporary British poets who write, after all, at least equally in response to their personal and social circumstances as in response to their conceptions of English poetic tradition. Particularly, one would imagine, an Irish poet. If metre and rhyme are not our sole considerations—and even indeed if they are—we need to discuss Heaney against the backgrounds of poetry and life in Ulster and the rest of Ireland. (And where, incidentally, fits Yeats into Hobsbaum's scheme?)

Philip Hobsbaum is rightly credited with having single-handedly galvanised Ulster poetry into its present vibrant state. The province's cultural debt to him is immense. Yet I wonder if the fact that so many of Heaney's poems are tight as clenched fists, coiled springs without emotional release, is not due in large part to the influence of The Group. It is an influence that has encouraged formal excellence (an essay could be written on Heaney's rhyme alone), but has had the side-effect of encouraging Heaney's Irish, perhaps Catholic Irish, impulse to keep self-revelation and emotional openness for situations other than poetic; perhaps too it has encouraged Heaney to be the "big-eyed Narcissus" he repudiated back in "Personal Helicon," staring into the recesses of the Irish landscape and past, cleverly rhyming simply to see himself, "to set the darkness echoing." If Heaney becomes the best Irish poet of his generation, it will be because he has remained true to as great an Irishness in diction, setting and theme as he has already achieved, while taking the emotional risks of his great antecedent Yeats and his contemporary Thomas Kinsella. His sure sense of miniaturist form, learned from the English poets of the 'fifties and 'sixties, is a solid foundation from which he needs to launch into a variety of modes. Time, shall we say, to lay aside the spade and bring out the heavy machinery. In the meantime, there is little contemporary poetry that has bettered the quality and fruitfulness of Heaney's solitary digging; few poets have enlivened their work with a more remarkable gift for seeing afresh the physical world around us and beneath us.

*Notes*

1. The volumes are: *Death of a Naturalist* (1966, 1969), *Door into the Dark* (1969, 1972) and *Wintering Out* (1972, 1973), all published in London by Faber and Faber; the second date is in each case that of the second or reprinted edition I have used.

2. Evans, *Irish Folk Ways* (London, 1957), p. 185; as background to "Bog Oak," cf. Evans's further remark: "In the past, too, considerable use was made of buried timber dug from bogs, of oak for roofing beams. . . ."

3. Evans, *Irish Heritage* (Dundalk, 1942), p. 24.

4. For an account of Irish well-worship, see W. G. Wood-Martin, *Traces of the Elder Faiths of Ireland* (London, 1902), II, Chapter III; Wood-Martin is invaluable background material for the reader of Heaney, illuminating such elements as the lough legendry in "A Lough Neagh Sequence" and the mandrake-root in "A Northern Hoard."

5. "The Blinker" appeared in *Fortnight: An Independent Review for Northern Ireland*, July, 1972.

6. Evans, *Irish Folk Ways*, pp. 304–305.

7. Benedict Kiely, "A Raid into Dark Corners: The Poems of Seamus Heaney," *The Hollins Critic* (Virginia), VII (October 1970). 1–12; the editor's biographical and bibliographical information in this article is unfortunately garbled.

8. G. L. Brook, *English Dialects* (London, 1963), p. 112.

9. Heaney implies that the velar fricative *gh* (pronounced *ch*[x]) was a native Irish rather than English sound that was adopted by the Scots planters, but in fact it was also an English sound that disappeared early in the Modern English period, J. Taniguchi, *Irish English* (Tokyo, n. Eng. d.), p. 240; according to J. Braidwood, the Scots spirant is stronger than the Irish, "Ulster and Elizabethan English," *Ulster Dialects*, ed. G. B. Adams (Holywood, Co. Down, 1964), p. 75.

10. The wild goose has not, of course, disappeared from Ireland as has the bittern, but this may be an allusion to the "wild geese," Irishmen who fled the island from the Elizabethan age onwards and who formed Irish Brigades in Continental armies.

11. Thomas Flanagan, *The Irish Novelists 1800–1850* (New York, 1959).

12. "The Present State of British Poetry," *Lines Review*, No. 45 (June, 1973).

13. "The Growth of English Modernism," *Wisconsin Studies in Contemporary Literature*, VI (1965), 105.

# A Decade of Seamus Heaney's Poetry

JOHN HILDEBIDLE*

Full of recollections and echoes, *Station Island* insists that it be taken as a retrospective view of Seamus Heaney's career. As such, it is very much of a piece with his prior work, which has from the beginning been regularly and productively visited by the ghosts of the past. But there is, I think, a more particular reason for looking at the book in the light of the three which precede it—*North* (1975), *Field Work* (1979), and *Sweeney Astray* (1984). The four volumes, taken together, represent a decade-long effort on Heaney's part to find or to create some coherence out of the varied "pasts" which have affected his life, and out of the peculiar present of Ireland as well. They amount to a sustained meditation on the place of the poet in the world, in the hope of resolving the cruel choice which Yeats proposed, a choice between the work and the life.

*North* is a book especially concerned with history; or rather with histories. There is the political history marked by the colonizations of Ireland by Danes, missionaries, Normans, and most importantly by the English, colonizations which are transformed into acts of sexual conquest in a sequence of poems ("Ocean's Love to Ireland," "Aisling," and "Act of Union") very near the center of the volume and which of course underlie the contemporary conflicts in the poems in Part II. The book as well incorporates the mythic cultural history of Heaney's Ireland, both in the "bog poems" that follow upon those in *Door into the Dark* and in the pair of poems "Antaeus" and "Hercules and Antaeus," which frame Part I of the book and which propose a fundamental image of conflict and rootedness. Heaney's effort to find or to define his own place in literary history becomes explicit in the evocation of writers as varied in time and character as Baudelaire, Walter Ralegh, Yeats, and Wordsworth, as well as in the dedication of many poems to Heaney's contemporaries. And finally, the personal history which had been the substance of so many of the poems in Heaney's first three books is at last drawn together, especially in the powerful long poems in the second half of *North*, which amount to

*Reprinted from *The Massachusetts Review* 28, no. 3 (Autumn 1987): 393–409. © 1987 *The Massachusetts Review*, Inc.

But categories quickly lose their distinctness, as for instance in "Funeral Rites," where the small necessary acts of burying one's own dead connect both with the Viking burial of the hero Gunnar and with the sadly repetitious and minimal ceremonies occasioned by "each neighbourly murder" in the Northern Ireland of the mid-1970's. To distinguish between various myths—personal, tribal, political, cultural, historical—is in fact to misrepresent the character of the book, which is fundamentally concerned with interconnection. The problem which dominates the book is how, and why, and to what end one may speak verse in a tragically interwoven world, one in which, as Heaney argues at several points in *Preoccupations*, even vowels and consonants have an apparent political import.

One might fairly define the theme of *North* by way of the borrowed dictum, "whatever you say, say nothing." The source is any Belfast shopwindow, where posters remind all sects that any speech is dangerous. Heaney slightly revises the line to "whatever you say, you say nothing," a version which does much to explain the particular darkness of *North*. Many of the voices to be heard in Heaney's later poetry, and especially in "Station Island," object to that dictum, seeing it both as an abdication of responsibility and as a simple untruth: in Ireland, even to say nothing is to take a side. In any case, for a poet who continues to speak (and Heaney's output has not flagged since *North*), the line will not serve as a resting-place. But the inevitable conflict between the sense of powerlessness which the line states and the effort in *North* as a whole to make "music" out of "what happens" (as Heaney puts it later, in "Song" in *Field Work*) is in fact the generative tension of the book, and of Heaney's work since.

The apparent solution to that conflict in *North* (and in Heaney's own life, since he is no longer a resident of the North) is to abandon the context in which the conflict exists—to seek a protective and yet still productive geographic estrangement. "Exposure," the final section of the concluding sequence "The Singing School," provides a richly open ending to the volume. Heaney has fled to his new (but, as a note in *Field Work* tells us. only temporary) home, in Co. Wicklow. The flight leaves him "an inner émigré"—which captures both Heaney's sense of being forced back on himself and his recognition that to move to the South is to move within, rather than truly between, lands. That new position brings a kind of freedom (he is "neither internee nor informer"), at least the freedom from making one sort of impossible choice. Thus he has perhaps been empowered; he has at least "grown . . . / thoughtful." The question which the poem propounds— and which, we realize, the whole book has tried to answer—is "How did I end up like this?" That question is complicated by the number of voices Heaney still hears, and which will come to dominate, indeed to determine the shape of, "Station Island": "I often think of my friends' / Beautiful prismatic counselling." But the question misrepresents the case, since

Heaney has not, at this point, "ended" anywhere. And what is he to do next?

Whatever relief the poem may offer—and it opens with a lovely evocation of the Wicklow landscape, in which the violent forces operating in so many of the prior poems seem blessedly absent—still this is no unequivocally comfortable place. The time is December and night, the place outdoors, the voice alone. The poem ends with a richly mixed image of a "wood-kerne," escaped and lost. Surely no escape can put to rest the itch of what Heaney a few lines earlier calls "my responsible *tristia*"; and the very title of the poem is a complex image. It would seem that Heaney has escaped that landscape in which he would be, still, exposed to what he calls in one of his essays "predatory circumstances." But too long a stay in this new outdoors could very well lead to the death-by-exposure which so many migrants suffer. He can hide—using "protective colouring"—but to do so may continue the restriction of his view. The goal of this escape is, perhaps, a different kind of exposure: an openness both to the new and to the significance of the old.

But what if that opportunity to confront the new involves a separation from all those things which have given rise to poetry? The question which the final lines of *North* necessarily leave moot is whether and how Heaney might still write once his poetic and geographic and familial roots are at some remove. He has, of course, never been strictly an admirer of the old ways. The much-anthologized "Digging," to take only one instance, had asserted a continuity between his poetic work and the labor of his fathers; but it is a continuity that contains as well an inescapable distance, since his digging with the pen will never be more than analogic to the digging he sees his father doing. But never, before "Exposure," had the distance been so absolute, or its risks so badly stated.

If *Field Work* is, in part, an answer to the conundrums of "Exposure," it is, to use a word Heaney himself uses in "Casualty," a "tentative" one. That tentativeness appears less in the manner of his speech (which confidently manipulates form and language) than the unsettlements in what is being said. The title of the book suggests a return to the rural, richly typological landscape of *Death of a Naturalist*, but Heaney's home-place is explicitly present only in "The Strand at Lough Beg." And that one return, which confronts "random sectarian killing," is anything but reassuring.

The landscape may still be full of familiars and relics, but what is clear even without the prior evidence of *North* is the degree to which escape is a necessary step. The sequence of memorial-poems to Colum McCartney ("The Strand at Lough Beg"), to Sean Armstrong ("A Postcard from North Antrim"), and to a nameless fisherman ("Casualty") emphasizes the murderous actuality of Heaney's former home; and worse yet the unpredictable intrusion of violence even into relatively unpolitical lives. One thing which distinguishes these poems from the attention paid to the contemporary Troubles in *North* is the relative clouding of sectarian lables. Heaney acknowledges his own politics, but only early on, in poems such as "The Toome Road" and "Triptych." Now the sects turn on themselves. The tribe which slays the fisherman is "ours"; bomber, victim, and elegist are all Catholic. In "Triptych," Heaney's sybil proclaims a dark fate for the whole of Ireland, including that part to which Heaney has "escaped": "Our island is full of comfortless noises."

Thus the nature and potential of Heaney's escape from the North is heavily qualified from the beginning; and the note of escape brings a counter-vailing sense of abandonment and betrayal, which culminates in Dante's story of Ugolino, with which Heaney closes the book. Ugolino's sin of betrayal places him very near the absolute bottom of hell, in the ninth circle. He suffers eternally just below the betrayers of kinsmen (a charge which Colum McCartney will level at Heaney himself in "Station Island"), just above the betrayers of friends (and Heaney, for all his affection for the dead fisherman, had, as he admits, "missed his funeral"), in the midst of those who have betrayed their nation.

Dante's curse falls not only on Ugolino but on his homeland; he calls down a purifying flood upon Pisa for including within its atrocity the deaths not only of the traitorous Ugolino but also of innocent children. The betrayal, in other words, is cruelly doubled: the person betrays the State, and the individual and often innocent human life is betrayed by the political forces within the State. Heaney uses the poem in part as a charge against Ireland (and surely not only the North), which has shed so much blood to no apparent effect. But the focus of the poem is on Ugolino himself, the collaborator, and thus a man who tried, in a term Heaney applies to Francis Ledwidge, to achieve an "equilibrium," albeit one which proves, in the end, to be "useless." Ugolino's punishment is eternal cannibalism; he "lives" in hell "soldered" to his arch-rival Archbishop Roger (we might observe that all parties to this violence are Catholic), "gnawing him where the neck and head / Are grafted to the sweet fruit of the brain."

It is not too far from that appalling image to the picture Heaney constructs of himself in the first poem in *Field Work*, "Oysters." There, what begins as an account of a friendly, if extravagant, meal turns unexpect-edly into a poem about anger, trust, and voracity. The oysters at first allow Heaney to step into a portentous star-scape like that which, at the close of "Exposure," he had feared losing. But his transport arises from victimization; the oysters are "alive and violated," "ripped and shucked and scattered." Heaney on the one hand can take pleasure in "toasting friendship, / Laying down a perfect memory" like a rare wine. Yet that human gesture brings him to anger.

The poem's final stanza is indeed enigmatic. The connection between poetry and freedom, both creatures of "clear light" and perhaps even of "repose," is an important foreshadowing of the Sweeney figure, an altogether (and yet rarely reposing) free singer. But the poem speaks of "poetry *or* freedom," as if the two were in fact at odds, as if the freedom from threat which is the altogether-recognizable human impulse behind Heaney's search for a new home may in fact be the foe, not the fellow, of art. The condition of repose and freedom is in any case denied, in large part by the poet's own learning and imagination; he cannot help imposing on the events of the day a bookish memory of an old, imperially Roman "glut of privilege." Ultimately, the poet here is an omnivore; the hope is not for memory or friendship but for a digestion (and gestation) into language. One wonders how "pure" any word so born could be said to be.

Often in *Field Work* Heaney suggests the dark, even traitorous character of the poetic vocation. In his elegy to Lowell, he defines "art's / deliberate, peremptory / love and arrogance." *Deliberate* takes us back to "Oysters"; and Heaney's frequent talk, in his poems and in his essays, of poetry as a kind of visitation should not blind us to the willed and crafted nature of his work. Even in his love-lyrics, which often depend upon a kind of incantation, one cannot escape the sense of the observing, recording, re-shaping poetic eye and hand. "Love and arrogance" can serve to label the doubleness of Heaney's position, at once attached and detached, at home (or wishing to be so) and astray (or hoping to remain so), both confident (about his art) and tentative (about the human connections it records).

Part of that doubleness shows in poems of marital disaffection. In "An Afterwards," the making of poetry is at the heart of the central figure's estrangement from his family—just as, in "Casualty," it is Heaney's role as poet that stands between him and the slain fisherman. As he will often do in *Station Island*, Heaney cedes the poem to an accusing other voice—his wife's?—who consigns the poet to the ninth circle of hell (where Ugolino suffers) and who insists that the "perfection of the work" has, as Yeats feared, led to a sacrifice of the (domestic) life. Worse yet, the betrayal of the home is only the first; neither art nor life is served in the end: "you left us first, and then those books, behind." The same note of accusation is sounded by a dream-consciousness in "A Dream of Jealousy"; there the wounded beloved cannot be healed by "these verses / Nor my prudence"—by either speech or silence, in other words. It is against the hard background of this self-imaging that the powerful love verse of such poems as "Field Work" must be read. And even there the poet's memory plays him false, misremembering in small ways the beloved.

To the poet-as-traitor and the poet-as-devourer must be added the poet-voyeur, as when "At my window over the hotel car park" Heaney watches young lovers, only to find himself "like some old pike." All these predatory versions of the "arrogance" of the artist are of course only part of the story.

But the recurrence of such unsettling images complicates the search throughout *Field Work* for a home; one wonders what place could serve to house this creature of love and threat.

Heaney places at the center of *Field Work* the sequence of Glanmore sonnets, which are the fullest account in the book of a home. Like many another such evocation in his work of the possibly comforting place, the sequence closes ambiguously, in a dream of love and death and a clear remembrance of "our separateness"—a memory which is placed "years ago in that hotel" and thus separate from the "home" landscape of the poems. In an earlier poem, he had posed a pained question: "How perilous is it to choose / not to love the life we're shown?" Now, as if in answer, he makes the substance of the sonnets from precisely what, almost accidentally, is before and around him: weather, trees, a rat at a window, even the litany of names from a radio weather forecast. The poems pronounce the relief to be sought and found in words, as when, in the seventh of the sonnets, the names of places and of vessels bring him to a sense of (momentarily) completed escape and comforting residence. But earlier in the sequence, words—even the apparently innocent "elderberry"—argue not for rest but for alienation and loss, which can only in part be overcome by a persistent verbal memory and the assertion that "We still believe what we hear." In any case moments of confident loud speech are offset by the defensiveness of such lines as "I won't relapse / From this strange loneliness I've brought us to," and by the intrusion of terror, haunting, and self-interrogation. Even having escaped, the poet still wonders, seeing a rat at the window, "Did we come to the wilderness for this?" Safely south, the habitual worries of the North remain: "What would I meet, blood-boltered on the road?" And again, "What is my apology for poetry?"—where *apology* captures both the defensive anxiety of the modern meaning of the world and the prideful assertiveness to be heard in the echo of Sidney's *Apology for Poetry*.

The first of the Glanmore sonnets can serve as a final *locus* of the complications of the book as a whole. The poem begins with language, even with sound ("Vowels ploughed into other"), and reminds us of the erotic power Heaney finds in the words which visit him. The image of ploughing is an old one for him, and one which as in "Digging," attaches his work as artist with the hand-work of his agricultural forebears, and thus to what he calls, in *Preoccupations*, "the ordinary rituals of life." There is a note of formal elegance as well in the way in which the vowels of the opening line— especially the varying *o* sounds—do persist in "ploughing" into the consonantal field throughout the poem, down to the final word. The poem is carefully placed in the present (as if the ghosts of memory had, for the time, been put to rest) and in a landscape which is general enough not to insist on its distance from Mossbawn. The season is mild and promising (very early spring), and all visible work points toward fruition. In this place Heaney can imagine both the "good life" and the paradigmatic congruence of art with the most natural of human acts.

But that imagining is only potential; it is what "could be," not what is. He is himself (as he wished to be in "Oysters") quickened; but he is as well "gorged," and while what provokes him is a Dantean rose, it is "redolent," as if with the odor of its own death. All that he can propose for now is to wait. Such waiting in part flies in the face of the oddity and temporariness of the landscape. In place of the music of what happens, there is an absence of sound, a silence which is vulnerable to the customary noises of farming. Heaney's own ploughing then is in its way at war with the actual ploughing that will allow the true fruition of this farmland.

What transpires is a visitation by yet more ghosts. They bear a clear force of ritual and religious meditation, taking up their stations as Heaney himself will in "Station Island." They too carry the promise of quickening, sowing their seeds. Yet those seeds are "freakish Easter snows": unseasonable, out-of-place, and (as snow) potentially deadly to any true growth. The ghosts are particularly "mine"—a statement of ownership perhaps, a sense of special vocation or, it may be, only of special torment. In any case the poem ends with Heaney in isolation, the communal sense hinted at in the word "our" now having, it seems, fallen away. It is no surprise to learn, in the poem which follows the sonnet sequence ("September Song"), that Heaney is now an émigré from Glanmore as well.

Heaney calls Glanmore his "hedge-school"—the old, surreptitious but indomitable culture of Celtic learning, long "staffed" with wandering bards. In *North*, he had called Belfast his singing school; that school, too, he had in the end abandoned. After four years at Glanmore, the record of which is both the sonnets and the book which contains them, he has perhaps finished his schooling altogether. But what then is to be done with what he has learned? If "the end of art is peace"—the motto at the heart of "The Harvest Bow"—then his art is, at the conclusion of *Field Work*, not yet at its end, either for the nation or for Heaney himself.

*Sweeney Astray* is, at first glance, the clearest outgrowth of Heaney's formal schooling. The introduction Heaney appends to his "version"—he is scrupulous in not presenting it as a straightforward translation—makes clear the particular complex of appeals which Sweeney's story offers to Heaney. Sweeney is, first of all, not strictly speaking a mythic figure at all, but rather "a literary creation" and thus—like the Heaney of North—"an historically situated character." His historical moment is, like the present, the locus of a sharp conflict, the "tension between the newly dominant Christian ethos and the older, recalcitrant Celtic temperament." Today, of course, the Christian and the Celtic—especially, the Catholic and the Celtic—are so identified that it takes an accurate historical consciousness to recall with what pain and violence that identity was achieved. The linking of Celtic and "recalcitrant" is important. It will, as we will see, give Heaney a possible key to the paradoxical wish to be "responsible" to his own Irishness while refusing, as one of the "Station Island" ghosts—also named Sweeney—advises him, to join any procession: the possibility, in other words, of being most true to the Celtic temperament precisely by remaining at odds with all sectarian definitions of it. Sweeney's tale, which exists at the intersection of history, literature, and myth, becomes in Heaney's version an exploration of that free escape which is, in his prior poetry, at most one side in a continuing war of the self.

Indeed, Heaney makes explicit the value of Sweeney as a figure of the artist (and especially, one suspects, the Daedalian artist), and does so in terms which with little revision could serve as a characterization of the central figure in *Station Island*: "displaced, guilty, assuaging himself by his utterance," which relief, for both Sweeney and his translator, is only momentary, and summoned most fully by the poetry of place and name, of landscape and language. Sweeney's troubled escape—or as we might call it, in terms that will apply to *Station Island*, his estrangement—is complete. Home, family, tribe, even the bodily shape of a man are all gone. In the person of Sweeney, the "creative imagination," which has often seemed in Heaney's poetry to be a kind of betrayal of the human and communal demands of life, can be set loose from "constraints of religious, political, and domestic obligation"—freed, in other words, from exactly those predatory circumstances which are at work in almost all of Heaney's poetry.

But the paradoxical appropriateness of that "escape" is that it represents, for Heaney, a simultaneous *meeting* of obligations. The act of translation represents Heaney's acceptance of a place in the ongoing, almost institutionalized recovery of the "Irish" past that has engaged the effort of writers from Synge and Yeats, through Frank O'Connor and Flann O'Brien, down to Kinsella and Montague; and the beauty of the translation serves as yet another demonstration of the particular richness of Irish poetry. That this recovery and transmission must occur by way of the imperial language might seem ironic, and might even today be politically suspect, if the point is to honor the recalcitrant Celtic temperament. But on the other hand the fact that Heaney can find a way reasonably to English in this poem suggests that there is a way to stop fighting the war of language, to rest more comfortably at last in the role of an Irish poet writing exclusively in English.

The poem serves in personal ways as well. There is a biographical and topographical connection, by way of "a family of tinkers, also called Sweeney, who used to camp in the ditchbacks along the road to the first school I attended"—a family which will return, twice, in *Station Island*. That persistence, into life, of the mythic Sweeney, is indicated by an accident of naming (but to Heaney, correspondences of language are never accidental) and a similarity of migration. It offers yet one more opportunity for Heaney to connect his own life to some indomitable tradition—but in this case one of unattached wandering, not respectable and settled farming. Sweeney is himself a singer of places, a talent for which his mobile life offers particularly rich material, and those places are Heaney's as well, both the North of his childhood and the Wicklow of *Field Work*.

If his account of his own childhood in the prose reminiscence "Mossbawn" is at all accurate, Heaney has long imagined himself as a Sweeney-figure, a wary watcher in the trees. And to that intimately personal web of connections is added an intriguing political possibility. For Sweeney may not be Irish at all, in the end; there is the chance that his tale is in fact "a development of a British original," making Sweeney a citizen of two mythic cultures, assumed usually to be inevitably at war. Counterbalancing the utterly free Sweeney, the untrammelled artist, is a thoroughly rooted Sweeney, and one who offers, Heaney tentatively suggests, a new and potentially useful kind of equilibrium: "Sweeney's easy sense of cultural affinity with both Western Scotland [the ancestral home of Ulster Protestantism] and southern Ireland [may be] exemplary for all men and women in contemporary Ulster."

Having broached that optimistic possibility, Heaney steps back from it, and indeed from the broad claims he has made for the poem, and argues that it "makes its immediate claims more by its local power to affect us than by any general implications we may discover in its pattern." *Local* here bears a nicely double weight, as place-within-the-poem and as place(s)-which-the-poem-names. We might observe that it is Heaney's version of the entire work that seems to need defense; certainly many of the individual lyrics within it will stand as poetry and incantation. But the larger patterns which Heaney both proposes and dismisses are in fact clearly visible in his "version" as a whole; and the tale stands as a representation of a mind in transit from the dislocations of *Field Work* to the meditations of *Station Island*, where Heaney will detach Sweeney from his traditional literary home and unashamedly use him as persona and metaphor. Even the modest prunings which Heaney the scholar acknowledges will not, to the modern eye, make Sweeney's tale a tidy one; his wanderings are circular and repetitious, characters like the mysterious hag appear and disappear, the whole story has two endings, and Sweeney himself, as the story advances, shows a disposition to go back and recapitulate. But the apparently loose threads of the tale cannot obscure the fundamental—to both Sweeney and Heaney—question of trust and responsibility. The word *trust* recurs throughout the poem, but in an oddly negative way, often in conjunction with its cousin *faith*: keeping the (new) faith and living up to (old) trusts are both to be avoided.

Sweeney's battle against the new priestly creed brings upon him a punishment that is both inward and outward; driven from his own kingdom and denied any permanent "natural asylum," he is at the same time "exiled from [him]self." In one sense, he pays the price of his "sin," and the Christian ethos wins out, not altogether convincingly, in the end, when he asks forgiveness (something Sweeney has not seemed to crave before) and wins a kind of sainthood. But through most of the poem, the moral weight is all behind the Celtic, the impious, and the irresponsible. The whole notion of trust (and "trust" was somehow a part of Heaney's anger in "Oysters") is a trap, a means by which Sweeney may be re-attached to human society, at the cost of his ability to sing. Again and again Sweeney's music draws his enemies: soldiers, priests, kinsmen, wife. From such approaches Sweeney must always flee, just as the poem must break away from lyric into prose narration. That flight allows him to sing again, even if all he has to sing about are the cruel winds of winter, as he does some nine times.

The movement of the hero in *Sweeney Astray* may seem, especially to one whose knowledge of Irish geography is sketchy, almost random, although he does return again and again to one adopted home, the edenic Glen Bolcain—a dangerous return, since his fondness for the place is what allows his deceitful kinsman Lynchseachan to find him. The crucial movement, however, is not geographical; and it is orderly, or at least falls into a pattern of movement back-and-forth, toward the human, toward memory, toward old attachments, and then rapidly away, to "freedom." For a bird-man with a hatred for the Church, Sweeney spends an astonishing amount of time near churches; that is in fact where his first flight, to Kilreagan, takes him, to "an old tree by the church," and so too does his last and fatal journey, to St. Mullins in Wicklow. Sweeney's place of refuge is not the open and unpopulated wild, but a tree at the edge, where he—like Heaney himself, as a child—finds a point of concealment and observation.

But the customary entanglements are never far away (Heaney's own tree was in sight both of a shrine of St. Patrick and of an occupying army). In Sweeney's tale, marriage is so sour as to be utterly poisonous. But now the betrayer is not the singer but the spouse: Eorann, Sweeney's wife, who prefers good sense and good manners to the demands of vocation, and who has "broken trust, / unmade it like a bed." Women in general in the poem— as so often in early Irish poetry—are sinister. More often than not they have a concealed net near at hand. But all domesticity is the real snare; however much Sweeney may "dread the cold space of plains," he knows too that his ancestral house is a place where he'll be tied and mocked. So also the "normal" domestic emotions: Lynchseachan's plot, the only snare which captures Sweeney, is based on that deceiver's ability to summon up Sweeney's love of parents, wife, and children.

In the person of Sweeney, then, the tension between art and life is, especially in domestic but also in political terms, played out, but with an absence of the guilt on the part of the singer which forms the substance of earlier poems like "An Afterward." The condition of exile from self, the role of inner émigré, however painful, is clearly necessary here. The rejection of the obligations of kinship, martial virtue, marriage, fatherhood, are vital and productive, even if not altogether voluntary. The figure of Sweeney, and the story his poem tells—not to mention the poetry his story includes— are, then, an elaborate exploration of one answer to the puzzles of "Exposure" and the sense of migratory rootlessness so common in *Field Work*. In Sweeney's estrangement the betrayals outlined in Heaney's verse autobiography since *North* are justified.

But that justification occurs only in a world long-dead and half-mythic; the answers which *Sweeney Astray* provides to Heaney's long argument with himself, and between himself and his element, are only metaphoric, only imagined. To find a way in which the metaphoric Sweeney may be brought "home" to the world of the actual, the world of contemporary Ireland, is, in large measure, the work which *Station Island* undertakes, in the context of an extended reconsideration of all of Heaney's work of the past decade, and indeed to a degree of his work *in toto*.

The book explicitly presents itself as a Dantean venture, a descent into "St. Patrick's Purgatory," the Irish devotional shrine at Lough Dearg. The movement down, spiritually and psychically, is at the same time a movement backwards in time, once again into Heaney's own life and into the history and myth of Ireland. The parallel to the *Divine Comedy* suggests that the descent will not be permanent, the purgatory not (for the poet-hero) a stopping-place but a field of transition, even a route out of Hell. The book's plot—to use a clumsy word term for it—involves not only a trip but a transformation; Heaney himself, the central figure in Parts One and Two, becomes in Part Three a revived Sweeney, now at large in a new, and indeed a modern, world. The Dantean hope of progress is thus complicated by the degree to which that third part of the exploration is, yet again, a return; but the return at least allows, indeed demands, a new vantage point, an adoption by Heaney of Sweeney's wary and perceptive marginality.

The complexities of movement are proposed in the very first poem, "The Underground," which begins as a memory, apparently a happy one, of a moment when Heaney and his wife, "honeymooning, moonlighting," rush up the stairs at a London Tube stop near the Albert Hall. The joy of the memory seems, on first reading, to prompt a kind of learned playfulness. The speaker of the poem manages to see himself, in a short space, as a nameless god and Hansel and Orpheus. But the priapic diety who appears first—"a fleet god gaining / Upon you before you turned to a reed"—is, in his way, rapacious and threatening; his embrace would bring not love but, for the beloved, a loss of all humanity. Thus the beloved's flight is as much away from as alongside the speaker. So too we should recall what a dark story "Hansel and Gretel" is—a tale for children, to be sure, but one which incorporates abandonment, foiled escape, and betrayal. And the final Orphean echo suggests that the beloved is permanently trapped in a nether region, an entrapment caused by the curiosity of an anxious husband.

The poem darkens considerably just about half way along, when the speaker shifts his attention from the marital *then* to the isolated "now." It is at this point that he becomes Hansel, "retracing the path back," only to find not a home (as Hansel hopes to) but a distinctly Eliotic purgatorial place, "a draughty lamplit station / After the trains have gone." There he stands, "bared [or, we might say, once again exposed] and tensed"—but at the same time, and by way of a pun, "all attention." What he awaits is "your step"; but he (or is it she?) would be "damned if I look back."

The topography of the poem has been utterly contorted. At that final moment, to look back would be to look in exactly the direction that was so breathlessly and promisingly forward in the opening stanza: prospect and retrospect are somehow now the same. And the possibility of damnation is all the more cruelly near if we keep in mind the fact that—chronologically— the poet just has looked back, and shortly will again. If hell is the price of such looking, he has already earned it, and his beloved's following footstep might take her there as well.

The whole first part of *Station Island* continues the theme of dangerous but necessary retrospect. Thus Heaney observes a dying man who is himself, apparently in the hope of comfort, re-viewing his home landscape and his past ("Looking Back"). And the poet looks repeatedly not only into his own past (the prevailing tense of these poems is the preterite), but further back still, by way of relics and topography, of imagined recreations of other lives and of mythic creatures. The degree to which he is at the same time looking back at his poetic life can be measured by the ease with which many of these poems place themselves alongside poems in earlier volumes. Thus "A Hazel Stick for Catherine Ann" recalls "The Diviner" in *Death of a Naturalist*; "The Sandpit" echoes so many of his poems of Mossbawn and digging, as well as his tributes to the "ordinary rituals" of work. "Remembering Malibu" repeats the mood and very nearly the location of "Westering" in *Wintering Out* and "The Skunk" in *Field Work*. "An Ulster Twilight" revisits the land of *North* and, in its consideration of sectarian division and the ominous figure of a policeman, particularly recalls "A Constable Calls" in that volume. And finally, "A Bat on the Road" is another of a long string of evocative, precise, and dark animal poems which stretches back to the title piece of *Death of a Naturalist*.

I do not mean to say that this part of *Station Island* is merely repetitous. Just as Heaney presumes, correctly, that his "glosses" on Sweeney in Part Three can stand apart from *Sweeney Astray*, so too these poems work individually without the burdens of their bibliographic past. In some cases Heaney is clearly revising—"An Ulster Twilight" moves carefully toward a *rapprochement* with at least one Ulster Protestant, and thus is in a way an answer to earlier poems like "Docker" or "Protestant Drums, Tyrone, 1966." There is often something reassuring in the echoes one hears in these poems. For Heaney, relics still function (and will continue to do so in Parts Two and

Three) as points of reference and as the focus of what Thoreau called "insight and far-sight." So too will attachments to friends and fellow writers and family, and the erotics of marriage and language. Heaney seems in these poems particularly to be searching for stability. He finds it more often in things than in people—sloes are "bitter / and dependable" (perhaps, in fact, dependable because bitter), a gourd is "reliably dense." But then too ghosts can be "reliable," as they are for Hardy. More clearly than ever, what stability there is can be found in small, repeated, painstaking acts of work and survival—wood-working, for instance, or ironing.

These points of anchorage stand out all the more clearly in a world of transition, which he calls at one point a "miasma of spilled blood." There, freedom is to be craved, no matter how hard it is to find and to sustain a "free state of image and illusion," no matter how much freedom (which is almost always a freedom of *movement*) may seem, as Heaney imagines it is for Chekhov, a "burden." Movement at least brings one into contact with an imaginative landscape in which "the deer of poetry" may not, for once, "scare." Heaney feels drawn two ways, attracted and repelled, encountering again and again "dream fears I inclined towards"; he addresses loving poems to his family but admires as well "a migrant solitude." He says, in apparent exasperation, "I still cannot clear my head / of lives in their element"—but the element is his as well as theirs. What is to be longed for, it seems, is persistence. Thus the migratory Brigid holds together her family on a voyage of exile that parallels Heaney's own, from the North to Wicklow ("A Migration"); thus Hardy stubbornly makes of his ghosts a body of work that can overcome speechlessness and "resist" the too-easy appeal of "the words of coming to rest" ("The Birthplace"); thus Chekhov on Sakhalin is, however hesitantly, at the threshold of work that is both socially useful (his monograph on convict life will prompt penal reform) and artistically great.

The woman whom Heaney recalls ironing embodies what he hopes for—she is at the same moment "dragged upon. And buoyant." So too is the self which Heaney at times achieves, most centrally in "Making Strange"—a self who can be a reliable guide because he can find a viable place of estrangement, especially in language, a place where he can be "adept and dialect" and communicative. But the final shape this figure takes is that of Sweeney, "The King of the Ditchbacks," who follows the Scriptural advice and abandons his riches to become a trespasser. As Part One closes, Heaney sees himself first in "the limbo of lost words," then stripped down and adopting a protective "dissimulation." At that point he is ready for the penitential encounters of Part Two.

The central poem-sequence "Station Island" is, in one sense, a long, ritualized self-accusation, a mortification of the artistic flesh, but it is also a vehicle by which Heaney controls and confronts his ghosts, and thus defines more particularly the heritage he wants to take on, which is not necessarily the one which his culture and upbringing, not to mention his adult experience as a poet, would apply to him. One of the many artifices of this sequence is to grant to the visiting ghosts most of the powerful lines. The poet himself seems to speak little, just as in the *Divine Comedy* the character Dante seems almost preternaturally (for a poet) silent and slow to learn.

The technical mastery of the poems is particularly important, because it allows Heaney implicitly to defend poetry of a highly crafted kind even while he hears (and allows us to hear) it being questioned. The homage to Dante which is apparent in the premise of the sequence is explicitly rebuked by McCartney, who accuses Heaney of having "whitewashed ugliness" by employing "the lovely blinds of the *Purgatorio*"; but it is supported both by translation (in poem VI) and by the frequent use of a supple English *terza rima*. McCartney's rebuke in poem VIII is itself, ironically, couched in a careful variation of the *ottava rima* stanza. The sequence as a whole is in fact very close to what Heaney says *Sweeney Astray* is, in the original—"a primer of lyric genres." The particular forms are recognizably Heaney's—stanzaic free verse in poem I, rhymed quatrains in poems III and X, blank verse in much of poem VIII, sonnets in poems VI and IX.

Against that array of what Heaney has in his essays called discipline, there is an increasing power of feeling in the first nine poems, moving to a "bottom" of self-doubt and self-loathing in poem IX. Each of the ghosts to that point has contributed to the descent, as have the two poems (III and VI) where Heaney confronts not shades but the memories of his own life. The various visitors recapitulate the guises apparently available to Heaney himself: the migratory tinker Simon Sweeney, an illiterate man of place and movement; the folklorist and "turncoat" Carleton, who insists on the virtue of memory; the young priest who has tried to carry an Irish faith into foreign parts; schoolmasters, who invoke as well the poet Kavanagh; an archaeocological bog-digger, a sectarian activist hunger-striker, and several sectarian victims. The ghosts raise again old questions of obligation and silence, rebuke the ignorance which remains in Heaney, despite his learning, and demand that he wonder whether any change is possible. And they propose renunciation, suggesting the curative effects of a "last look" at Catholic Ireland. But they also ask to what place Heaney might flee, as if in answer to the young priest's charge in poem IV, that Heaney's visit to Lough Deargh is false in the extreme.

The accusation which marks the crisis is McCartney's—the charge that Heaney's apparent effort (in particular, in "The Strand at Lough Beg") to fulfill, poetically, his obligations to home, family, and tribe, has actually been an avoidance. That calls into question all the rich bulk of elegiac record in Heaney's poems, and it is directly after that that Heaney touches bottom— and begins to rise. But in a sense Heaney has already defended himself— has, in a new way, kept his eye on the facts, while still making music—in poem IV, which gives speech to the bloody victim of a night-killing. In that poem Heaney's attention is not on the poet's response but on the victim himself, and not on the life but on the death. For the first time, I think, in Heaney's long career as an elegist, the poem ignores the metaphoric healing to be sought in a placing of a life in its element, in order to keep its eye and ear on the direct and painful account of the ugly, deforming wound. Certainly there is no whitewashing. And interestingly, the particular party—if any—of which the victim is a member, is not a part of the record. We may presume the man is Catholic but we are not told so; he is no more and no less than an individual being wakened in the night to be shot for no explicit reason. That is, I think, the furthest Heaney has yet gone in making poetry (and in form, it is Dantean poetry) of the omnivorous modern world. In so doing he has finally been true to the dictum, borrowed from Willa Cather, which had been offered to him as long ago as 1962: "Description is revelation!"

Heaney's way back up is both a movement forward and a circling back. The vehicles of restoration are, not surprisingly, relics: an old brass trumpet in poem IX, a mug in poem X. And the penance is an abandonment, briefly, of his own voice, by way of a translation from John of the Cross in poem X. Having fulfilled the ritual, in poem XII he meets—now on the ground of the real world, a tarmacked car-park—one last tutelary figure: Joyce. The ghost is a relatively new one for Heaney, who in his essays, for instance, has focused his attention, understandably, on Hopkins, Wordsworth, Yeats, and Kavanagh. Joyce urges (rather deceptively, given the retrospect in his own works) not memory but forgetfulness, and more importantly, independence and an abandonment of the formulae of Irish poetic / political rhetoric—a message which recovers the wisdom offered at the beginning of the sequence by tinker Sweeney: "Stay clear of all processions."

Joyce is in fact a kind of literary Sweeney, a polymathic, highly schooled, and yet thoroughly grounded king of the ditchbacks, whose physical distance from his home sharpened, rather than obscured, his view both of the fact and the whole. Heaney, by having Joyce speak in Dante's *terza rima*, conjoins those two masters—two more schoolmasters, really. And both can serve as exemplars of a new stance in relation to the historical situation. We should recall that Dante—as Heaney himself remarks in *Preoccupations*— was immersed in, and indeed plagued and exiled by, the political conflicts of his own time, and as well a poet who had moved through the more "personal" utterance of the *Vita Nuova* to the vision of the *Divine Comedy*. Similarly, Joyce may be said to have progressed from the autobiographical (in *Stephen Hero* and *Portrait*) into something more objective. And just as Sweeney takes to his tree in part to have an unobstructed view, Dante and Joyce both made of their exile the opportunity to record—and to transform— the minutiae of an historical moment. By a similar kind of straying Heaney may hope at last and less painfully to see and to say something more than nothing.

*Station Island* explicitly moves, in Part Three, to Sweeney—but only to Sweeney's voice. In other words, it is a shift of perspective and speech rather than of material, since the substance of the "Sweeney Redivivus" poems remains recognizably the material of Heaney's life: one more climb up the childhood tree ("In the Beech"), the recognition of the "murders and miscarriages" of Irish life ("The First Kingdom"), of the pressures of life amid the "spiteful vigilance of colonies" ("Drifting Off"), of the hand of clerics and schoolmasters with their seductive weapons of language ("The Cleric," "The Masters," "In Illo Tempore"). What Sweeney's voice empowers Heaney to do is to articulate most directly his answer and his rejection of the self, of trust and obedience ("Alerted"), in favor of a figure which is made explicit in "The Artist," where the virtues are "anger," "obstinacy," "coercion / of the substance from green apples," a "hatred of his own embrace," and finally "fortitude." The estrangement laid out in these poems is not, however, complete; Sweeney's flights are balanced by "Sweeney's Returns," and the richness of landscape remains, as in "Holly," a powerful rooting, as do the relics of the past ("The Old Icons"). But now at least those elements of betrayal so worrisome earlier are to be praised as "dear-bought treacheries grown transparent now, and estimable."

In the book's final poem, "On the Road," Heaney, in Sweeney's voice, offers one (temporarily) last assessment of things as they are. He is once more (or should we say, still?) in motion, but no longer so concerned with arrival, since "all roads [are] one." Shades still visit him, but now the question (a Biblical one: "What must I / do to be saved?") has an answer ("Sell all you have"). He recalls one more ascent, made as a child climbing a chapel roof, protectively, we suspect, outside the sanctuary itself; that is the way of "scaling heaven." But it is also, when it needs to be, a route of return. The latter part of the poem shifts to the future and the conditional; "would" is now the ground-note. Heaney has long returned, roosted, migrated, mediated, but not by way of a verb-form that carries with it so much force of choice, intention, and control. There is now a road yet to be travelled, not just a road back; what is at hand is now "a book of changes."

It would be presumptuous in the extreme to predict where Heaney / Sweeney will go next. But at the least this final poem answers "Exposure" by proffering a way out of the limits of self-consciousness. The old powers will not be abandoned, but the poet is now abroad in a slightly more hopeful landscape, one which is outside the self and in which the "deer of poetry" is no longer "dumbfounded," no longer stricken by silence, but ready to break cover into a new life.

The song of the self has, for more than a decade, been a richly productive terrain for Heaney. Yet it is one that it may be he has at last exhausted (I do not mean the word judgmentally). All along, aware that, as he puts it in *Preoccupations*, "poetry is secret and natural, [but] it must make its way in a world that is public and brutal," to the work of healing the self Heaney has added the task of healing the community, of encompassing fully and directly a culture which seems, especially to those outside of it, incurably riven, eccentric, even mad. But attention to the nightly news prompts the reflection that Ireland may, in its contour if not its details, be truly "normal" and representative. Whatever shifts in vantage point he may have undertaken, it is hard to imagine that Heaney has yet finished with the question of how to live, as individual and poet—how to live *usefully*, in a torn and contentious world of exposure, exile, murderously politicized speech, and irreconcilable obligation.

# Seamus Heaney's New Voice in *Station Island*

ALASDAIR MACRAE*

In the opening paragraph of his lecture "The Three Voices of Poetry," delivered in 1953, T. S. Eliot explains the meaning of his title:

> The first voice is the voice of the poet talking to himself—or to nobody. The second is the voice of the poet addressing an audience, whether large or small. The third is the voice of the poet when he attempts to create a dramatic character speaking in verse; when he is saying, not what he would say in his own person, but only what he can say within the limits of one imaginary character addressing another imaginary character. The distinction between the first and second voice, between the poet speaking to himself and the poet speaking to other people, points to the problem of poetic communication; the distinction between the poetic communication; the distinction between the poet addressing other people in either his own voice or an assumed voice, and the poet inventing speech in which imaginary characters address each other, points to the problem of the difference between dramatic, quasi-dramatic, and non-dramatic verse.[1]

Later in the lecture, he declares that he does not see these voices as "mutually exclusive"; "for me the voices are most often found together—the first and second, I mean, in non-dramatic poetry; and together with the third in dramatic poetry."[2]

Eliot's discussion engages with basic questions concerning a poet's relationship not just with a potential audience but also with the society of which he is a member. In Western literature such questions were first articulated by Plato in his consideration of the role of the poet in his Republic. Shelley, in *A Defence of Poetry*, which was, of course, a defence of poetry as a force for morality, offers the most celebrated formulation of Eliot's first voice: "A poet is a nightingale, who sits in darkness and sings to cheer its own solitude with sweet sounds; his auditors are as men entranced by the melody of an unseen musician, who feel that they are moved and softened, yet know not whence or why."[3] Yet Shelley did not consider the poet as cocooned from his society nor did he see poetry as a private, impotent indulgence. He

*Reprinted from *Irish Writers and Society at Large*, ed. Masaru Sekine (Buckinghamshire: Gerrards Cross, Colin Smythe Ltd, 1985), 122–37.

himself wrote poems of solid political commitment and he propounded the highest claims for the influence of poetry: "Poets are the hierophants of an unapprehended inspiration; the mirrors of the gigantic shadows which futurity casts upon the present; the words which express what they understand not; the trumpets which sing to battle and feel not what they inspire; the influence which is moved out, but moves. Poets are the unacknowledged legislators of the world."[4] Certainly, over the past two centuries, the relation of a poet to his society has become a vexed problem. In earlier bardic societies and societies where the poet was a member of the court, his position was established by tradition and he wrote in a manner appropriate to that position; in modern European societies no such position exists. The problem for the modern poet is not lessened if he belongs to a smaller country: the pressures of loyalty, expectation and censure are stronger in a smaller community where there is no escape afforded in the anonymity of a cosmopolitan metropolis.

It is unnecessary here to rehearse the bickerings and bitternesses of Irish intellectual life or to call a roll of the literary wild geese who have fled the island of their birth on every tide. In Seamus Heaney's case, since the publication of his first book, *Death of a Naturalist*, in 1966, he has had constant and contradictory advice and admonishments from critics eager that he should write of Ireland in accordance with their views of the situation. In an introductory note to his fourth collection, *North*, in 1975, Heaney wrote: "During the last few years there has been considerable expectation that poets from Northern Ireland should 'say' something about the 'situation,' but in the end they will only be worth listening to if they are saying something about and to themselves."[5] By and large, in the first five collections, he seemed to work according to his own counsel and ranged himself with Shelley's nightingales who sing in Eliot's first voice. Looking back through these earlier volumes, the reader finds few examples of poems in Eliot's second and third voices. It is particularly rare for Heaney to address an audience directly; possibly the only case is in *An Open Letter* (Field Day, Derry, 1983). Instances of dramatic poems, poems delivered through devised voices, would include: "For the Commander of the 'Eliza' " in *Death of a Naturalist*; "Requiem for the Croppies," "Undine," "The Wife's Tale," and "Mother" in *Door into the Dark*; "A Northern Hoard" (possibly) and "Shore Woman" in *Wintering Out*; "Antaeus," "The Digging Skeleton" (after Baudelaire), "Bog Queen" and "Freedman" in *North*; and "Ugolino" (translated from Dante) in *Field Work*. These do not constitute a large proportion of his work and it could be argued, therefore, that neither Heaney's interest nor his talent lie in the dramatic mode. On the other hand, it could be suggested that his attempt to re-enact imaginatively the lives of the bog people, mainly in *North*, demonstrates an eagerness to construct characters. In *Field Work*, however, which followed *North* there are no poems using a dramatic persona, with the doubtful exception of "Ugolino," Dante's creation.

Thus, with this view of Heaney as a rather undramatic poet firmly in our minds, we look at his new work with considerable surprise. In Britain, his two new books, *Station Island* and *Sweeney Astray*, have been published simultaneously. (*Sweeney Astray*, a translation from the medieval Irish *Buile Suibhne*, was first published in Ireland in 1983 by Field Day). The remainder of this essay will focus on *Station Island* but some comments are called for on *Sweeney Astray* even if only by way of introduction to the new collection.

What attracted Heaney to Sweeney? In the introduction to his translation, he suggests that the primary connection was "topographical": the seventh century Sweeney had inhabited the area close to where Heaney spent the first thirty years of his life. He offers, however, some further reflections on the story of Sweeney and its relevance to contemporary readers, particularly in Ireland. After emphasising that Sweeney was an historically based character, he further explores the figure and situation of the poem:

> The literary imagination which fastened upon him as an image was clearly in the grip of a tension between the newly dominant Christian ethos and the older, recalcitrant Celtic temperament. The opening sections which recount the collision between the peremptory ecclesiastic and the sacred king, and the closing pages of uneasy reconciliation set in St. Moling's monastery, are the most explicit treatment of this recurrent theme. This alone makes the work a significant one, but it does not exhaust its significance. For example, insofar as Sweeney is also a figure of the artist, displaced, guilty, assuaging himself by his utterance, it is possible to read the work as an aspect of the quarrel between free creative imagination and the constraints of religious, political and domestic obligation. It is equally possible, in a more opportunistic spirit, to dwell upon Sweeney's easy sense of cultural affinity with both western Scotland and southern Ireland as exemplary for all men and women in contemporary Ulster, or to ponder the thought that this Irish invention may well have been a development of a British original, vestigially present in the tale of the madman called Alan
>
> (Sections 46–50).

With certain obvious adjustments, Heaney's identification with Sweeney is clear and provocative. Does he really, even if in an "opportunistic spirit," entertain a vision of a new Goidelic federation as a solution to the problems of Northern Ireland? Of course, what is most telling in relation to this essay, is how Heaney sees Sweeney as a *poète maudit* and is able to feel with and through him. The king cursed to live as a wild bird, Sweeney as an exile in his own kingdom, the wordsmith condemned to speak only to himself—these are powerful, dramatic images.

A reading of *Sweeney Astray* as a preliminary to *Station Island* is extremely useful, possibly even necessary. *Station Island* consists of three parts: Part One (untitled); Part Two: "Station Island"; Part Three: "Sweeney Redivivus." In his note to Part Three, the poet says "The poems in this section are voiced for Sweeney . . . Many of them, of course, are imagined in contexts far removed from early medieval Ireland." "Voiced for Sweeney" is an odd phrase, symptomatic of some ambivalence in his conception of the persona; and this ambivalence is further exposed in the second half of his comment. Some of the poems in this section are rather opaque even when the reader has the advantage of knowing what Heaney trusts is unnecessary, "the support system of the original story." Most of the newspaper reviewers passed over this section as if they felt unconfident as to how to handle it, and, yet, it is so noticeably meshed and cross-referenced with the other two sections that a just consideration of the whole volume has to give due attention to these poems "voiced for Sweeney." For example, the note to "The King of the Ditchbacks," the final poem of Part One, refers the reader to the author's note on Part Three and the poem has a fuller meaning when the reader is able to run together Sweeney, the tinker from the ditchbacks, and King Sweeney. The opening poem of "Station Island" also concerns Simon Sweeney, the tinker outcast, and, making him the first familiar ghost on the island, creates a bridge across the whole collection and, more particularly, between the personal world of Heaney's childhood and the less personal persona of the Sweeney figure adopted by Heaney as an adult. In "The King of the Ditchbacks," he remembers how the tinkers had contrived his camouflage:

> they dressed my head in a fishnet
> and plaited leafy twigs through meshes
>
> so my vision was a bird's
> at the heart of a thicket
>
> and I spoke as I moved
> like a voice from a shaking bush.

Simon Sweeney, whom the young Heaney had willed himself to become, speaks as a ghost to the pilgrim poet: "I was your mystery man / and am again this morning." Later, when Heaney writes as the bird-man in "Sweeney Redivivus," he confesses with surprise: "And there I was, incredible to myself, / among people far too eager to believe me / and my story, even if it happened to be true." To say that the disguise has become complete and successful is not accurate; the poet has become aware that the Sweeney character, is an aspect of himself, an aspect that has struggled to emerge for a long time, but, up till now, had not discovered a mode of expression. The title of the sequence "Sweeney Redivivus," contains this sense of uncovering what was there.

It may be that as the bird-man, Sweeney-Heaney has found a way to fly free from a locale that was in danger of becoming poetically restrictive, a way to enlarge his territory. "The Cleric" concludes with Sweeney conceding victory to St. Roman but also finding recompense:

> History that planted its standards
> on his gables and spires
> ousted me to the marches
>
> of skulking and whingeing.
> Or did I desert?
> Give him his due, in the end
>
> he opened my path to a kingdom
> of such scope and neuter allegiance
> my emptiness reigns at its whim.

Some critics are apprehensive lest Heaney should desert the quarry from which he has sculpted so many marvellous poems but, in *Station Island*, he demonstrates that his hand has not lost its cunning to continue and develop that skill. There is manifested in the volume, however, a new, acute awareness of dangers, tensions, questions in writing the kind of poems he has. In essays, lectures and interviews he has explored notions of poetic development; it would be strange if such enquiries did not enter into his poems. Two of his declared masters, Wordsworth and Yeats, present him with very different examples of how poets may or may not survive middle age. Although he wrote some wonderful dramatic poems in *Lyrical Ballads*, Wordsworth did not develop this mode and his apologetic comment on *The Prelude* that, "it was a thing unprecedented in literary history that a man should talk so much about himself," acknowledges the narrowness, the exhaustibility, of the vein of the child's development into artistic manhood, what theorists of the novel call *Künstlerroman*. Yeats's theory of Masks and of Primary and Antithetical gyres has clear implications for his poetry, a development of dramatic poetry with voices devised appropriate to the particular Mask. Wordsworth stagnated as a poet; Yeats enjoyed amazing aggrandisement in the second half of his career.

In *Station Island*, is it significant that the title of the final poem is "On the Road"? Interspersed in the images of travelling, exile, migration, exploration are the question and answer from St. Matthew's Gospel: "Master, what must I do to be saved? Sell all you have and give to the poor. And follow me." Sweeney has been reduced to the most abject poverty and, in the end, dies as a Christian (according to *Sweeney Astray*). In Heaney's case, are the question and instruction to be interpreted in religious terms or in artistic terms? If the whole collection has been read in order, the reader comes on this interpretative problem with some preparation provided by pointers in the final poems of Parts One and Two. "The King of the

Ditchbacks" ends with a masked Heaney, "a rich young man / leaving everything he had / for a migrant solitude." James Joyce, the ultimate ghost and adviser to confront Heaney on his pilgrimage, reprimands him and then directs him:

> "You are raking at dead fires,
>
> a waste of time for somebody your age.
> That subject people stuff is a cod's game,
> infantile, like your peasant pilgrimage.
>
> *You lose more of yourself than you redeem*
> *doing the decent thing.* Keep at a tangent.
> When they make the circle wide, it's time to swim
>
> out on your own and fill the element
> with signatures on your own frequency,
> echo soundings, searches, problems, allurements,
>
> elver-gleams in the dark of the whole sea."
> [my italics]

Again, it can be seen how the collection works as a whole, with poems commenting on each other, reinforcing or challenging propositions offered in individual poems and creating a sense of debate or dramatic dialogue.

If a change in the ground of his poetry is being intimated, Heaney is keenly aware of the difficulties involved in such a manoeuvre. He reconstructs in "Chekhov on Sakhalin" the experience of the Russian writer travelling to the convict island of Sakhalin off the Pacific coast in 1890 and examines whether Chekhov found release in his venture. Himself the grandson of a serf, Chekhov is confused between images of freedom and images of bondage. The ringing sound of his smashed cognac glass blurs into the rattle of the convicts' chains; he, a free observer, is burdened with his very freedom when confronted with the sufferings in the prison island. The luxury of the cognac, the luxury as a writer, "To try for the right tone—not tract, not thesis—/ And walk away from floggings," these luxuries cannot be afforded by his conscience. Against the therapeutic ambition of writing the inherited ailment may prove too tenacious: "He who had thought to squeeze / His slave's blood out and waken the free man / Shadowed a convict guide through Sakhalin."

Something of the dilemma presented through the figure of Chekhov is reproduced in Heaney's own person in the following poem, "Sandstone Keepsake," where as a casual stroller on a beach in the Irish Republic he faces across to the Detention Camp at Magilligan in Northern Ireland. The poem opens casually with a typically scrupulous description of a stone picked up on the beach. Equally casually, it seems, the perimeter lights of the camp across the water come on. A literary memory in the form of a question is suggested by the wet reddishness of the stone: "A stone from Phlegethon, / bloodied on the bed of hell's hot river?" and Heaney muses on the story in Dante of Guy de Montfort consigned to suffer in the Phlegethon for his murder of Prince Henry of England in 1270. The poem has shifted from the casual to a serious tone. Although Heaney apologises for his extravagant allusion, "but not really . . . Anyhow," the simple stone has become a venerated heart and we remember that the Phlegethon is a river of boiling blood in Dante's *Inferno* where those who committed acts of violence against their neighbours are condemned to suffer. In the final two stanzas, the casual tone appears to be restored with a pun on "free state" and the poet identified as, "a silhouette not worth bothering about, / out for the evening in scarf and waders." There is, however, an excessiveness in his final description of himself as, "one of the venerators," which sends ripples back across the poem to Prince Henry's heart, "long venerated" and alerts the reader to a quiet irony exerted by Heaney against his position as a passive observer in his "free state of image and allusion."

In "Away from it All," he speaks of how quotations come to the mind "like rehearsed alibis" and he quotes from Czeslaw Milosz, the exiled Polish writer:

> I was stretched between contemplation
> of a motionless point
> and the command to participate
> actively in history

The questions raised in some of the poems in Part One regarding the poet's relation to events and an audience provide an introduction to the concerns of the middle part of the collection, the sequence called "Station Island." One of the most dramatic encounters in the sequence occurs in the second half of section VIII where Heaney is confronted by his cousin, Colum McCartney, for whom he had written an elegy in *Field Work*, "The Strand at Lough Beg." The elegy uses some of the features of a traditional pastoral elegy; Heaney imagines that, after his cousin has been the victim of a random sectarian murder, he leads him to the shore of their native Lough Beg where he cleans his wounds with moss and dew before laying him out. Colum now appears to Seamus Heaney and accuses him of having failed to fulfil his obligations of kinship and of having romanticised his death in the elegy:

> "You confused evasion and artistic tact. The
> Protestant who shot me through the head I accuse
> directly, but indirectly, you who now atone perhaps
> upon this bed for the way you whitewashed ugliness and

> drew the lovely blinds of the *Purgatorio* and
> saccharined my death with morning dew."

Of course, self-rebuke is not new to Heaney. "An Afterwards" in *Field Work* sees all poets condemned by his wife to the ninth circle of hell for backbiting. She makes some allowance for him: " 'You weren't the worst. You aspired to a kind, / Indifferent, faults-on-both-sides tact.' " Earlier, in "Punishment" in *North*, Heaney accuses himself of being "the artful voyeur . . . who would connive in civilised outrage." It could be argued that he is being poetically indulgent not just with death but also with his guilt, that the measured, rhymed metres, albeit in the mouth of his cousin, ensure that guilt is rendered palatable. It is at this point that the scheme of the poem (and beyond the central poem, the scheme of the collection) may help to rescue the poet from such an accusation.

The conception of "Station Island" is based on the traditions of the pilgrimage to Station Island (or St. Patrick's Pilgrimage) in Lough Derg, County Donegal. Heaney, who went on the pilgrimage three times as a schoolboy, explains the nature of the penitential ritual in his note to the poem. As a result of the communal religious atmosphere, the fasting, the lack of sleep, the repetitions of prayers, confessions, renunciations, circuits of the "beds," it is highly probably that pilgrims will enter a strange usually unvisited zone of awareness where hallucination is indistinguishable from actuality. Heaney exploits this foundation as MacDiarmid used a different foundation in his long, free-ranging poem *A Drunk Man Looks at a Thistle*. It allows him to range beyond his personal history and have imaginary conversations with any figures who have impressed themselves in his consciousness although he rations himself to those who can reasonably be connected with the purpose of his pilgrimage. He is intent on establishing where he has come to in the middle of his life and to sift the emotional and spiritual and artistic accretions to ascertain what should be jettisoned.

The process of self-examination is conducted in a serious manner but his interlocutors are not chosen for any glibly reverential attitude. The sequence opens with Simon Sweeney, "an old Sabbath-breaker," whose first words are " 'Damn all you know' " and whose parting shout of advice is, " 'Stay clear of all processions!' " At the far end of the vigil, James Joyce turns on Heaney irascibly:

> "You are fasted now, light-headed, dangerous.
> Take off from here. And don't be so earnest,
>
> Let others wear the sackcloth and the ashes.
> Let go, let fly, forget.
> You've listened long enough. Now strike your note."

William Carleton, the author of "The Lough Derg Pilgrim," a caustic story about the pilgrimage, and a convert from Catholicism, is appalled to learn that the poet is on his way to the island and explodes: " 'O holy Jesus Christ, does nothing change?' " Patrick Kavanagh makes a brief appearance and announces that in his time, " 'the odd one came here on the hunt for women.' " In section VII, a shopkeeper relates how he was killed in the middle of the night by " 'shites thinking they were the be-all and the end-all' "; when, after hearing the man's account, Heaney embarrassedly blurts: " 'Forgive the way I have lived indifferent—/ forgive my timid circumspect involvement' " the shopkeeper interrupts: " 'Forgive / my eye,' he said, 'all that's above my head.' " Some reviewers have complained that Heaney himself sounds sometimes ponderous, sometimes unsure of himself, sometimes taking more than what they see as a fair share of the conversation. None of these behaviours seems particularly surprising if the oddity of the situation is borne in mind. If Heaney had presented himself as confident, balanced, sure of his stance, the emotional and spiritual core of the sequence would have been uninteresting and dramatically unviable: it is Heaney's pilgrimage, embarked on precisely because of an unsureness about his stance.

Not all the sections of the sequence consist of conversations with characters. Some are communings with aspects of his self, areas of memory, vulnerable points in his psyche. In his comments . . . on the origins of the poem, *Buile Siubhne*, he sees the seventh century Sweeney as marking the breaking-point or overlap between the old Celtic and the new Christian dispensations. These dispensations are not tidily limited to religious doctrines but include hierarchies of power and obedience, ownership of land, concepts of social order and justice, attitudes to the natural world. In his earlier volumes, Heaney has shown a special interest in old orders giving way to new; people, implements, trades, language becoming redundant. In the twentieth century, organised Christianity in many part of Europe has been atrophied by secular thought and, in Ireland, the authority of the Catholic Church has certainly slackened. Language is often slower to change than ideologies and secular ideas are presented and discussed in a diction with a strong religious flavour. In *Station Island* it is difficult to gauge how vexed Heaney is by religious scruples; what is evident is that the language of the collection has powerful residual elements of a faith that seems open to serious challenge. Having chosen the device of the penitential vigil, it would be impossible to avoid all language associated with such religious exercises and, anyway: "When you are tired or terrified your voice slips / back into its old first place and makes the sound your / shades make there." As this quotation from "The Loaning" makes clear, Heaney is aware of a residual strain in his language and the poem is partly an exploration of this strain in his mind:

> And I knew
> I was in the limbo of lost words.

> They had flown there from raftered sheds and crossroads,
> from the shelter of gable ends and turned-up carts . . .
> Then I knew why from the beginning
> the loaning breathed on me

The word "loaning" itself is probably in a limbo for most English speakers. He coaxes a number of words out of their customary limbo, words such as: "japped," "mirled," "slub," "flensed," "welted," "tines," "soft-deckled" and "scrabs." The sequence of "Station Island" is much concerned with what he calls in section III, "habit's afterlife," but Heaney has memories and ghosts which do not allow him to luxuriate in such a condition. When he tries to impress on Carleton how similar their backgrounds have been, the novelist butts in impatiently: " 'I know, I know, I know, I know,' he said, / 'but you have to try to make sense of what comes.' " Even where the figure who appears seems, as in section IV, to represent the traditional dedication to the faith, this illusion is quickly dispelled. Heaney has set the scene carefully: he is in the penitential position, about to say the words "I renounce the world, the flesh and the devil"; he is aware of photographs of "newly ordained faces," he hears " 'Father' pronounced with a fawning relish," the young priest, his school friend, is immaculate, "glossy as a blackbird." The missionary priest had trained obediently, "doomed to the decent thing." When he tells his story, however, it is a confession of failure and disenchantment, his faith broken by the life in the jungle. Heaney acuses him of having, in his student days, protected the people's spurious religiosity and helped them to ignore the facts around them: " 'You gave too much relief, you raised a siege / the world had laid against their kitchen grottoes / hung with holy pictures and crucifixes.' " In retaliation, the priest demands to know what the poet is doing at Lough Derg: " 'But all this you were clear of you walked into over / again. And the god has, as they say, withdrawn. / / What are you doing, going through these motions?' " The section ends on a muted note but the final word "visiting" has a chiding sharpness because it connects Heaney with the empty "Visiting neighbours" of which he had accused the young priest. The priest's earlier self-defence, "I at least was young and unaware / that what I thought was chosen was convention," operates against Heaney as he presents himself in the poem because he may not yet be able to distinguish between what he thinks is his choice and what is merely his tradition, spiritually and artistically.

Likewise the joys and fulfilments experienced in "Station Island" owe little to religious enlightenment or divine intervention. Section XI opens with an image Heaney had tried out before in his group of prose poems, *Stations* (Ulsterman Publications, Belfast, 1975): a child's kaleidoscope was plunged into muddy water and emerged brilliant but spoiled. A monk confessor urges him: "re-envisage / the zenith and glimpsed jewels of any gift / mistakenly abased." Is Heaney thinking of his gifts as a poet and that he has misused them? He is instructed by the monk to "read poems as prayers" and, as a penance, to translate something by Juan de la Cruz. The piece he translates develops his own opening image and contrasts the pure, eternal and hidden fountain with the dark night in which we live. There is no comment offered on the Spanish poem and again Heaney has resorted to a voice not necessarily indentifiable with himself. Furthermore, the translated poem, as is common with Juan de la Cruz, proffers images which are free of doctrine and can be interpreted in a non-religious way. The other instance of pleasure in the sequence occurs in section VI and seems categorically unreligious. He remembers the slow arrival of sexual satisfaction and while he plays back the tape of his memory he resists the penitential demands of the island: "I shut my ears to the bell." The "beds of Saint Patrick's Purgatory" are overlaid in his mind with idyllic images of Horace's Sabine farm. In contrast to the "breathed-on grille of the confessional" was the revelation of the body of his loved one and "I inhaled the land of kindness."

As Heaney returns to the mainland, sensing "an alien comfort as I stepped on ground," he meets Joyce and, in answer to what the reader as well as the poet has in his mind to ask, he pronounces:

> "Your obligation
> is not discharged by any common rite.
> What you must do must be done on your own
>
> so get back in harness. The main thing is to write
> for the joy of it. Cultivate a work-lust
> that imagines its haven like your hands at night
>
> dreaming the sun in the sunspot of a breast."

If Heaney accepts the advice, and, of course, it is he who, in a sense has offered it, has the penitential vigil been a waste of time? A "work-lust" implies poetry and sexuality, not religious observance, and "haven" sounds dangerously like a secularised heaven.

The scheme of the sequence allows Heaney to investigate from different angles questions of concern to him. Although, because the ground plan of the poem is founded on a religious ritual, the terms of the investigation are religious, the poem is not narrowly or even primarily religious. Because he has found a device in which so many voices can be accommodated, Heaney is freed from attempts to pin him down to one consistent, stable stance. He begins the sequence with questions; he does not conclude with solutions. The Sweeney poems which follow the sequence may be seen to act out Joyce's instruction but to insist that they do is to curtail the freedom Heaney hopes to find.

"Station Island" has dark, troubled areas and if the sequence stood on its own there would be a chilly quality undispelled at the end. Powerful images remain sour in the reader's mind:

> A cold draught blew under the kneeling boards.
> I thought of walking round
> and round a space utterly empty,
> utterly a source, like the idea of sound;
> like an absence stationed in the swamp-fed air
> above a ring of walked-down grass and rushes
> where we once found the bad carcass and scrags of hair
> of our dog that had disappeared weeks before.

These final stanzas of section III anticipate and answer his cousin's accusation in section VIII. The sequence, however, does not stand on its own but is encountered after some wonderful, warm lyrics in Part One.

In "The Birthplace" Heaney describes a visit to the house of Thomas Hardy. The poem switches about in time, reconstructing Hardy from his furnishings, remembering reading Hardy thirty years before, and recalling the day of the visit and a sexual episode intricately connected with Hardy and his house. Through the shifts from descriptive to private to meditative runs an attempt to re-enact in Hardy's birthplace what Hardy stood for in Heaney's mind. In the end he has a success, in that, "I heard / roosters and dogs, the very same / as if he had written them." We are reminded of Coleridge's memorable comments on Shakespeare's persuasive power, where the reader becomes a co-creator with the poet: "If I should not speak it, I feel that I should be thinking it; the voice only is the poet's, the words are my own."[6] Heaney has that power to draw the reader by the justness of his language into a collaborative activity where the reader's recognition is so total that he feels that he must have written the poem himself. In the poems of childhood awareness and poems commemorating objects with introjective acuteness Heaney has few contemporary peers. That ability to partake in himself of the character of an object or a creature or a place, to animate without distortion, to perceive without imposition, is a rare artistic tact. "A Kite for Michael and Christopher" has:

> But now it was far up like a small black lark
> and now it dragged as if the bellied string
> were a wet rope hauled upon
> to lift a shoal.

Such animations are not unrelated to a dramatic skill although the voice remains the voice of Heaney. In "Making Strange" there is a problem of voice. Heaney finds himself standing between a sophisticated incomer:

>           with his travelled intelligence
>           and tawny containment,
>           his speech like the twang of a bowstring
> and
>
>           another, unshorn and bewildered
>           in the tubs of his wellingtons

The difficulty of communication between the two and what they represent
is solved when "a cunning middle voice" advises him to " 'be adept and
dialect.' " In the end:

>       I found myself driving the stranger
>
>       through my own country, adept
>       at dialect, reciting my price
>       in all that I knew, that began to make strange
>
>       at that same recitation.

Whether there are three persons and the voice in the poem or only Heaney
in different guises and the voice, is not a necessary question to answer. What
is significant is that "the cunning middle voice" advocates not a choice
between the adept and the dialect but a combination of them:

>       call me sweetbriar after the rain
>       or snowberries cooled in the fog.
>       But love the cut of this travelled one
>       and call me also the cornfield of Boaz.

Heaney's voice has achieved a wider range to "Go beyond what is reliable."
It is noteworthy how many of the poems in Part One are composite, con-
structed of several units which allow him to alter his focus and perspective.
Looking across the whole collection, we see that each Part is differently
organised and, when examined in more detail, the Parts are seen to comment
on and complement each other. It is not a question of which Part is the
centre or fulcrum but rather that a new dimension has been devised by
Heaney to allow him to speak in a more dramatic voice. Although the focus
of his poetry is still in his native Northern Ireland, although the pull of
emotion is still to something behind him and much of his language manifests
"habit's afterlife," his adoption of the dramatic mode promises a different,
more oblique attitude to his own background. In his previous volumes,
poems written in a foreign locality seemed like postcards sent home to
reaffirm his connection with his familial and tribal base. Now he may be
able to renegotiate his relations with his original society and include in his

poetry the wider perspectives his travelling has given him. "The First Flight" concludes with what may signal his new direction:

> I was mired in attachment
> until they began to pronounce me
> a feeder off battlefields
>
> so I mastered new rungs of the air
> to survey out of reach
> their bonfires on hills, their hosting
>
> and fasting, the levies from Scotland
> as always, and the people of art
> diverting their rhythmical chants
>
> to fend off the onslaught of winds
> I would welcome and climb
> at the top of my bent

The bird-man, Sweeney Heaney, is no longer a nightingale.

*Notes*

1. "The Three Voices of Poetry," the eleventh annual Lecture of the National Book League, delivered in 1953. Included in *On Poetry and Poets*. London: Faber and Faber (1957), p.89.

2. *Ibid.*, p.99.

3. *Shelley's Prose*, ed. David Lee Clark. Albuquerque: University of New Mexico Press (1954), p.282.

4. *Ibid.*, p.297.

5. *Poetry Book Society Bulletin*, 85 (Summer 1975), p.1.

6. *Coleridge on Shakespeare*, edited by Terence Hawkes, Harmondsworth: Penguin Books (1969), p.161.

# Second Thoughts
## [On *The Haw Lantern*]

HELEN VENDLER*

Here are thirty-two new poems by Seamus Heaney —the yield since *Station Island* (1985). Heaney is a poet of abundance who is undergoing in middle age the experience of natural loss. As the earth loses for him the mass and gravity of familiar presences—parents and friends taken by death— desiccation and weightlessness threaten the former fullness of the sensual life.

The moment of emptiness can be found in other poets. "Already I take up less emotional space / Than a snowdrop," James Merrill wrote at such a point in his own evolution. Lowell's grim engine, churning powerfully on through the late sonnets, did not quite admit the chill of such a moment until *Day by Day*: "We are things thrown in the air alive / in flight . . . / our rust the color of the chameleon." It is very difficult for poets of brick and mortar solidity, like Lowell, or of rooted heaviness, like Heaney, to become light, airy, desiccated. In their new style they cannot abandon their former selves. The struggle to be one's old self and one's new self together is the struggle of poetry itself, which must accumulate new layers rather than discard old ones.

Heaney must thus continue to be a poet rich in tactile language, while expressing emptiness, absence, distance. *The Haw Lantern*, poised between these contradictory imperatives of adult life, is almost penitentially faithful to each, determined to forsake neither. Here is the earlier Heaney writing fifteen years ago about moist clay:

> They loaded on to the bank
> Slabs like the squared-off clots
> Of a blue cream. . . .

> Once, cleaning a drain
> I shovelled up livery slicks
> Till the water gradually ran

*Reprinted with permission from *The New York Review of Books*, 28 April 1988, 41–45. Copyright © 1988 NyRev, Inc.

> Clear on its old floor.
> Under the humus and roots
> This smooth weight. I labour
> Towards it still. It holds and gluts.[1]

Image and sound both bear witness here to the rich fluidity of the natural world. Now, in *The Haw Lantern*, Heaney finds he must, to be truthful to his past, add manufacture to nature. When he looks with adult eyes at his natal earth, he finds machinery there as well as organic matter; and he writes not with fluidity but with aphoristic brevity:

> When I hoked there, I would find
> An acorn and a rusted bolt.
>
> If I lifted my eyes, a factory chimney
> And a dormant mountain.
>
> If I listened, an engine shunting
> And a trotting horse. . . .
>
> My left hand placed the standard iron weight.
> My right tilted a last grain in the balance.

"Is it any wonder," the poet asks, "when I thought / I would have second thoughts?" ("Terminus").

*The Haw Lantern* is a book of strict, even stiff, second thoughts. Such analytical poetry cannot permit itself a first careless rapture. No longer (at least, not often) do we follow the delightful slope of narrative: "And then, and then." Instead, we see the mind balancing debits and credits. "I balanced all, brought all to mind," said Yeats, using a scale to weigh years behind and years to come. A poet who began as luxuriously as Heaney could hardly have dreamed he would be called to such an audit. The need for adult reckoning must to some degree be attributed to his peculiar internal exile. Born among the Catholic minority in British Protestant Ulster, he came young to social awareness; now removed to the Catholic Republic of Ireland, he is part of an Ulster-bred minority substantially different in culture and upbringing from the majority.

The poetry of second thoughts has its own potential for literary elaboration. *The Haw Lantern* is full of parables and allegories, satires of Irish religious, social, and political life. The blank verse of these allegories is as far from the opulent rhymed stanzas of Heaney's sensual, Keatsian aspect as from the slender trimeters and dimeters of his "Irish" side. The strangest poem in *The Haw Lantern*, a blank, verse piece called "The Mud Vision," arises from Heaney's desire to respect amplitude, even in an analytic poem.

I don't find the effort wholly successful, but I see in it the way Heaney is willing to flail at impossibility rather than divide his believing youth from his skeptical middle age.

This religious-political-social poem begins with a bitter satiric portrait of an unnamed country dithering between atavistic superstition and yuppie modernity. The landscape displays a thin layer of industrial modernization over a desolate rural emptiness; in a typical scene, terrorist casualties are carried, in a heliport past the latest touring rock star:

> Statues with exposed hearts and barbed-wire crowns
> Still stood in alcoves, hares flitted beneath
> The dozing bellies of jets, our menu-writers
> And punks with aerosol sprays held their own
> With the best of them. Satellite link-ups
> Wafted over us the blessings of popes, heliports
> Maintained a charmed circle for idols on tour
> And casualties on their stretchers. We sleepwalked
> The line between panic and formulae, . . .
> Watching ourselves at a distance, advantaged
> And airy as a man on a springboard
> Who keeps limbering up because the man cannot dive.

In that last image, Heaney catches the "advantaged and airy" complacency of an impotent nation congratulating itself on political flexibility as a way of concealing indecisiveness. The despair brilliantly hidden in this sketch casts up a compensatory vision. What if a dispossessed country could believe not in its useless statues of the Sacred Heart nor in its modern veneer of restaurants and heliports, but in its own solid earth? In the "mud vision" of the title, a whirling, rainbow-wheel of transparent mud appears in the foggy midlands of this unnamed country, and a fine silt of earth spreads from it to touch every cranny. Heaney tries to catch the vision and its effect on those who see it:

> And then in the foggy midlands it appeared,
> Our mud vision, as if a rose window of mud
> Had invented itself out of the glittery damp,
> A gossamer wheel, concentric with its own hub
> Of nebulous dirt, sullied yet lucent.
>                . . . We were vouchsafed
> Original clay, transfigured and spinning.

The poem runs out of steam trying to imagine how the "mud vision" banishes traditional religion (bulrushes replace lilies on altars, invalids line up for healing under the mud shower, and so on). Eventually, of course, the vision disappears in the "*post factum* jabber" of experts. "We had our chance," says the speaker, "to be mud-men, convinced and estranged," but in hesitation, all opportunity was lost.

"Vision" is meant in the entirely human sense, as we might say Parnell had a vision of a free Ireland, or Gandhi a vision of a free India, but "The Mud Vision" puts perhaps a too religious cast on clay. Can a vision of the earthy borrow its language from the conventional "vision" of the heavenly ("a rose window . . . lucent . . . original . . . transfigured")?

"The Mud Vision" puts many of Heaney's qualities on record—his territorial piety, his visual wit, his ambition for a better Ireland, his reflectiveness, and his anger—and attempts somehow to find a style that can absorb them all. However, "The Mud Vision" has none of the *sprezzatura* and firm elegance of other poems in *The Haw Lantern*, such as "Wolfe Tone." In this posthumous self-portrait, the speaker is the Irish Protestant revolutionary (1763–1798) who attempted a union of Catholics and Protestants against England, and was captured in 1798 after his invading fleet was defeated off Donegal. Tone committed suicide in prison before he could be executed for treason. He symbolizes the reformer estranged by his gifts, his style, and his daring from the very people he attempts to serve:

> Light as a skiff, manoeuvrable yet outmanoeuvred,
>
> I affected epaulettes and a cockade, wrote a style well-bred and impervious
>
> to the solidarity I angled for . . .
>
> I was the shouldered oar that ended up
> far from the brine and whiff of venture,
>
> like a scratching post or a crossroads flagpole,
> out of my element among small farmers.

Though the first two lines of "Wolfe Tone" owe something to Lowell's *Day by Day*, the poem has a dryness and reticence all its own. The force of the poem lies in the arid paradox—for reformers—that authentic style is often incompatible with political solidarity with the masses (a paradox on which Socialist Realism foundered). The desolate alienation of the artist / revolutionary is phrased here with the impersonality and obliqueness of Heaney's minimalist style (of which there was a foretaste in *Station Island's* "Sweeney Redivivus").

I hope I have said enough to suggest where Heaney finds himself morally at this moment, poised between the "iron weight" of analysis and "the last grain" of fertile feeling, between cutting satire and a hopeful vision of possibility. Besides the blank-verse political parables I have mentioned. *The Haw Lantern* contains several notable elegies, among them a sequence of eight sonnets ("Clearances") in memory of Heaney's mother, who died in 1984. To make this hardest of genres new, Heaney moves away from both stateliness and skepticism. Borrowing from Milosz's "The World," a poem in which a luminous past is evoked in the simplest, most childlike terms, Heaney writes a death-sonnet that imagines all Oedipal longings fulfilled:

> It is Number 5, New Row, Land of the Dead,
> Where grandfather is rising from his place
> With spectacles pushed back on a clean bald head
> To welcome a bewildered homing daughter
> Before she even knocks. "What's this? What's this?"
> And they sit down in the shining room together.

Such felicity brings Milosz's "naive" effect fully into our idiom, and displays the self-denying capacity of the son to write about his mother as ultimately her father's daughter.

But "Clearances" also touches on the irritability, the comedy, and the dailiness of the bond between sons and mothers. In one of its best sonnets son and mother are folding sheets together; and here I recall Alfred Kazin's recent memoir of his youth in the Thirties, when he wrote for a freshman English class at City College "an oedipal piece about helping my mother carry ice back to our kitchen, each of us holding one end of a towel": "This was such a familiar and happy experience for me in summer that I was astonished by the young instructor's disgust on reading my paper. He was a vaguely British type, a recent Oxford graduate . . . who openly disliked his predominantly Jewish students. My loving description of carrying ice in partnership with my mother seemed to him, as he tightly put it, "impossible to comprehend."[2] It is useful to be reminded how recently literature has been open to such experiences. Here is Heaney with his mother folding the sheets:

> The cool that came off sheets just off the line
> Made me think the damp must still be in them
> But when I took my corners of the linen
> And pulled against her, first straight down the hem
> And then diagonally, then flapped and shook
> The fabric like a sail in a cross-wind,
> They made a dried-out undulating thwack.

Petrarch or Milton could hardly have imagined that this might be the octave of a sonnet. Yet the pretty "rhymes" echo tradition, as *line* stretches to *linen* (the clothesline and the sheets), and as *them* shrinks to *hem* (a folded sheet in itself). Frost, Heaney's precursor here, would have recognized the unobtrusive sentence-sounds; the line "Made me think the damp must still be in them" could slip into "Birches" without a hitch. (The "dried-out undulating thwack," though, is pure Heaney; Frost's eye was more on Roman moral epigram than on sensual fact.)

The seven-line "sestet" of the sonnet closes with a muted reference to the writing of the poem (the poet is now inscribing his family romance on a different set of folded sheets), but this literary marker is almost invisible in Heaney's intricately worked plainness:

> So we'd stretch and fold and end up hand to hand
> For a split second as if nothing had happened
> For nothing had that had not always happened
> Beforehand, day by day, just touch and go,
> Coming close again by holding back
> In moves where I was x and she was o
> Inscribed in sheets she'd sewn from ripped-out flour sacks.

Taut lines and folded sheets connect mother and son, in art as in life.

Like "Clearances," the other elegies in this volume combine the density of living with the bleakness of loss, preserving the young, tender Heaney in the present stricken witness. "The Stone Verdict" is an anticipatory elegy for Heaney's father who has since died; other poems commemorate his young niece Rachel, dead in an accident; his wife's mother ("The Wishing Tree"); and his colleague at Harvard, Robert Fitzgerald. Heaney affirms that the space left in life by the absence of the dead takes on a shape so powerful that it becomes a presence in itself. In the elegy for his mother, Heaney's emblem for the shocking absence is a felled chestnut tree that was his "coeval"—planted in a jam jar the year he was born. Cut down, it becomes "utterly a source." "Its heft and hush become a bright nowhere. / A soul ramifying and forever / Silent, beyond silence listened for." Heaney's sharply etched "nowhere" is a correction not only of Christian promises of heaven, but also of Yeats's exuberant purgatorial visions of esoteric afterlifes. It returns Irish elegy to truthfulness.

Heaney has said that because people of any culture share standards and beliefs, the artist's "inner drama goes beyond the personal to become symptomatic and therefore political."[3] To ascribe immense and unforgettable value to the missing human piece, simply because it is missing, is to put the power to ascribe value squarely in the human rather than in the religious sphere. Since institutional ideology everywhere reserves to itself alone the privilege of conferring value, it is all the more important for writers to remind us that control of value lies in individual, as well as in collective, hands.

Heaney directly addresses the question of value in "The Riddle," the poem placed last in this self-questioning book. His governing image here is the ancient one of the sieve that separates wheat from chaff. Such sieves are no longer in use, but the poet has seen one:

> You never saw it used but still can hear
> The sift and fall of stuff hopped on the mesh,
> Clods and buds in a little dust-up,
> The dribbled pile accruing under it.
>
> Which would be better, what sticks or what falls through?
> Or does the choice itself create the value?

This is the poem of a man who has discovered that much of what he has been told was wheat is chaff, and a good deal that was dismissed as chaff turns out to be what he might want to keep. Coleridge, remembering classical myths of torment, wrote, "Work without hope draws nectar in a sieve"; Heaney, rewriting Coleridge, thinks that the endless labors of rejection and choice might yet be a way to salvation. He asks himself, at the close of "The Riddle," to

> . . . work out what was happening in that story
> Of the man who carried water in a riddle.
>
> Was it culpable ignorance, or was it rather
> A via negativa through drops and let-downs?

The great systems of dogma (patriotic, religious, ethical) must be abandoned, Heaney suggests, in favor of a ceaseless psychic sorting. Discarding treasured pieties and formed rules, the poet finds "drops and let-downs," and he refuses to take much joy in the task of sifting, though a middle couplet shows it to be undertaken with good will: "Legs apart, deft-handed, start a mine / To sift the sense of things from what's imagined." In Heaney's earlier work, this couplet would have been the end of the poem, breathing resolve and hope. Now he ends the poem asking whether his sifting should be condemned as "culpable ignorance" (the Roman Catholic phrase is taken from the penitentials) or allowed as a *via negativa*. The latter phrase, which is also drawn from Catholicism, is a theological term connected to mysticism, suggesting that we can know God only as he is not.

The elegiac absences and riddles of *The Haw Lantern* are balanced by powerful presences, none more striking than the emblematic winter hawthorn in the title poem. This poem, by dwelling throughout on a single allegorical image, displays a relatively new manner in Heaney's work. In the past, Heaney's imagery has been almost indecently prolific: readers of *North* (1975) will remember, for instance, the Arcimboldo-like composite of the exhumed cadaver called Grauballe Man:

> The grain of his wrists
> is like bog oak,
> the ball of his heel
>
> like a basalt egg.
> His instep has shrunk
> cold as a swan's foot
> or a wet swamp root.
>
> His hips are the ridge
> and purse of a mussel,
> his spine an eel arrested
> under a glisten of mud.[4]

It is hard for a poet so fertile in sliding simile to stay put, to dwell on a single image until it becomes an emblem; it means going deeper rather than rippling on. "The Haw Lantern," doing just this, fixes on the one burning spot in the blank landscape of winter—the red berry, or haw, on the naked hawthorn branch. At first the poet sees the berry as an almost apologetic flame, indirectly suggesting his own quelled hopes as a spokesman. He goes deeper into self-questioning by transforming the haw into the lantern carried by Diogenes, searching for the one just man. The stoic haw, meditation reminds the poet, is both pith and pit, at once fleshy and stony. The birds peck at it, but it continues ripening. In this upside-down almost-sonnet, the stern haw lantern scrutinizes the poet scrutinizing it:

> The wintry haw is burning out of season,
> crab of the thorn, a small light for small people,
> wanting no more from them but that they keep
> the wick of self-respect from dying out,
> not having to blind them with illumination.
> But sometimes when your breath plumes in the frost
> it takes the roaming shape of Diogenes
> with his lantern, seeking one just man;
> so you end up scrutinized from behind the haw
> he holds up at eye-level on its twig,
> and you flinch before its bonded pith and stone,
> its blood-prick that you wish would test and clear you,
> its pecked-at ripeness that scans you, then moves on.

Like other poems in Heaney's new volume, "The Haw Lantern" reflects a near despair of country and of self.

Heaney's burning haw can bear comparison with Herbert's emblematic rose, "whose hue, angry and brave, / Bids the rash gazer wipe his eye." Forsaking topical reference, the artist writing in such genres as the emblem-poem' ("The Haw Lantern") and allegory ("The Mud Vision") positions himself at a distance from daily events. Such analytic, generalized poetry hopes to gain in intelligence what it loses in immediacy of reference. (The greatest example of such an aesthetic choice is Milton's decision to write the epic of Puritan war, regicide, reform, and defeat by retelling Genesis.)

Heaney has several times quoted Mandelstam's "notion that poetry—and art in general—is addressed to . . . 'The reader in posterity' ": "It is not directed exploitatively towards its immediate audience—although of course it does not set out to disdain the immediate audience either. It is directed towards the new perception which it is its function to create."[5] The social, historical, and religious perceptions of *The Haw Lantern*, if they should become general in Ireland, would indeed create a new psychic reality there. Such a prospect seems so unlikely now that it is only by believing in "the reader in posterity" that a writer can continue to address Irish issues at all.

I have saved the best of this collection for the last: two excellent poems about the life of writing. The first, "Alphabets," written as the Phi Beta Kappa poem for Harvard, presents a series of joyous scenes that show the child becoming a writer. The alphabets of the title are those learned by the poet as he grew up: English, Latin, Irish, and Greek. They stand for the widening sense of place, time, and culture gained as the infant grows to be a youth, a teacher, and a poet. Against Wordsworth's myth of a childhood radiance lost, the poem sets a countermyth of imaginative power becoming fuller and freer with expanding linguistic and literary power.

With great charm, "Alphabets" shows us the child in school mastering his first alphabet:

> First it is "copying out," and then "English"
> Marked correct with a little leaning hoe.
> Smells of inkwells rise in the classroom hush.
> A globe in the window tilts like a coloured O.

Learning Irish, with its prosody so different from those of English and Latin, awakens the boy's Muse:

> Here in her snooded garment and bare feet,
> All ringleted in assonance and woodnotes,
> The poet's dream stole over him like sunlight
> And passed into the tenebrous thickets.

The boy becomes a teacher, and the verse makes gentle fun of his self-conscious and forgivable vanity: "The globe has spun. He stands in a wooden O / He alludes to Shakespeare. He alludes to Graves."

"Alphabets" closes with a hope for global vision, based on two exemplary human images. The first is that of a Renaissance humanist necromancer who hung from his ceiling "a figure of the world with colours in it," so that he could always carry it in his mind—"So that the figure of the universe / And 'not just single things' would / meet his sight / / When he walked abroad." The second figure is that of the scientist-astronaut, who also tries to comprehend the whole globe:

> . . . from his small window
> The astronaut sees all he has sprung from,
> The risen, aqueous, singular, lucent O
> Like a magnified and buoyant ovum.

Heaney implies that whatever infant alphabet we may start from, we will go on to others, by which we hope to encompass the world. Ours is the first generation to have a perceptual (rather than conceptual) grasp of the world as a single orbiting sphere—"the risen, aqueous, singular, lucent O"; and the almost inexpressible joy of sensuous possession lies in that line, a joy Heaney sees in the cultural and intellectual possession of the world, whether by humanist or scientist. "Alphabets" combines a humorous tenderness of self-mockery with an undiminished memory of the vigilant vows of youth, proving that middle age need not mark a discontinuity in life or writing.

The other brilliant poem here, "From the Frontier of Writing," offers a *vie de poète* altogether different from that of "Alphabets." Written in an adapted Dantesque terza rima, "The Frontier" retells a narrow escape from a modern hell. It takes as its emblem the paralyzing experience—familiar even to tourists—of being stopped and questioned at a military roadblock in Ireland. The writer, however, has not only to pass through real roadblocks but to confront as well the invisible roadblocks of consciousness and conscience. In either case, you can lose your nerve: in life, you can be cowed; in writing, you can be tempted to dishonesty or evasion. I quote this report from the frontier in full.

> The tightness and the nilness round that space
> when the car stops in the road, the troops inspect
> its make and number and, as one bends his face
>
> towards your window, you catch sight of more
> on a hill beyond, eyeing with intent
> down cradled guns that hold you under cover

and everything is pure interrogation
until a rifle motions and you move
with guarded unconcerned acceleration—

a little emptier, a little spent
as always by that quiver in the self,
subjugated, yes, and obedient.

So you drive on to the frontier of writing
where it happens again. The guns on tripods;
the sergeant with his on-off mike repeating

data about you, waiting for the squawk
of clearance; the marksman training down
out of the sun upon you like a hawk.

And suddenly you're through, arraigned yet freed,
as if you'd passed from behind a waterfall
on the black current of a tarmac road

past armour-plated vehicles, out between
the posted soldiers flowing and receding
like tree shadows into the polished windscreen.

This poem is so expressive of the present armed tension in Ireland that it is political simply by being. It produces in us an Irish weather—menacing, overcast, electric—so intense that for a while we live in it. It has the allegorical solidity of the *déjà vu*, and the formal solidity of its two twelve-line roadblocks.

But formal solidity is not the only manner in which Heaney composes good poems. He has always had a talent and an appetite for the organic (growing and decaying at once), for which he invented the "weeping" stanzas of the bog poems. The elusive short couplets in "Wolfe Tone" and "The Riddle" suggest a third temper in Heaney, one represented neither by commanding masonry nor by seeping earth but rather by rustling dust, leaves, and feathers. The epigraph to *The Haw Lantern* epitomizes this third manner as the poet waits for a sound beyond silence listened for: "The riverbed, dried-up, half-full of leaves. / Us, listening to a river in the trees." In deprivation, the poet trusts the premonitory whisper from the stock of unfallen leaves. *The Haw Lantern* suggests the trust is not misplaced.

*Notes*

1. "Bann Clay," *Poems: 1965–1975* (New York: Farrar, Straus and Giroux, 1980), 83–84.

2.   From *An Apple for My Teacher*, Louis Rubin, Jr., ed. (Algonquin Press), quoted in *The New Times Book Review*, June 24, 1987, 23.

3.   Seamus Heaney, comments during a symposium on art and politics at Northeastern University, 1986, printed in *Working Papers in Irish Studies*, issued by Northeastern University, 1986, 33.

4.   *Poems: 1965–1975*, 190.

5.   *Working Papers*, 36.

# Critic as Heaney

## HAZARD ADAMS*

The last several decades have witnessed the academization of criticism, its enormous growth in volume, and radical changes from what might be called critical discourse focusing on literary texts or literary careers to theoretical discourse calling elaborate attention to its own problems and internal interests. The cultural, including academic, reasons for this development are many and varied and cannot be discussed here, as interesting they are. Nevertheless, it is possible and necessary to note that the critical discourses of poets today are not taken very seriously in academia, where theory reigns. Indeed, it is difficult to discover theorists well acquainted with such discourses. And it is a little more difficult than an outsider might think to discover a theorist highly interested in poetry. This last phenomenon has to do with the politicization of theoretical discourse and the resultant impatience of many theorists with literary values and techniques that seem to them irrelevant to political content or at least difficult to assimilate to it. All of this is by no means entirely the fault, if one thinks it a fault, of academicians. There has been a tendency in recent times, fostered in the United States at least, to categorize writers as either novelists, dramatists, poets, or critics (theorists). The academic professors in creative writing have been complicitous in this development. People have been encouraged for a variety of reasons to *make a commitment* in one of these directions, to the virtual exclusion of the others.

Through the time of T. S. Eliot most of the principal critical and theoretical statements written in English that we value highly were made by poets, novelists and dramatists, tacitly or explicitly defending what they regarded as their own practices. As any anthology of criticism and theory will show, the situation is now radically different. Hardly any poet, dramatist, or novelist now gains entry into the academic anthologies of criticism and theory, and the estrangement between poets and theorists is pronounced except in a few special cases where a writer has created works that live tantalizingly on the border. All this has occurred in spite of assertions by many theorists that the line between "literature" and theoretical discourse

---

*This essay was written specifically for this volume and is published here for the first time with permission of the author.

has been effectively erased. It is notable that theorists make this statement (I don't know of any poets who do), which suggests that the line may have been only *theoretically* erased and that what has been happening among some theorists is the attempt to develop a new and different sort of theoretical discourse—a new category, but one that seems more hermetically sealed and specialized even as it seems to claim the disappearance of all boundaries. Here Derrida's *Glas* comes to mind. His work has been called obscure as has Joyce's *Finnegans Wake*, but the obscurities are of quite different orders.

Seamus Heaney is certainly one of the foremost poets of our time. He does not fit easily into the scene I have described. He has published three collections of critical essays: *Preoccupations: Selected Prose, 1968–1978* (1980), *The Government of the Tongue* (1988), and *The Place of Writing* (1989). All of the essays have been written during the last two and one-half decades, during which the developments to which I have referred have taken place. It does not seem to me, however, that these developments have been nearly as intense in Ireland as in the United States. Four reasons may account for this: (1) There are far fewer academic positions available in Ireland from which to write theoretical criticism; (2) the tradition of the more or less journalistic or bellettristic essay survives there; (3) poets generally command more respect, or at least more respect across a greater range of the populace, and (4) there is a fairly long tradition of the poet's deep involvement with the issues of the day and a broader recognition that poets may have something to say about them. Much of this can be traced back to Yeats, and even beyond him. Although in recent years Heaney has spent a certain amount of time in the United States (principally as Boylston Professor of Rhetoric and Oratory at Harvard), his criticism reflects the Irish situation, though he is well aware of the more general issues and trends in contemporary criticism and theory. Indeed, it is the strenuous relation between his sense of vocation as poet and the depressing political events in Ireland that gives his critical essays a thematic center that is sometimes directly, sometimes tacitly expressed. His criticism is *engaged*, though as I shall try to show he is always cautionary about the nature of that engagement, and his cautionary statements are frequently directed at other Irish critics, even if they are clearly also meant as comments on the general situation of critic and poet beyond purely local concerns.

There is very little reference to recent critical and theoretical discourse that would be familiar to American academics in Heaney's essays, and almost no use of its jargon, though what little there is indicates some acquaintance with the work of Roland Barthes and deconstruction in general. One indirect reference to Barthes occurs in a discussion of a poem of Patrick Kavanagh, in which Heaney describes his own response: "What was being experienced was not some hygienic and self-aware pleasure of the text but a primitive delight in finding world become word" (*GT*, 8). This is not, I think, meant to be critical of Barthes's assumptions about reading so much as to try to isolate Kavanagh's particular value (about which more later). Schiller's old distinction between naive and sentimental poetry is recast, not at the expense of the sentimental, so much as in the interest of expressing a need in Irish poetry that Kavanagh fulfilled, or at least nearly fulfilled. Barthes is also more recently invoked in support of Heaney's own long meditation on the stressful relation of poetry to politics, and of poetic form to the world (*PW*, 37).

The other references or implied allusions to recent theory involve deconstruction and are rather general and loose with respect to our rigorous understanding of theoretical practices. In a discussion of Yeats and others in *The Place of Writing*, Heaney views Yeats as an heroic deconstructionist of sorts, arguing for his process of unwriting his previous writings and indicating that "any writing is to some extent an unwriting not only of previous writings but even of itself" (*PW*, 56). He observes that since this has always been the case, the elaboration of unwriting into "systems of reading" has largely resulted in new critical procedures rather than new perceptions (*PW*, 56). Many deconstructionists would regard this view as unexceptionable, even though there is a little edge to it, similar to R. P. Blackmur's bemoaning the decline of the New Criticism into mechanical method. Heaney is nothing if not evenhanded in such remarks. He is even deliberately somewhat self-effacing in the foreword to *Preoccupations* when he characterizes his own critical work as "the slightly constricted utterance of somebody who underwent his academic rite of passage when practical criticism held great sway in the academy" (*P*, 13–14). In *The Government of the Tongue* he praises the critical procedures of Geoffrey Grigson on Auden. They are not so up-to-date as Stan Smith's deconstructive readings of Auden which, he observes, "yield many excellent insights," for Grigson is not so strictly analytical. Nevertheless, his kind of activity is "not to be superseded, because it is so closely allied, as an act of reading, to what happens during the poet's act of writing" (*GT*, 120). I shall return to this as exemplary of an interest Heaney never abandons, but first I will observe that his account of Yeats in *The Place of Writing* (the Richard Ellmann Lectures given at Emory University in 1988) is difficult to imagine apart from the critical climate in which deconstruction was a significant force. This is true even though Heaney's account emerges from consideration of some remarks by Ellmann, hardly a postmodernist, on Yeats. In the end, though, it is more important to see Heaney's discussions of Yeats in the context of the debates about him that have recently raged in Ireland and are highly politically motivated. Heaney's thesis in the Ellmann lectures is twofold: "that the poetic imagination in its strongest manifestation imposes its vision upon a place rather than accepts a vision from it; and that this visionary imposition is never exempt from the imagination's antithetical ability to subvert its own creation. In other words, once the place has been brought into written existence, it is inevitable that it be unwritten" (*PW*, 20).

There is nothing nostalgic about Heaney's praise of Grigson and no implied criticism of deconstructive methods, but clearly what interests Heaney and what he regards as "not to be superseded" is a criticism that is centered on the problems of the writer. For him, these problems are to a large extent technical and "expressive." By "expressive," Heaney does not quite mean what M. H. Abrams in *The Mirror and the Lamp* characterized as typically romantic self-expression. It involves technique and the "genetic laws" of poetry; these are the matters that poets, and presumably critics as well, should put first.

As a result, one of the major themes of Heaney's critical writings is the relation of art to life, a theme he obviously inherited from Yeats but which is made more specific in relation to Heaney's own time and place, every bit as much as Yeats made it relevant to his own. The place is Northern Ireland, and the time is that of the recent troubles. Most specifically, it is the summer of 1969: "From that moment the problems of poetry moved from being simply a matter of achieving the satisfactory verbal icon to being a search for images and symbols adequate to our predicament" (P, 56).

"Predicament" in this case suggests the notion of place and time that plays so great a part in Heaney's criticism as well as in his poetry. But place is not invoked merely because of the political situation. Place has a deeper yet connected significance, in that Heaney does not think of poetry without the implication of rootedness or displacement. His accounts of Kavanagh, Montague, and Hewitt, Mahon, Muldoon, and Longley, to say nothing of Yeats, begin with an assessment of each poet's relation to place. He discriminates among them on the basis of this relation. Not only is the matter of place more or less explicitly political; it also, and more fundamentally, is a ground for feeling and identification with a natural environment even prior to words. It is where poetry finds its "entry into the buried life of the feelings" (P, 52) and provides a point of exit or expression for them in the form of a personal mythology. Place is never far from Heaney's discussion of the roots of poetry, which he says begins in crucial "unconscious activity at the pre-verbal level" (P, 62). His criticism covers a range that moves from what he admits is the "slightly predatory curiosity of a poet interested in the creative processes of another poet" (P, 79) to his deep concerns with what he calls "the tail-end of a struggle in a province between territorial piety and imperial power" (P, 57). As for poetry itself, "on the one hand, [it] is secret and natural, on the other hand it must make its way in a world that is public and brutal" (P, 34). I shall return to these matters. Here I can remark that the opposition Heaney sets forth is not one he can easily resolve, for though he is clearly against "imperial power," he has deep reservations about Irish "territorial piety" and those sacred mysticisms believed in and exploited by the IRA. His own sense of place, and his notion of a poet's proper sense of it, has nothing to do with such mystifications. Nevertheless, for him, poetry is a sort of "divination, . . . a revelation of

the self to the self, . . . [9] restoration of the culture to itself' (P, 41).
Poems are "elements of continuity." In emphasizing place, Heaney identifies
himself with continuity. The Celtic sensibility, he observes, has a strain
that expresses "love of place and lamentation against exile" (P, 184), and
he notes that the Irish God of the monasteries has for poets always shared
importance with "another god in the tree, impalpable perhaps but still
indigenous" and with which early Irish poetry affiliated itself (P, 186). The
early poets especially made the sense of place "more or less sacred" (P, 132),
performing a "marriage between the geographical country and the country
of the mind" (P, 132). Heaney's identification with these early poets is an
expression of his search for *poetic* roots. In one essay he speaks of his desire
to "see how far we can go in seeking the origins of a poet's characteristic
'music' " (P, 61). Elsewhere he insists that the power of poetry emerges
from a depth always below "declared meaning," as a force that is "elusive,
archaic and only half-apprehended by maker and audience" (P, 186). He
wishes to go far deeper than patriotism or nationalism or the programmatic
tendencies that are revealed in conscious applications of Gaelic techniques
to poetry, to take one example (P, 36).

Heaney sees himself in relation to a place and what has happened in
it, but he recognizes the complexity of that relation in Ireland. He has found
himself "symbolically placed between the marks of English influence and
the lure of the native experience" (P, 35), between the demesne and the
bog, as he put it in 1972. And he has found himself between the political
and cultural traumas of Ireland and the world beyond them. He observes
that one identifies with "a place, an ancestry, a history, a culture," but there
are quarrels with the self in which the "voices of [one's] education," as
Lawrence put it, figure decisively (P, 35). All of the Irish poets upon whom
Heaney comments are seen in the light of one or more of these oppositions.

Yet the overriding thesis of Heaney's criticism is the more traditional
and universal theme of the relation of his art to life. Both *Preoccupations*
(1978), the title of which indicates the theme's importance, and *The Government of the Tongue* (1988), with its political ambiguity, begin by stating this
theme; the second tacitly acknowledges the stress of Northern Irish political
conditions that has required Heaney to reaffirm certain principles. In 1978
Heaney asks simply how a poet should live and write, and what his relation
to his own voice, his place, his literary heritage, and the world should be
(P, 13). In 1988 his views on these matters have not changed, but the stress
is greater and the discussion more intense. Can art, should art, go on
under the conditions of violence being experienced in the North? Heaney
remembers lecturing on Wilfred Owen some twenty years earlier, and his
awareness on the one hand of Owen's tendency to "over-write" as against
the sense that "the need to call for verbal restraint felt prissy and trivial
when you considered what lay behind the words" (GT, xv). Poets, too, not
just critics, are in most situations embarrassed by their art, for "lyric poetry,

however responsible, always has an element of the untrammeled about it. There is a certain jubilation and truancy at the heart of an inspiration. There is a sense of liberation and abundance which is the antithesis of every hampered and deprived condition. And it is for this reason that, psychologically, the lyric poet feels the need for justification in a world that is notably hampered and deprived" (*GT*, xviii). The poetic model Heaney chooses to help overcome this embarrassment is Osip Mandelstam, for whom obedience to the poetic impulse was identical with obedience to conscience. Heaney has some trouble defining what "obedience to the poetic impulse is," but the example of Mandelstam goes some way toward this. It is the "urge to sing in [one's] own way" (*GT*, xx), and this may involve being a "witness" (*GT*, xvi), where the "compulsion to identify with the oppressed becomes necessarily integral with the act of writing itself" (*GT*, xvi). In such situations—Owen's, for example—the poet may feel compelled to abjure conventional artistic expression and assert his freedom to employ the language, but in any case his art, if at all genuine, will involve an expression of the determination to speak freely. Yet that freedom requires a certain detachment from one's own emotions, through which the poet fleetingly achieves a relation of equidistance from both self-justification and self-obliteration.

Early on, Heaney saw his own generation of poets in a particular place and time. Much of what was happening was blatantly clear and did not require working out, appraisal, revelation or even accusation: "Sectarian prejudice, discrimination in jobs and housing gerrymandering by the majority, a shared understanding that the police were a paramilitary force." (*GT*, xxi). His generation, he thinks, saw itself as part of a possible change for the better: "The fact that a literary action was afoot was itself a new political condition, and the poets did not feel the need to address themselves to the specifics of politics because they assumed that the tolerances and subtleties of their art were precisely what they had to set against the repetitive intolerances of public life" (*GT*, xxi). For Heaney there are moments in which the tongue rejects governance by the conditions of obeisance to one loyalty or another: "It gains access to a condition that is unconstrained and, while not being practically effective, is not necessarily inefficacious" (*GT*, xxii).

But this faith is constantly tried, and Heaney makes the stress upon it central to his essays. The pages of *The Government of the Tongue* restate the propositions about poetry that appeared ten years earlier in *Preoccupations* (1978). "They are," he now says, "symptomatic of an anxiety that in arrogating to oneself the right to take refuge in form, one is somehow denying the claims of the beggar at the gate" (*GT*, xxii). Yet, with the example of Mandelstam before him, he chooses that freedom.

The theme has taken Heaney to repeated meditations on his great predecessor Yeats, who, most notably in his poem "Ego Dominus Tuus," distinguishes between men of action and poets and who makes the poet's relation to action one of his many subjects in his ambitious sequence "Meditations in Time of Civil War." Poets of the generation after Yeats and before Heaney were certainly preoccupied with Yeats, who for them represented a spectral force of overwhelming power. Heaney is neither a slavish follower of nor an Orcan rebel against Yeats. He is astonishingly free of Yeats, free enough to point to him as an example. Yet, as an example of what? Thus the question mark appears in the title of the essay "Yeats as an Example?" It is not just a question of what Yeats represents as an example. It is also a question of whether Yeats can serve as an example without being overwhelming. Yeats is not present in Heaney's essays as a stylistic influence or an object to be opposed at any cost. But as a certain kind of example Yeats is everywhere. As an object of meditation he appears twice in *Preoccupations* and very strongly in *The Place of Writing*.

There is no doubt that the example of Yeats as a stylist had at last to be overthrown in Ireland, as many of Yeats's most cherished cultural strategies also need to be. Heaney knows that a great poet can be "a very bad influence on other poets" (*P*, 109). The example of Yeats to be deeply respected was his stubbornness on behalf of the poetic and of "creative action," his deliberate assertion of freedom. In Heaney's view, Yeats, who worried the anxiety of the relation of art to life into some of his greatest poems, managed to make the two into one: "I admire the way that Yeats took on the world on his own terms, defined the areas where he would negotiate and where he would not, the way he never accepted the terms of another's argument but propounded his own. I assume that this peremptoriness, this apparent arrogance, is exemplary in an artist, that it is proper and even necessary for him to insist on his own language, his own vision, his own lines of reference" (*P*, 101). To the practicing poet Yeats offers the example of "labour, perseverance" (*P*, 110). These remarks seem to me entirely on target. It is to be noted that they do not engage in the Yeats-bashing that at about the same time began to appear in the remarks of Seamus Deane, Declan Kiberd, and others. The difference is grounded first on Heaney's respect for Yeats's commitment to the "absolute validity" of the artistic process (*P*, 99) and second on Yeats's "large-minded, whole-hearted assent to the natural cycles of living and dying" (*P*, 110). For Heaney, Yeats's intransigence and commitment to both of these things evokes a great admiration that runs entirely counter to a fairly common tendency in Ireland, among Catholic intellectuals at least, to treat Yeats as "poor silly Willie" or to regard him as a bit cracked. Finally, Heaney sees Yeats as an example to others in "the way his life and work are *not* separate but make a continuum, the way the courage of his vision did not confine itself to rhetorics but issued in actions" (*P*, 100). Heaney's Yeats was well aware of and thematized the problem of life and art, and plied "the effort of the individual work into the larger work of the community as a whole" (*P*, 106). For Heaney the popular notion of Yeats as an impractical dreamer is belied by the facts not only of his life but also of his poetry and drama. His intransigence and commitment were directed toward an ideal goal, from which he seldom wavered: a campaign "with the idea of conquest, not of territory perhaps but of imagination" (*P*, 104).

This is Heaney's Yeats of a 1978 lecture. Ten years later, in *The Place of Writing*, the question of place is paramount. Yeats as poet who imposed his own vision on a place—Thoor Ballylee—and thereby revealed a "country of the mind" is contrasted to Thomas Hardy, whose country seemed to have created his mind and whose houses somehow defined *him*. But this notion of imaginative domination and making is given a further twist, with the idea that Yeats finally unwrote the place he made his ground, or at least unwrote its ultimate efficacy as insurance against the absurd. For Heaney this is Yeats's greatest triumph—the acknowledgment, indeed the necessary embrace, of limitation, the return to earth, the rejection of the temptation of triumph itself. Heaney's Yeats possesses an implacable artistic drive that shapes and disciplines his materials, always trying out new voices, assuming theatrical masks, overcoming difficulties. He is contrasted to a Wordsworth who seems mesmerized by his own voice and by natural forces, and prescribes a wise passivity.

But the poet whom Heaney most contrasts to Yeats—in an entirely different way—is Patrick Kavanagh. In *Preoccupations* it seems as if the essay on Yeats generates one on Kavanagh. Ten years later Heaney looks at Kavanagh again and feels that he has come to better understand why he is drawn to Kavanagh's work. Heaney contrasts Kavanagh to Yeats, but unlike Seamus Deane in *Celtic Revivals*, not at the expense of a Yeats deemed irrelevant, a Yeats who must be overthrown in order to get on with the task of an Irish cultural politics that would transcend nationalism. Kavanagh has a strong appeal to critics and poets of the radical Left in Ireland for at least two reasons. First, he rejected the "matter of Ireland," he refused to serve the traditions and forms of the Irish Literary Revival, of which he was entirely suspicious. They have been suspect on the Left because of their alleged connection with middle-class culture and nationalist jingoism. Second, as Heaney points out, Kavanagh expressed "a hard buried life that subsisted beyond the feel of middle-class novelists and romantic nationalist poets" (*P*, 116). Kavanagh was a "new, authentic and liberating" voice (*P*, 116) and spoke for a consciousness that had not previously been articulated. Kavanagh's *The Great Hunger* was a rebuke to the idea of the peasant as a noble savage and a dramatization of what its author called "the usual barbaric life of the Irish country poor" (*P*, 124). For Heaney, Kavanagh expressed social commitments in spite of himself, even as he rejected any form of nationalism. Yet his work "probably touches the majority of Irish people more immediately and more intimately than most things in Yeats" (*P*, 137).

Nevertheless, the essay in *Preoccupations* expresses some reservations about Kavanagh's work. I shall turn to these after observing that ten years later, in the essay in *The Government of the Tongue*, Heaney somewhat revises his opinion. In the earlier essay Heaney values Kavanagh for bringing an aspect of Irish life to expression. In the later essay Heaney identifies himself to some extent with that life. "One felt less alone and marginal as a product of that world now that it had found its expression" (*GT*, 9). He describes himself as responding to Kavanagh from a "comparatively bookless background," presumably like Kavanagh's own. Heaney also values Kavanagh's work because, though it was deliberately anti political in intention, it had political effect, an effect, I might add, that Kavanagh probably would have hated. "Whether he wanted it or not, his achievement was inevitably co-opted north and south, into the general current of feeling which flowed from and sustained ideas of national identity, cultural otherness from Britain and the dream of a literature with a manner and a matter resistant to the central Englishness of the dominant tradition" (*GT*, 9–10). It is ironic that Kavanagh, then, has been read in the light of the aims of the Irish Literary Revival, which he had called "a thoroughgoing English bred lie."

The result in the second essay is an assertion of a high personal evaluation. Heaney sees Kavanagh as having achieved a style appropriate to "his universal ordinariness" (*GT*, 14). He would now rewrite the conclusion to his earlier essay: "I said then that when Kavanagh had consumed the roughage of his Monaghan experience, he ate his heart out. I believe now that it would be truer to say that when he had consumed the roughage of his early Monaghan experience, he had cleared a space where, in Yeats's words, "the soul recovers radical innocence." (*GT*, 14). Yet Heaney admits even here, I think, Kavanagh's definite limitations and alludes to his too often "wilful doggerel, writing which exercised a vindictiveness against the artfulness of art" (*GT*, 14). Thus Heaney, though appreciating Kavanagh, does not abandon the criticism he makes in the earlier essay, where he distinguishes between technique and craft and faults Kavanagh for a paucity of the latter. This is an opposition that runs through much of Heaney's criticism, along with other oppositions: masculine/feminine and active/passive. It is by manipulating one or more of these sets that Heaney frequently achieves his characterizations of poets. Only his use of the first set seems to imply a value judgment, though in Kavanagh's case it is tempered. The other two oppositions are more or less descriptive, though Heaney's personal preference is for the masculine and active.

By technique Heaney means a way with words, meter, rhythm, and verbal texture in general. "Technique is what allows that first stirring of the mind round a word or an image or a memory to grow to articulation" (*P*, 48). But this also involves a stance toward life, toward one's own reality, and the act of discovering ways to "raid the inarticulate" (*P*, 47). Craft, on the other hand, involves what one can learn from other verse; it is skill. What Heaney calls "poetic music" he identifies with technique more than with craft (*GT*, 109). Craft is for Heaney what William Blake called the learning of the "language of art." Though Blake hated imitation of nature, he argued that all artists copied a great deal. It was part of learning the language.

Heaney's second essay on Kavanagh finally maintains his judgment with respect to this distinction: "There is, we might say, more technique than craft in his work, real technique which is, in [Kavanagh's] own words, 'a spiritual quality, a condition of mind, or an ability to invoke a particular condition of mind . . . a method of getting at life,' but his technique has to be continuously renewed, as if previous achievements and failures added up to nothing in the way of self-knowledge or self-criticism of his own capacities as a maker" (P, 116). In spite of a failure of craft, Kavanagh is still to be admired. Other poets whose work is admirable in Heaney's eyes suffer from a similar lack. Stevie Smith's "literary resources are not adequate to the sombre recognitions, the wounded *joie de vivre*, the marooned spirit we sense they were destined to express" (P, 201). Theodore Roethke shows the opposite weakness when he is not in full possession of his emotion and "employs the artificer's resources" (P, 193). Heaney might have added that where this happens Roethke most sounds like an ephebe of Yeats. Hugh MacDairmuid's genius turns into bore when earnestness takes over and his capacity for parody fails.

Heaney praises the early Auden for both technique and craft. Auden displayed poetic authority and in the process "caught native English poetry by the scruff of the neck, pushed its nose sharply into modernity, made it judder and frolic from the shock." (GT, 110). But in Heaney's view, English poetry did not take Auden's route and settled into a sort of provincialism, from which it emerged only under foreign influences—principally through translation. A kind of provinciality of person is the problem in Sylvia Plath's poetry, a domineering theme of "self-discovery and self-definition" (GT, 168). For Heaney, the best work is the result of a "certain self-forgetfulness" denied to her. Perhaps, for him, this self-forgetfulness is distributed among both technique and craft, but surely the discipline of craft, though not assuring self-forgetfulness, contributes very strongly to it.

Heaney opposes Hopkins and Keats in terms of what he calls the masculine and feminine. Hopkins' rhythm "alerts us to perceive" (P, 85). Keats's narcotic rhythm "woos us to receive" (P, 85). Clearly Heaney himself values the masculine more highly, but he resists a clear judgment. The poet's truth to his or her own sensibility is more important. In *Preoccupations* a personal statement on behalf of his own way seems half-apologetic in the context of Northern Ireland's political troubles: "It would wrench the rhythms of my writing procedures to start squaring up to contemporary events with more will than ways to deal with them" (P, 34). Ten years later in the essay on Plath, he is less apologetic for poetry, more forthright in defending the necessity of the poet's hard-won freedom, even as he recognizes the tension between art and politics. By this time he is convinced that poetic commitment must come first, and the ethical, moral, or political vision must be fashioned within it, for better or worse. He concedes the danger. "I do not in fact see how poetry can survive as a category of human consciousness if it does not put poetic considerations first—expressive considerations, that is, based upon its own genetic laws which spring into operation at the moment of lyric conception. Yet it is possible to feel all this and still concede the justice of Czeslaw Milosz's rebuke to the autocracy of such romantic presumption" (GT, 166). These dangers acknowledged, Heaney nevertheless frequently returns to the assertion that poets must be faithful to the demands of the "poetic event" in spite of what they feel they must "concede to the corrective pressures of social, moral, political, and historical reality" (GT, 101). Poets must stand by what they write, "stand [their] ground and take the consequences" (GT, 39). Heaney is explicitly critical of "poets who dwell in the conditional" and comments on the frequency of such poetry, particularly in the United States (GT, 38–39).

It is worth returning for a moment to Heaney on Yeats, to the connection between Yeats's life and art that Heaney perceives, and the relation of that connection to Yeats's aggressively creative tendencies. Yeats, he observes in *Preoccupations*, started and carried through a countercultural movement at which it is now fashionable to smile indulgently. But it was grounded, for Yeats, in place, a place he actively made, though it also involved what he considered to be a restoration of a body of legends and folklore. Yeats attempted to create a "new country of the mind" (P, 135). Yeats has come under attack from the materialist critics for the falseness of this country. Heaney does not make this attack. He is interested in the accomplishment rather than its content and relevance to today's situation. He therefore has no explicit quarrel with Deane and others over Yeats. Nevertheless, he has issued warnings against judgments so completely centered on political ideology and the situation of the moment. "We live here in critical times ourselves, when the idea of poetry as an art is in danger of being overshadowed by a quest for poetry as a diagram of political attitudes. Some commentators have all the fussy liberalism of an official from the ministry of truth" (P, 219–20). He has also attacked the politicians of poetry itself, who live with "anxious over-the-shoulder" glances in a world of grants, fashions, and schools (GT, 40). Poets in his view should not consciously respond to a "demonstrable literary situation," lest their brains be turned into "butterfly nets" (P, 190). Heaney holds out against fashionableness, a certain literary politics, ideological commitments oversimplified by the pull and stress of the moment and, perhaps above all, the jingoism of the extremists on all (both) sides. From the outset of his career, or at least from the moment when he defined his task as the "search for images and symbols adequate to our predicament" (P, 56), he has held to the notion that he could be a poet and, with the implied artistic commitments, "encompass the perspectives of a humane reason, and at the same time . . . grant the religious intensity of the violence its deplorable authenticity and complexity" (*P*, 56–57). Ten years later, in *The Government of the Tongue*, he insists that if no lyric poem has ever stopped a tank, it still ought to be possible to write poetry that is like "the writing in the sand in the face of which accusers and accused are left speechless and renewed" (*GT*, 107).

I have entitled this essay "Critic as Heaney" because it seems to me that today we need more critics behaving as Heaney does. His criticism is what I would call a "writerly" criticism as compared to that academic criticism that has been readerly and descriptive and has given way in the academy to a theoretical discourse that tends to dwell incessantly on its own problems or an ideological discourse that has little patience with the niceties of what Heaney calls craft. Over and over in his critical writings Heaney utters a paragraph about a particular poet or particular lines which achieves what is lacking in most discussions of literature—a truly creative insight into another's work, a capacity to edge up to it in words without burying it in either paraphrase or jargon.

Like Yeats before him, Heaney has been actively involved in the cultural politics of Irish life, not alone in his involvement with the Field Day Theatre and its publications, to an extent that no critic or literary theorist I know of in this country has. When with the credentials of his experience he returns to an insistence on the necessity of art's having its own role generated and regenerated by the poet's properly stubborn commitment to a special sort of freedom, we should listen and admit this sort of discourse—antithetical as it may be to our cherished methods and jargons—to our various specialized worlds.

*Works Cited*

*G: The Government of the Tongue: The 1986 T. S. Eliot Memorial Lectures and Other Critical Writings*. 1988. London and Boston: Faber and Faber, 1989.

*P: Preoccupations: Selected Prose 1968–1978*. 1980. London and Boston: Faber and Faber, 1984.

*PW: The Place of Writing*. Atlanta: Scholars Press, 1989.

# CULTURAL AESTHETICS

◆

# Facing *North* Again: Polyphony, Contention

PAUL SCOTT STANFIELD*

Much of Seamus Heaney's recent work bears traces of a vacillation between the wish to perfect his art and the obligation to speak for his community—the dilemma outlined in the sentence of Czeslaw Milosz quoted by Heaney in "Away from It All": "I was stretched between contemplation of a motionless point and the command to participate actively in history."[1] His interest in this question crops up even in his work as a translator, for in his introduction to his English version of *Buile Suibhne* Heaney claims that the mad King Sweeney enacts just such a vacillation: "insofar as Sweeney is also a figure of the artist, displaced, guilty, assuaging himself by his utterance, it is possible to read the work as an aspect of the quarrel between the free creative imagination and the constraints of religious, political, and domestic obligation."[2] Putting the point more familiarly in an interview with Seamus Deane, Heaney said: "There is a sort of schizophrenia in him. On the one hand he is always whinging for his days in Rasharkin, but on the other he is celebrating his free creative imagination," and went on to call the myth of Sweeney an "objective correlative" for "feelings in myself I could not otherwise find words for."[3]

Some of Heaney's best poems succeed precisely because of the exactness with which they re-create the tension of this ambivalence. "Casualty," for instance, both convinces us of the deep instinctive power of community, felt by the poet at the funeral of Bloody Sunday's thirteen dead, and makes us admire the independence of the fisherman killed in the republican bombing of a curfew-violating pub, whose work is implicitly likened to the poet's in its dependence on rhythm, remoteness, and freedom.[4] Similarly, "Exposure" gives us the poet in Wicklow, physically and psychologically removed from his native terrain and its sorrow, stretched between contemplation of the "diamond absolutes" of the raindrops—Milosz's "motionless point," perhaps—and the wish to glimpse the arching, blazing, but momentary "once in lifetime portent, / The comet's pulsing rose"—historical crisis, perhaps.[5]

The dilemma is an old one. We might think of Yeats, at times hoping to be "True brother of a company / That sang to sweeten Ireland's wrong,"at

*Reprinted from *Éire-Ireland* 23, no. 4 (Winter 1988): 133–44.

at other times blaming himself for heeding "The seeming needs of my fool-driven land." From a common-sense point of view, Heaney deserves no blame for not solving this dilemma—how could anyone solve it?—yet in his recent work he often becomes his own accuser on this score, taking responsibility for his vacillation as if for a sin.

"An Afterwards," a strange and moving poem in *Field Work*, finds the poet and all his fellow-poets consigned to the ninth circle of Dante's Hell for "backbiting in life" (thus fulfilling, according to the poem, a wish of the poet's wife).[6] The poet's wife appears, "aided and abetted by Virgil's wife," and these damned, like Dante's, immediately and self-interestedly ask for news: "Who wears the bays / In our green land above . . .?" Her summation of her husband's posthumous reputation runs: "You weren't the worst. You aspired to a kind, / Indifferent, faults-on-both-sides tact"—faint praise that seems literally to damn, as if tact and ambivalence, in the poet's circumstances, were tantamount to betrayal, landing him all too justly in the infernal circle created for traitors.

The sin the poet hopes to expiate by his pilgrimage in the sequence "Station Island," as Seamus Deane has suggested,[7] seems to be exactly this ambivalence-as-betrayal. To the ghost of a friend of his youth, who has just told the story of his "execution" by unidentified terrorists, the poet blurts: "Forgive the way I have lived indifferent—/ forgive my timid circumspect involvement."[8] The ghost of the poet's cousin, another victim of political violence and the subject of a beautiful elegy in *Field Work*, attacks the very beauty of that elegy as a betrayal of the truth of his ugly murder: "You confused evasion and artistic tact."[9] Soon follows the poem's crisis, in which the poet's "softly awash and blanching self-disgust" materializes as a "strange polyp" afloat on a "mucky, glittering flood," and he names his sin: "I repent / My unweaned life that kept me competent / To sleepwalk with connivance and mistrust."[10]

This remorse may have arisen from the poet's dissatisfaction not only with his handling of the conflict between the free imagination and public duty but also with his handling of another conflict within the first. When, as in *North*, Heaney inclined away from the pole of the free creative imagination towards the pole of community obligation, he found himself faced by another opposition: "At one minute you are drawn towards the old vortex of racial and religious instinct," he wrote in 1972; "at another time you seek the mean of human love and reason."[11] Here we are stretched between the effort to clear from our minds, consciously and rationally, the community's archetypal patterns of fear and desire so as to prepare the ground for a humane, practical, consensus solution; and the pull, too deep or genuine to ignore, of those same patterns—in Heaney's case, the familiar matrix articulated by Catholicism, republicanism, the Irish language, an ur-Irish racial inheritance.

A feeling that he had mistaken his ground in this conflict may have led Heaney to meditate in his later work on the more inclusive conflict of artistic imagination and public duty and to accuse himself of having wrongfully hesitated in making intellectual choices or wrongfully chose to feign the innocent ignorance of a sleepwalker. Many readers, indeed, have found fault with *North* precisely because it seems to them to hesitate in condemning tendencies it ought unambiguously to condemn. The reputation of the volume is hardly in ruins, but it nonetheless strikes me that a minor effort at rehabilitation has become needful. I wish to argue here that in much of *North* Heaney artistically encompassed his vacillation in such a way that the word "vacillation"—which slides so easily into tut-tutting near-synonyms like timidity, circumspection, evasion, indifference—does not do his stance justice.

Consider the much-discussed and somewhat controversial "Punishment," in which the poet contemplates the remains of a young woman killed for adultery by her community in Iron Age Jutland, buried in a peat bog, and unearthed by archaeologists centuries later in a state of near-perfect preservation.[12] Likened both to the woman taken in adultery (John 8: 3–11) and to the Catholic women in Northern Ireland abused by their own community for dating British soldiers, the young woman becomes a touchstone for the poet to measure his responses to barbarism—a word in which I must ask the reader to detect not only savagery or cruelty but also a dominant culture's designation of a dominated alien culture.

As the poem begins, the poet is virtually one with the imagined living woman as she faces her executioners; emphasizing her fragility and vulnerability, the poet seeks to make her victimage his own, or our own:

> I can feel the tug
> of the halter at the nape
> of her neck, the wind
> on her naked front.

When the imagery of the second stanza becomes more visual than tactile[13]—

> It blows her nipples
> to amber beads,
> it shakes the frail rigging
> of her ribs

—it reminds us that the poet and we ourselves are not victims but her observers, a shift confirmed in the opening of the third stanza ("I can *see* her drowned / body in the bog" [my emphasis]) and heightened by a dislocation in time which puts before us not the imagined living woman but her exhumed corpse ("oak-bone, brain-firkin").

When the poet returns to imagining the living woman, "flaxen-haired," under-nourished," she is emphatically object to the poet's subject, made distinct from him by apostrophe ("Little adulteress") and the startling confession: "I am the artful voyeur," and half-participant abstracting from observation the emotions of the experience itself. The crucial twist in "Punishment" comes with the revelation that the poet half-participates as well in the other dimension of punishment, that of the crowd, the community that feels itself wronged. Had he been present at the execution, the poet admits, he "would have cast, I know, / the stones of silence"—would have made himself partly responsible by a failure to intervene, as he had when, standing

> dumb
> when your betraying sisters,
> cauled in tar,
> wept by the railings,

he had been one who "would connive in civilized outrage," civilized outrage apparently being as much a tacit consent, a disguised participation, as silence and inaction.

The poem's last two lines push this admission further. The poet participates not only negatively by inaction but also positively in that he is bound by kinship to the crowd, "understand[s] the exact / and tribal, intimate revenge." As the poem began by identifying with the victim, an identification gradually dissipated by the poet's self-consciousness first of his voyeuristic relation to the woman and then of his passive connivance with the crowd, so it ends by identifying with the crowd.

That the poem's closing lines seem to have been sucked into "the old vortex of racial and religious instinct" has disturbed some readers who feel that Heaney, by granting the traditional code of the community a power seemingly unbreakable by pity, reason, or conscience, is suggesting that "even if we do understand the past we may still be condemned to repeat it"[14] or is insisting on the "helplessness and inescapability" of the Northern troubles.[15] By finding such historical or ancestral antecedents for modern political violence, Blake Morrison has argued, Heaney grants that violence a "respectability which is not granted in day-to-day journalism: precedent becomes, if not justification, then at least an 'explanation.' "[16] Ciaran Carson argued in a 1975 review of *North* that the poem and the volume misinterpret, even mystify history, ignoring "the real differences between our society and that of Jutland in some vague past," expressly to make political violence forgivable because comprehensible, to turn understanding of that violence into its absolution by placing it in "the realms of sex, death, and inevitability."[17]

Seamus Deane seems backhandedly to confirm Carson's suspicions when, in interviewing Heaney, he praises *North* while calling Conor Cruise O'Brien's "humanism" an "excuse to rid Ireland of the atavisms which gave it life even though the life itself may be in some ways brutal,"[18] or when, in writing on Heaney, he concludes: "In his writing . . . we are witnessing a revision of our heritage which is changing our conception of what writing can be because it is facing up to what writing, to remain authentic, must always face—the confrontation with the ineffable, the unspeakable thing for which 'violence' is our helplessly inadequate word."[19]

But it is a mistake, I feel, to see in the poem so complete a surrender to race, community tradition, or violence—a mistake arising from privileging closure, allowing the poem's conclusion the right to outshout the rest of the poem. Certainly the poet's identification with the vindictive emotions of the crowd surprises us and perhaps pricks us where our political conscience, if we are liberals, are most sensitive. But does it wholly overthrow the poet's identification with the victim's body that opens the poem or the tenderness of "Little adulteress, . . . my poor scapegoat, I almost love you," or the evocation (in the image of casting stones) of Christ's intervention in similar circumstances, the rational, humane, and timely question that deflected another crowd's vengeance? I think not; each movement of feeling in the poem is equally real, equally intense, equally genuine. They contend, but none finally dominates. This is the poem's peculiar virtue.

Noting that the poem takes the point of view both of the victim and of the crowd, Edna Longley has asked: "But can the poet run with the hare and hunt with the hounds?"[20] Yes; I would answer, following James Lafferty who has praised the poem's "double perspective"[21] and following John Westlake who has defended the poem's "equivocal position" as part of its "transparent honesty."[22] My reading, however, departs somewhat from Lafferty, who writes of "painful ambivalence" and "vacillation," and from Westlake," who writes of "ambiguity," and from another of the poem's defenders, Neil Corcoran, who describes "empathetic pity for the victim" as "the poem's predominant emotion."[23] Instead, I would urge that we see the poem not as in dubious battle with itself but as precisely mapping the emotional possibilities of a particular intersection of the personal and the political.

I say "mapping" with a purpose, for I would suggest that we see the poem spatially rather than temporally not as a progression but as a spectrum. We might compare what "Punishment" does to what Dostoevsky's novels do, as described by the great Russian critic Mikhail Bakhtin: "The fundamental category in Dostoevsky's mode of artistic visualizing was not evolution, but *coexistence* and *interaction*. He saw and conceived his world in terms of space, not time. . . . In contrast to Goethe, Dostoevsky attempted to perceive the stages themselves in their *simultaneity*, to *juxtapose* and *counterpose* them dramatically, and not stretch them out into an evolving sequence. For him, to get one's bearings on the world meant to conceive all its contents as simultaneous, and *to guess at their interrelationships in the cross-section of a single moment*."[24] Heaney conflates different times in the poem by making the punished young woman, her museum-housed remains, her "betraying sisters" in Northern Ireland, and the woman taken in adultery all co-exist in the one plane, as it were, of a single moment; and by making a graduated variety of emotional responses (identification with victim, remote participation with victim via voyeurism, remote participation with crowd via connivance, identification with crowd) co-exist in the single sustained moment of the poem. This method risks confounding real historical differences, as Carson has noted, and risks having one dimension of the poet's emotional response taken as its totality, but when it succeeds it lets us see all at once, as in a cross-section, the historical and emotional strands that become entangled in the knot of the present.

By concentrating on showing how these strands co-exist and interact rather than on making one or another dominate, Heaney approaches the "polyphony" Bakhtin ascribes to Dostoevsky's novels, in which no character, no voice among the contending voices, is granted ultimate authority. Were we to conceive of an "upside-down" version of this poem—beginning with an identification with the crowd, succumbing to the same mingled currents of self-consciousness in the center, and ending with an identification with the victim—we would have a poem that probably would have disturbed fewer readers but, according to my argument—even so—much the same poem since the spatial encompassing is what matters most and not the temporal progression.

It may seem inappropriate to use the term "polyphony"—created to describe a kind of novel—in regard to a lyric poem which we think of as necessarily governed by a single voice; it may seem doubly inappropriate to use it of a poem by Heaney whose *"timbre*, a sound so familiar that it could border on self-parody, left little room for tone, the assumption of new voices or the adjustment of voice to audience," according to at least one perceptive critic, Dillon Johnston.[25] I feel, however, that the deliberate symmetry of the juxtapositions in "Punishment," the clarity and immediacy with which it represents irreconcilable movements of thought, deserve to be called polyphonic rather than ambivalent.

In the later "Station Island" sequence we see a plainer attempt at internalized drama and hear a host of voices other than Heaney's—not incorporated with the virtuosity of Kinsella's "Nightwalker," perhaps, or the panache of Muldoon's "7, Middagh Street," but still tellingly and powerfully, especially in sections VII and VIII. The possibility of this development is already present in "Punishment" and other poems in *North*, such as "Viking Dublin: Trial Pieces." The poet is suspended between humane reason and old loyalties, figured by victim and crowd in "Punishment." This suspension appears again in "Viking Dublin" complicated by another opposition, that between his wish to contemplate from an aesthetic distance and the obligation to participate. Reason and loyalty, contemplation and duty, co-exist and interact by means of opposing metaphors: on the one hand, figures pertaining to excavation, penetration and containment, reach downwards and inwards; on the other, those pertaining to flight, escape, head upwards and outwards.[26]

We learn in the poem's second section (there are six, of four quatrains apiece) that the object of the poet's attention is an archaeological relic, a "trial piece," a bone fragment upon which a Viking artisan, perhaps a child, has carved for no other purpose, apparently, than to practice his hand: "the craft's mystery / improvised on bone." The poem itself imitates the improvisational, experimental character of the trial piece, the indefinable pattern inscribed on the bone undergoing a succession of metamorphoses as the poet tries out metaphors: an eel, a bird, a fish, a longship, among others. The poem only *imitates* improvisation, however, for soon enough we see that the shifts of metaphor are not governed by whim. Take these examples from the first section:

> . . . a small outline
>
> was incised, a cage
> or trellis to conjure in.
> Like a child's tongue
> following the toils
>
> of his calligraphy,
> like an eel swallowed
> in a basket of eels,
> The line amazes itself
>
> eluding the hand
> that fed it,
> a bill in flight,
> a swimming nostril.

The criss-crossings of the pattern are both a cage—obviously suggestive of confinement—and a trellis which enables the plant to grow upward and outward. A similar opposition of containment with escape is discernible between the image of the eel absorbed into the community of eels and those of the flying bird and the swimming fish escaping their origins, slipping past nets—Joycean nets, as we shall see. Intertwined with the opposition is the act of writing itself, which both depends on continuity with the past (the conventions the child is struggling to learn) and which represents a foray into the future, a gamble, a departure.

When the opposition shifts the figures in the second section, historical dimensions begin to appear. The cage or trellis becomes "the netted routes / of ancestry and trade," the nostril "a migrant prow / sniffing the Liffey": that is, a Viking longship. Routes of trade mean expansion and the opening of possibilities, but we must note they are "netted"—these routes helped bind Ireland into a particular history. The "migrant prow" suggests freedom and movement, but we see it in the act of entering (being contained by) first the Liffey and then the earth itself. Here, Heaney ingeniously telescopes time to show us the ship turning to buried relics simultaneously with its arrival:

> swanning it up the ford,
> dissembling itself
> in antler-combs, bone pins,
> coins, weights, scale-pans.

The opening of the third section recapitulates the image of the longship's free movement becoming something contained and immobilized, this time complicating the historical dimension of the figure with overtones of violence and sexuality, conquest and domination:

> Like a long sword
> sheathed in its moisting
> burial clays,
> the keel stuck fast
>
> in the slip of the bank . . .

This penetration then metamorphoses into the delving of the archaeologist ("And now we reach in . . . the mother-wet caches") who discovers the trial-piece which, once unearthed, accomplishes another revolution of the figures, its inscribed outline becoming a sign of departure and escape: "a longship, a buoyant / migrant line."

In the fourth section, the opposition (down and in *vs.* up and out, digging *vs.* flight, memory *vs.* imagination) that has been swirling and re-inventing itself throughout the poem again participates in the act of writing, this time that of the poet himself as first-person singular pronouns appear for the first time. The migrant line "enters my longhand," becoming "a worm of thought / I follow into the mud." The imagery of escape again spins upon its axis and becomes the imagery of digging and entering. "I am Hamlet the Dane," he declares, like Hamlet enmeshed in costly inherited obligations to his community ("pinioned by ghosts / and affections), like Hamlet addressing those obligations in a way so indirect it looks like shirking ("skull-handler, parablist . . . dithering, blathering"), like Hamlet—though here, perhaps, the parallel strains—wondering whether there may be no way out but the way in, that understanding, enlightenment, and serene detachment may be attainable only by impulse, instinct, pursuit: "coming to consciousness / by jumping in graves."

But the jump into the grave and the worm followed into the mud transmute, in the fifth section, into flight as Hamlet, thanks to canny literary echoes, transmutes into the would-be-airborne Stephen Dedalus, never one to suffer being pinioned by ghosts and affections. The section's first line: "Come fly with me," may remind us less of the fabulous artificer than of Frank Sinatra, but whatever humor there may be in this note of exultation evaporates as the invitation continues: "come sniff the wind / with the expertise / of the Vikings."

As the sniffing of the migrant prow led to its entombment in the Irish earth, so our wind-sniffing flight lands us in the bog of origins, for the Vikings are so described as to be hardly distinguishable from modern Ulstermen ("neighbourly, scoretaking / killers, . . . hoarders of grudges and gain") and, in a kind of ancestor-worship prayer, are petitioned in the section's final quatrain:

> Old fathers, be like us.
> Old cunning assessors
> of feuds and of sites
> for ambush or town.

At the same moment that Heaney bends the knee to these ancestors, "old fathers" and "cunning" encode Stephen Dedalus into the poem, making him retrospectively visible in the "bill in flight," in the poem's evocations of Dublin, in Hamlet, and even in "come fly with me," and establishes the Joycean theme of separation and artistic independence in counterpoint to the poet's rooting out of origins. As the mutually exclusive rights of victim and crowd polyphonically co-exist and interact in "Punishment" so, in "Viking Dublin," Heaney's favorite metaphor—digging / unearthing / excavating—co-exists and interacts with the opposed and distinct metaphor of flight. I believe this suggests that the poet's wish to get to the bottom of mysteries of blood, origin, and tribe also combines with a wish for an enabling transcendence, a Joycean desire to go beyond the constraints of blood, origin, and tribe in order to elucidate the mind of one's nation, create its conscience, make it known to itself. Just as I have argued that the poet's identification with the crowd in "Punishment" does not cancel his identification with the victim, so I would argue that "Viking Dublin"'s fascination with the power and violence that created the past does not cancel the poem's wish to be free of that past by understanding it, knowing and naming it—to come to consciousness by jumping in graves. The poem succeeds not by the containment of opposing metaphors within an *ad hoc* unity but by letting them contend with each other.

With this appropriate polyphony, the poem's final section gives us the voice not of Heaney but of Synge's Jimmy Farrell of *The Playboy*. Asked by Philly whether the authorities will not come across Old Mahon's skull and realize a murder has been committed, Jimmy answers by asking how the authorities could possibly conclude that the skull belonged to a recently-murdered man rather than to an "old Dane, maybe, was drownded in the flood."[27] Jimmy Farrell's remark is a comic version of Heaney's own enterprise, a compounding of past and present that confounds historical differences—what Oliver MacDonagh, in *States of Mind*, has argued to be a definitive trait of the Irish historical imagination. Quoting Jimmy Farrell at the poem's end simultaneously asserts both the absurdity and the legitimacy of such a compounding / confounding. The act of writing—

> My words lick around
> cobbled quays, go hunting
> lightly as pampooties
> over the skull-capped ground

—thus does justice both to the tribe's insistence on a history of "absolute repetitive form"[28] and to the rational intellect's insistence on difference, both the plunge into the soil and the effort to rise clear of it.

Many readers have found *North* flawed because they feel the volume is marked much more by the plunge than by the rise and—so it would seem—is, for that reason, politically dangerous not to say vicious. In addition to the criticisms of Morrison and Carson referred to previously, we might cite Alan Shapiro, who feels "the language only sanitizes the violence it appears to articulate so unflinchingly," or Edna Longley, who feels that "by plucking out the heart of his mystery and serving it up as a quasi-political mystique he temporarily succumbs to the goddess [i.e. Cathleen ni Houlihan, the Shan Van Vocht]," or George Watson, who feels that "Heaney's reading of the Northern Irish crisis through these mystical spectacles . . . assumes deeply sinister overtones" and that "the virtuous philosopher must register his perturbation in the face of this ritualised obeisance to a fatalistic historicism."[29]

Even sympathetic accounts of Heaney's career—Blake Morrison's in *Seamus Heaney*, Dillon Johnston's in *Irish Poetry after Joyce*, Robert Garratt's in *Modern Irish Poetry*—seems to pass with audible relief from *North* to *Field Work*. As my readings of "Punishment" and "Viking Dublin" indicate, I do not feel *North* in fact privileges what I have called *the plunge* over what I have called *the rise*; what may shock, or frighten, or repulse some readers is that it refuses to privilege the rise over the plunge, the voice of the individual reason over that of the community's instinct, instead letting these two voices co-exist, interact, contend without declaring a victor. This is not to mythologize or explain away violence but merely to grant it the reality and immediacy that our newspapers daily witness and to let us know it to the bone as newspapers never possibly could. It is, in a word, *truthful*—truthful in a way it could never be did it not let the tribe's jealous, all-demanding matrix of loyalties speak in its own unimpeded voice.

Heaney himself may have doubts about *North*; of the four volumes that went into his *Selected Poems* no other was so thoroughly trimmed, and the dominant style of the volume—the short two- or three-stress line, the knotty syntax, the racy archaicisms of diction—has been abandoned in his later work. Heaney told Frank Kinahan in 1981:

> The line and the life are intimately related, and that narrow line, that tight lie, came out of a time when I was very tight myself. Especially the poems in *North*. I remember looking at them when I was just going to send them in and saying: This is a very habit-formed book—these little narrow lines. Can I open this? And I wrote out a couple of poems in long line, and the sense of constriction went; and when the constriction went, the tension went. I felt that I'd come through something at the end of *North*; there was some kind of appeasement in me.[30]

One readily sees that such a change was necessary, readily admits that it has been fruitful. Like the Yeats who had completed *The Wind Among the Reeds*, the Heaney who had completed *North* found himself with a style so thoroughly mastered that it had nowhere to go except self-parody; accordingly, he went about re-inventing himself.

Yeats, Heaney wrote in 1978, "bothers you with the suggestion that if you have managed to do one kind of poem in your own way, you should cast off that way and face into another area of your experience until you have learned a new voice to say that area properly."[31] Even though it was outgrown by its maker, *The Wind Among the Reeds* remained, however, unique, irreplaceable, in its own way unsurpassed; so, I would argue, does *North*. The constriction and tension that Heaney mentions are part of the book's concentration and strength; the fear it inspires is part of its truth. Its concentration and strength appear in the vatic confidence of its assertions ("I am Hamlet the Dane," "This centre holds," "I would restore / the great chambers of Boyne") and of its imperatives ("And you, Tacitus, / observe how I make my grove . . .")—remote indeed from the burden of guilt assumed in "Station Island"—and its truth lies in what I have called its polyphony. If Heaney has "come through something," like Dante and Vergil laboring up Satan's thigh into a different world with a different, penetential light, he did not come through it without uttering its difficult truth permanently.

*Notes*

1. Seamus Heaney, *Station Island* (New York: Farrar, Straus, Giroux, 1985), p. 16.
2. Seamus Heaney, *Sweeney Astray*. (New York: Farrar, Straus, Giroux, 1984), second page of unpaginated introduction.

3. Seamus Deane, "Unhappy and at Home: Interview with Seamus Heaney," in *The Crane Bag Book of Irish Studies (1977–81)* (Dublin: Blackwater Press, 1982), p. 70.

4. In Heaney's *Field Work* (New York: Farrar, Straus, Giroux, 1979), pp. 22–24.

5. Seamus Heaney, *North* (London: Faber and Faber, 1975), p. 73. I here follow the lead of Blake Morrison, who thinks the poet's failing to glimpse the comet means he "has missed the opportunity to observe a unique historical moment in the North" (*Seamus Heaney* [London and New York: Methuen, 1982], p. 71). Other readers have disagreed with this. Edna Longley suggests the comet may be "some personal and poetic revelation" (" 'North': 'Inner Emigré' or 'Artful Voyeur'?" in Tony Curtis, ed., *The Art of Seamus Heaney* [Bridgend, Mid Glamorgan: Poetry Wales Press, Dufour Editions, 1985], p. 91), and Robert Garratt feels the unglimpsed comet indicates "a disorientation in poetic sensibility and vision" (*Modern Irish Poetry: Tradition and Continuity from Yeats to Heaney* [Berkeley: Univ. of California Press, 1986], p. 245).

6. Seamus Heaney, *Field Work* (New York: Farrar, Straus, Giroux, 1979).

7. Seamus Deane, "A Noble, Startling Achievement," rev. of *Station Island* by Seamus Heaney, *Irish Literary Supplement* 4.1 (Spring 1985): 1.

8. Heaney, *Station Island*, p. 80.

9. Heaney, *Station Island*, p. 83.

10. Heaney, *Station Island*, p. 85.

11. Seamus Heaney, *Preoccupations: Selected Prose 1968–1978* (New York: Farrar, Straus, Giroux, 1980), p. 34.

12. Heaney, *North*, pp. 37–38.

13. This shift in the poem's imagery has been noted by John H. J. Westlake, "Seamus Heaney's 'Punishment': An Interpretation," *Literatur in Wissenschaft und Unterricht* 18:1 (1985): 52.

14. Morrison, p. 68.

15. Kieran Quinlan, "Unearthing a Terrible Beauty: Seamus Heaney's Victims of Violence," *World Literature Today* 57.3 (1983): 367.

16. Morrison, p. 68.

17. Qtd. in Longley, pp. 78, 81.

18. Deane, "Unhappy and at Home," p. 69.

19. Seamus Deane, *Celtic Revivals: Essays in Modern Irish Literature 1880–1980* (Winston-Salem: Wake Forest U. P., 1987), p. 186.

20. Longley, p. 78.

21. James J. Lafferty, "Gifts from the Goddess: Heaney's 'Bog People'," *Éire-Ireland* 17:3 (Winter 1982): 135.

22. Westlake, p. 56.

23. Neil Corcoran, *Seamus Heaney* (London: Faber and Faber, 1986), p. 117.

24. Mikhail Bakhtin, *Problems of Dostoevsky's Poetics*, ed. and tr. Caryl Emerson, Theory and History of Literature: Vol. 8 (Minneapolis: University of Minnesota Press, 1984), p. 28; Bakhtin's emphasis.

25. Dillon Johnston, *Irish Poetry after Joyce* (Notre Dame, Indiana: Univ. of Notre Dame Press; Mountrath, Ireland: Dolmen, 1985), p. 149.

26. *North*, pp. 21–24.

27. J. M. Synge, *Collected Works*, ed. Ann Saddlemyer (London: Oxford U. P., 1968) IV: 133.

28. Oliver MacDonagh, *States of Mind: A Study of Anglo-Irish Conflict 1780–1980* (London: Allen and Unwin, 1983), p. 9.

29. Alan Shapiro, "Crossed Pieties," *Parnassus* (Fall/Winter 1983 & Spring/Summer 1984), p. 347; Longley, p. 93; George Watson, "The Narrow Ground: Northern Poets and the Northern Ireland Crisis," in Masaru Sekine, ed., *Irish Writers and Society at Large*, Irish

Literary Studies 22 (Gerrards Cross: Colin Smythe; Totowa, N. J.: Barnes and Noble, 1985), pp. 212, 214.

30. Frank Kinahan, "Artists on Art: An Interview with Seamus Heaney," *Critical Inquiry* 8:3 (1982): 411–12.

31. Heaney, *Preoccupations*, p. 110.

# Heaney and the Politics of the Classroom

LUCY MCDIARMID*

At least since the Tudor and Stuart monarchs began suppressing monastic and "popish" schools in Ireland, the Irish classroom has been a site of ideological conflict. A debate in the *Irish Times* during the summer of 1916 about whether Irish schoolteachers had caused the Rising formed part of a long tradition. Ignoring altogether the notorious headmaster of St. Enda's, whose name never entered the discussion, letter writers such as the Provost of Trinity College offered the evidence "of those who lived through the whole insurrection in Dublin that it was deliberately planned . . . by the careful instilling of revolutionary principles in the teaching of so many of our primary schools."[1] One respondent, a wag signing himself "Warning Voice," suggested that it was the Commissioners of Education, not the teachers, who were to blame, because they had listed *Kidnapped* as required reading. And *Kidnapped*, insisted "Warning," is "the best text-book on sedition ever published. Alan Breck is an avowed rebel, and his efforts to sow the seeds of sedition are presented to the reader with all the insidious glamour of a master writer. I can scarcely believe that any of the Commissioners have read this book in the light of recent happenings in Ireland. . . ."[2] Later in the debate, Bishop O'Dwyer of Limerick complained that a pamphlet issued by the Commissioners under the title "Patriotism" was "in reality a recruiting manifesto," and contained not a word "about Grattan, or Emmet, or O'Connell, or Butt, or Parnell."[3] Irish teachers must now "revert to the days of Whately, and teach their pupils to bless the goodness and the grace that made them happy English children."

Only two years earlier, Joyce had published the classic scene of this *topos* in *A Portrait of the Artist as a Young Man*, Stephen's discussion with the Dean of Studies about the provenance of the word "tundish." "The language in which we are speaking is his before it is mine. . . . His language, so familiar and so foreign, will always be for me an acquired speech. . . . My soul frets in the shadow of his language" (189). And twenty-five years later Flann O'Brien would write it again in *An Beal Bocht* (*The Poor Mouth*), where the youngster who "had only Gaelic as a mode of expression and as

*This essay was written specifically for this volume and appears here for the first time with permission of the author.

a protection against the difficulties of life" is beaten by the English-speaking schoolmaster and given the same name as all the other little boys: "I fainted from that blow but before I became totally unconscious I heard him scream: 'Yer nam, said he, is Jams O'Donnell!' " (30).

English classrooms may be just as politicized, but the argument is rarely over the transmission of culture. Stephen Spender's "An Elementary School Classroom in a Slum" criticizes the dissemination of high culture to poor, sick children, but his concern is for feeding the children and not for taking Shakespeare back from the teacher. In a Scottish variation, Muriel Spark's *Prime of Miss Jean Brodie*, Miss Brodie links the high culture she disseminates with Mussolini's fascism, but the school fires her for her politics; it's her ideology, not theirs, and the novel shows the school as an institution dissociating itself from her.

Auden's 1937 poem "Schoolchildren," written from a 1930s leftist point of view, offers an instructive contrast to the Irish classroom. Like Irish writers, Auden sees the school as a place where power is exercised, a microcosm of class relations in the society outside it:

> Here are all the captivities; the cells are as real:
> But these are unlike the prisoners we know . . .
> For they dissent so little, so nearly content
> With the dumb play of the dog, the licking and rushing . . .
> Yet the tyranny is so easy. The improper word
> Scribbled upon the fountain, is that all the rebellion?
> The storm of tears wept in the corner, are these
> The seeds of the new life?
>
> (52–53)

Auden's vocabulary—captivities, tyranny, rebellion—insists that the classroom is a miniature state; the children play the role of political prisoners to the masters' jailers. Their attempt at "rebellion," a dirty word scribbled in a public place, mimics the chalking of slogans on a wall. Although the situation is a political one, the children themselves are only protopolitical, growing between the quasi-animal physicality of affectionate dogs and the tears and "new life" of a mature consciousness; they cry in a corner but do not experience conversions.

The political vision represented in Auden's poem sets in relief the distinctly Irish nature of the Irish schoolroom tradition. There, the classroom is not simply a place where a weaker class of beings is oppressed by a stronger, a site where rebellion is squelched; it is a site where the transmission of culture and information is a political activity, and where pedagogy has a cultural edge. Paul Muldoon's "Anseo" (1980) offers a more recent Irish example. As in the Flann O'Brien example, the students' confrontation with authority is a culturally charged moment. The primary school children in the poem call back "Anseo" ("Here") when their names are called on the roll, and "Anseo," writes Muldoon, "Was the first word of Irish I spoke." His fellow student Joseph Mary Plunkett Ward is made conspicuous by his failure to answer to his name. Regularly beaten for his truancy, he makes a fine art of choosing the stick he is to be whipped with, sanding and polishing it, "altogether so delicately wrought / That he had engraved his initials on it." Grown up, Joe Ward becomes a Commandant in the Provos, and "every morning at parade / His volunteers would call back *Anseo.*"

Here again, linguistic difference is associated with authority and corporal punishment, and (as Althusser would have put it) with the interpellation of individuals as subjects. The culture that is disseminated in the classroom is inseparable from the exercise of power; though of course there is no single, hegemonic "culture" disseminated in all Irish schoolroom literature. In the passage from *An Beal Bocht*, the child who has only Gaelic as a protection is not protected enough; his Irish name must be Anglicized. In Muldoon's poem, the Irish language serves first as a form of tyranny and later as a form of resistance, when the discipline associated with it is transferred from the classroom to the IRA.

Even when the Irish classroom-poem is set in England, the familiar pattern obtains. In Eavan Boland's "An Irish Childhood in England: 1951," England, by synecdoche, "was the teacher in the London convent who / when I produced 'I amn't' in the classroom / turned and said—'you're not in Ireland now' " (51). In "Fond Memory," the poem that follows this one in *The Journey*, Boland situates the child between *two* countries' versions of themselves, both embodied in cultural forms. The English version is foreign and considers her inferior; but the Irish national ideal, at least according to Boland's Thomas Moore, is sentimental and nostaglic and doesn't offer her anything substantial with which to identify. In the same English convent school, where the children cry at the announcement that the King has died, Boland "dressed in wool as well, / ate rationed food, played English games and learned / how wise the Magna Carta was." She goes home to hear her father at the piano

> sit down and play the slow

>> lilts of Tom Moore while I stood there trying
>> not to weep at the cigarette smoke stinging up
>> from between his fingers and—as much as I could think—

>> I thought this is my country, was, will be again,
>> this upward-straining song made to be
>> our safe inventory of pain. And I was wrong.

(52)

The poem expresses the separation of her own consciousness from any state treating her as a subject, whether it is identified with the British culture she receives in official form at school, or the Irish culture transmitted, benignly and patriarchally, through her father and Thomas Moore.

In postpartition poetry, on both sides of the border, questions about the control of cultural forms—accent, language, literature—arise in classrooms again and again: who owns these things and what can they be made to mean? Speech and writing appear ideologically unfixed, and the State, embodied in the teacher and sometimes linked with the Church, attempts to appropriate culture, to speak with authority about it and to silence opposition. So in John Montague's Co. Tyrone classroom, the pain of his mother's death returns to him

> . . . in a schoolroom
> where I was taunted by a mistress
> who hunted me publicly down
> to near speechlessness.
>
> *So this is our brightest infant?*
> *Where did he get that outlandish accent?*
> *What do you expect, with no parents,*
> *sent back from some American slum:*
> *none of you are to speak like him!*
>
> (91)

And so in the Free State Christian Brothers school that Thomas Kinsella recalls in *Nightwalker*, the teacher's authoritative voice, quoted at length, sounds forth reappropriating native culture:

> And the authorities
> Used the National Schools to try to conquer
> The Irish national spirit, at the same time
> Exterminating what they called our "jargon"
> —The Irish language; in which Saint Patrick, Saint Bridget
> And Saint Columcille taught and prayed!
> Edmund Ignatius Rice founded our Order
> To provide schools that were national in more than name.
> Pupils from our schools played their part,
> As you know, in the fight for freedom. And you will be called
> In your different ways—to work for the native language,
> To show your love by working for your country.
> Today there are Christian Brothers' boys
> Everywhere in the Government—the present Taoiseach
> Sat where one of you is sitting now.
>
> (110)

This classroom poem recalls the history of contested classroom space; Brother Burke complains about colonial control of the curriculum, but not about colonial pedagogy, because his own is identical with it. The British had used the schools to legitimate their Empire and educate its denizens, as the Irish use their schools to keep the state functioning. The school—quite unapologetically—trains civil servants. Brother Burke's syntax implies that "to work for the native language" and to "work for your country" are identical functions.

Seamus Heaney's series *Singing School* (from *North*) treats all Ireland as the school in which Heaney learned how to be a poet. The six-poem series opens with the naive belief that literature exists in a nonpolitical, uncontested, "free" space, but concludes with the acknowledgment that every poem assumes some kind of relation to the State, whether oppositional, complicit, or escapist. As a child Heaney discovers in the school a civic world, with its repressions and compulsions; in later poems he observes the political resonance in all cultural forms.

In its original context, Yeats's "Sailing to Byzantium," the title of this series signified the discipline and professional training (like an M.F.A. program) that the artist needs for his trade; an intense, almost monastic separation from the world. But Heaney's series implies that the kind of "singing school" that taught him offered its lessons not by escape from the ordinary life of his native land but by immersion in it. Reinforcing this point, the epigraphs from Wordsworth and Yeats suggest the simultaneous origin of aesthetic and ideological awareness, or the ideological nature of the emergent literary talent. Describing the "growth of a poet's mind," Wordsworth says he "grew up / Fostered alike by beauty and by fear." *Fosterage* is of course the traditional Irish method of educating children, and the particular mixture of beauty and fear available in midcentury Northern Ireland determines young Heaney's poetic sensibility. The prose passage from Yeats's *Autobiographies* states unambiguously the politicized nature of the young Yeats's aesthetic. In a kind of primal scene, he describes the poems that gave him the "pleasure of rhyme for the first time," a "book of Orange rhymes" that he read in the hayloft with the stableboy. Their effect was immediate: he wanted to "die fighting the Fenians." Those particular sympathies didn't last, we all know, but the inextricably political and partisan nature of literary taste is suggested at the beginning of Heaney's series.

Wordsworthian "fear" permeates the first poem and is projected onto two institutions, the (Catholic) secondary school, St. Columb's, and the (British) Northern Irish State. The title, "The Ministry of Fear," derives from Graham Greene's 1943 novel, where it designates the Nazi surveillance apparatus, of which a character (himself a Nazi, and untrustworthy) says, "They formed, you know, a kind of Ministry of Fear—with the most efficient undersecretaries. It isn't only that they get a hold on certain people. It's the general atmosphere they spread, so that you can't depend on a soul" (121). Such, by implication, was the atmosphere spread by the school and the RUC (Royal Ulster Constabulary), which the poem's vignettes associate with each other. The school memory begins with an unattributed insult, indicating the atmosphere outside the classroom: " 'Catholics, in general, don't speak / As well as students from the Protestant schools.' " A new student at St. Columb's, the "individual" Heaney is interpellated as a subject:

> "What's your name, Heaney?"
> "Heaney, Father."
> "Fair
> Enough."
> On my first day, the leather strap
> Went epileptic in the Big Study,
> Its echoes plashing over our bowed heads . . . (64)

As in *An Beal Bocht*, Muldoon's "Anseo," and the pandy-bat episode of *Portrait of the Artist*, the act of interpellation is linked with corporal punishment, as, student by student, the school creates its miniature state.

This association is repeated in the public world of the State, as the somewhat older Heaney, sitting in a car with a girlfriend, is interrogated by the RUC:

> policemen
> Swung their crimson flashlamps, crowding round
> The car like black cattle, snuffing and pointing
> The muzzle of a sten-gun in my eye:
> "What's your name, driver?"
> "Seamus . . ."
> *"Seamus?"*
> (64)

Civic space, like classroom space, is threatening, dominated by a "Ministry of Fear." Whether the apparatus is Catholic or Protestant, school or state, it creates an atmosphere in which every action seems guilty. When schoolboy Heaney throws over a fence the "biscuits left to sweeten my exile," even that childish act becomes "an act of stealth" (a phrase Edna Longley finds "archly literary" [71]).

Perhaps the whole poem is "archly literary"; poetry, young Heaney thinks, exists in a personal world, separate from school and state. The first juvenile literary efforts Heaney mentions here are sent from Seamus Deane to Heaney, "bulky envelopes arriving / In vacation time." They are outside institutional time and notebooks, "ripped from the wire spine / Of your exercise book." Heaney's metaphors for the poems place them beyond the reach of ideological apparatus: "Vowels and ideas bandied free / As the seed-pods blowing off our sycamores." With their beauty and freedom they attract him, and so, says Heaney,

> I tried to write about the sycamores
> And innovated a South Derry rhyme
> With *hushed* and *lulled* full chimes for *pushed* and *pulled*.
> Those hobnailed boots from beyond the mountain
> Were walking, by God, all over the fine
> Lawns of elocution.
>
> (63–64)

Poetry is presented as realm in which elements can be "bandied free," in which innovation is possible, in which the limits of class can be escaped. The rough country boy can participate in the elite activity of the leisured classes.

By the end of this first poem, the literary realm is less free. After describing the RUC incident, Heaney recalls another time he was stopped:

> They once read my letters at a roadblock
> And shone their torches on your hieroglyphics,
> "Svelte dictions" in a very florid hand.
>
> Ulster was British, but with no rights on
> The English lyric: all around us, though
> We hadn't named it, the ministry of fear.
>
> (65)

So the private friendship that the poem celebrates is spied up on; first the poems had to be ripped from notebooks and sent outside of school time, and now the letters are read by the RUC. In the last three lines, poetry is rather momentously defined as existing beyond the State's power; Ulster has "no rights on / The English lyric." The phrase suggests that even people who don't think of themselves as British can read and write English poetry and feel it is their own culture; the state apparatus alone is British; the "culture" is English. But the political autonomy of literature and of culture generally is cast in doubt by the poem, because the pervasive "ministry of fear" politicizes everything it touches. If the young Heaney feels like an intruder in the cultural domain of another class, walking in his boots on fancy lawns; if Deane's svelte dictions can be opened and read by the enemy, then nothing literary was ever really "bandied free," and all cultural forms— names, accents, languages—came already permeated by politics.

The next two poems show the obtrusive Northern Irish state as it is manifested in taxes and parades. The constable who calls to assess the family's taxes works for some ministry of fear, inspiring the young boy's anxiety that his father is hiding other root crops. And the "orange drums," like the constable's bicycle, fill the air with aggression. "Summer 1969" is the first poem to suggest the possibility that the realm of poetry might be used to oppose the State. When the Troubles begin again in 1969, Heaney is in Madrid, reading in the "life of Joyce" about a writer who stands as a model of minding his own aesthetic business in spite of Irish troubles. But the kind of voice that always appears in Heaney's poems to tell him what to do (like the longboat's swimming tongue in "North," or the ghost of Joyce at the end of *Station Island*) urges political engagement: "Go back . . . try to touch the people." Heaney's reaction is typically cautious: he "retreated to the cool of the Prado" to look at paintings of political events, such as Goya's *Shootings of the Third of May*. In lines Edna Longley calls the "elementary stuff from the proven matador" (71), Heaney characterizes painting as activism: "He painted with his fists and elbows, flourished / The stained cape of his heart as history charged." The unconvincing diction suggests that this possibility is rejected even as it is articulated.

"Fosterage," the next poem, offers another option in another absolute voice: " 'Description is revelation.' " Heaney's former teaching colleague, the writer Michael McLaverty, dominates a classroom in the same singing school, a room somewhat closer to Byzantium: " 'Listen. Go your own way. / Do your own work.' " Quoting Katherine Mansfield and citing Hopkins, neither of whom are notably engagé writers, McLaverty "gripped my elbow" and "fostered me and sent me out." Fosterage offers a more affectionate and personal mode of teaching than the priest with his whip, a mode that situates the relation of teacher to student in the private space of friendship rather than the civic space of the RUC. McLaverty's recommendation of artistic autonomy suggests that the poet can define his relation to ideologies in any way he desires. It's significant, however, that "fosterage" does not take place in an actual classroom but outdoors on a weekend ("Royal / Avenue, Belfast, 1962, / A Saturday afternoon." The surrounding walls of a classroom would be inconsistent with such a liberating view.

"Exposure," the final and best poem in *Singing School*, begins in a private, contemplative moment: "It is December in Wicklow." In exile like Ovid, Heaney sits "weighing and weighing / My responsible *tristia*." He appears to have taken McLaverty's advice but to have discovered that it isn't possible to "go your own way" as if ideological conflict could be ignored. Even in retreat in the southern part of Ireland, "escaped," responsibility weighs him down; so, like Yeats, he makes poetry out of ambivalence and guilt. Heaney's position is a position, even though he is "neither internee nor informer." Exposed to all the ideological winds, he writes a poetry that is neither passionately activist, "like a slingstone / Whirled for the desperate," nor romantically independent, with "Vowels and ideas bandied free." The image of poetry as sparks the wood-kerne has blown up "for their meagre heat" implies a limited poetry, written for comfort and satisfaction but of no public importance: not oppositional, not autonomous, but evasive. Focussing his attention on the probably-not-worthwhile process of creating, he makes sparks that distract from the grander, brighter sight of the lost comet.

*Singing School* makes the politics of the other Irish classroom poems explicit; it shows the birth, in the classroom, of the dissident, oppositional poet, who learns early on the state's attempt to control cultural forms. In all these poems, the teacher's attempted political and cultural authority over pupils reproduces the state's authority over its subjects. The pupil's delayed responses to his teachers take the form of dissident classroom poems. In "A Flowering Absence" Montague follows the moment of classroom humiliation with an aetiology of his poetic career:

> Stammer, impediment, stutter:
> she had found my lode of shame,
> and soon I could no longer utter
> those magical words I had begun
> to love, to dolphin in.
>
> And not for two stumbling decades
> would I manage to speak straight again.
> Grounded for the second time
> my tongue became a rusted hinge
> until the sweet oils of poetry
>
> eased it and light flooded in.
>
> (91)

Kinsella, after the scene in the Christian Brothers school, hears a seamew calling, *"Eire, Eire . . . is there none / To hear? Is all lost?"* Kinsella attributes to the bird his own concern that Irish culture has become "lost" in bureaucracy. I think another response to Br. Burke and his ilk was *An Duanaire*, the dual language edition of colonial Irish poems put out by Kinsella and Sean O'Tuama in 1981. It is oppositional not, like Br. Burke, to the British, but to the Irish state's takeover of Irish culture, especially the Irish language. Dissident classroom poems are loosely linked to other cultural projects in contemporary Ireland. In a similar way, those poems and letters in which (according to the first poem of *Singing School*) Heaney and Deane maintained a literary friendship blossomed, years later, into *Field Day*, with its theatre company, publishing company, and anthology. Boland's classroom poems hint at the way, years later, she would redefine through feminist opposition the patriarchal national culture she was "wrong" about as a child.

Classics like *A Portrait of the Artist as a Young Man*, Yeats's "Among School Children," Brian Friel's *Translations*, and many other fictional and poetic classrooms have made the Irish classroom a major modern Irish *topos*. It may be, however, that its days are numbered. In the Republic of Ireland

and in the North, schoolchildren now encounter a world with more ideological stripes than they did half a century ago. Feminist politics cut across sectarian and geographic divisions, and the membership of both Irelands in the European Community adds another complicating internationalist element to national identity. And in a state headed by Mary Robinson, dissidence is not what it used to be. Cultural gossip columns in southern Irish papers show photographs of TDs (*Teachtaí Dála*, elected members of the Irish Government's Lower House), ministers, and journalists happily mingling with prizewinning "dissident" writers.

A recent poem by Nuala Ní Dhomhnaill suggests a new configuration of culture, society, and institutions in Ireland. In "An Mhuruch Agus Focail Airithe" ("The Mermaid and Certain Words") a threatening Irish schoolmaster makes a cameo appearance; he is the type encountered by Kinsella, Montague, or Muldoon, one who made the learning of Irish a form of punishment. But this schoolmaster, the fictitious creation of a deceptive mermaid, is used to camouflage a deeper knowledge of Irish folklore than any taught in schools. Ní Dhomhnaill's mermaid denies any knowledge of the sea, or the "life under the wave," or "those superstitions," but Ní Dhomhnaill finds her out in her life:

In the Department of Irish Folklore there is a full manuscript,
from the Schools Compilation, written in her hand, written in water
with a quill pen, on a tassel of seaweed as parchment.
There are thirteen long stories and parts of others, as well as
charms, old prayers, opinions and certain other things to be aware of.
From her father and from her grandmother she took down the most of them.

She denies it entirely: "The schoolmaster gave it to us for homework a
long time ago back in the primary school. We had to do it. We had no
way out of it."
A nosebleed would be wasted before she would ever admit to being the
originator.

                                    [translation by Michael Durkan]

In this vignette of the generic Irish schoolteacher, Ní Dhomhnaill does not suggest a dichotomy between "the state" and "the people," or a struggle over cultural forms. Instead, the school is cited—by the mermaid!—as an institution disseminating a weakened, *safe* form of dangerous material. The mermaid considers it common knowledge that anything learned about folklore in an Irish primary school will not be very potent.

The "ownership" of cultural forms is complicated here: the mermaid "originated" the material that is in the record, she "took" it "down" from her father and granny, the Folklore Commission recorded it, the UCD (University College, Dublin) Department of Irish Folklore acts as steward over it; and in however debased a form, schoolmasters teach it. Irish language and beliefs exist in a diffuse field: they can be found, in varying degrees of authenticity, in persons and institutions, families, schools, governmental commissions, and university departments. Ní Dhomhnaill's poem represents the Irish culture taught in school as an outdated, merely official transmission of ancient traditions, too large, too momentous, and too threatening to be owned by anyone.

*Notes*

1. *Irish Times*, 17 May 1916, 6.
2. *Irish Times*, 30 June 1916, 6.
3. "The Teaching of Patriotism: Bishop O'Dwyer's Latest Outburst," *Irish Times*, 7 August 1916, 7.

*Works Cited*

Auden, W. H. *The Collected Poetry of W. H. Auden*. New York: Random House, 1945.

Boland, Eavan. *The Journey and Other Poems*. Dublin: Arlen House, 1987.

Greene, Graham. *The Ministry of Fear*. 1943. London: Penguin, 1974.

*North*. London: Faber and Faber, 1975.

Kinsella, Thomas. *Poems, 1956–73*. Winston-Salem: Wake Forest University Press, 1979.

Longley, Edna. "*North*: 'Inner Emigré' or 'Artful Voyeur'?" in *The Art of Seamus Heaney*, ed. Tony Curtis. Mid Glamorgan: Poetry Wales Press, 1982, 63–95.

Montague, John. *The Dead Kingdom*. Portlaoise and Winston Salem: Dolmen and Wake Forest University Press, 1984.

Muldoon, Paul. *Why Brownlee Left*. Winston Salem: Wake Forest University Press, 1980.

Ní Dhomhnaill, Nuala. "An Mhuruch Agus Focail Airithe: A New Poem," *The Irish Reporter* 11 (third quarter 1993): 13. (Unpublished translation by Michael Durkan.)

# "Pap for the Dispossessed"
## [Heaney and the Postcolonial Moment]

DAVID LLOYD*

1

And when we look for the history of our sensibilities I am convinced, as
Professor J. C. Beckett was convinced about the history of Ireland generally,
that it is to what he called the stable element, the land itself, that we must
look for continuity.

— Heaney, "The Sense of Place"

Since his earliest volumes, Seamus Heaney's writings have rehearsed all the
figures of the family romance of identity, doubled, more often than not, by
an explicit affirmation of a sexual structure in the worker's or the writer's
relation to a land or place already given as feminine. A certain sexual knowingness accounts in part for the winsome quality of such poems as "Digging,"
"Rite of Spring," or "Undine" in the early volumes.[1] The winsomeness and
the knowingness are compounded by the neatness with which the slight
*frissons* produced by the raised spectres of patricide, rape or seduction are
stilled by *dénouements* which stress the felicities of analogy or cure the implied
violence of labour and sexuality with a warm and humanizing morality. That
such knowledge should be so easily borne and contained makes it merely
thematic, and renders suspect the strenuousness of that "agon" which Harold
Bloom seems to identify in Heaney's work as the effort to evade "his central
trope, the vowel of the earth."[2] Bloom here correctly identifies a crucial
theme in Heaney's work, and one which indeed organizes his preoccupation
with the establishment of poetic identity. The relevant question, however,
is whether that "agon" ever proceeds beyond thematic concerns, and, further,
whether it could do so without rupturing the whole edifice within which
the identity of the poet, his voice, is installed.

To be sure, Heaney makes much play, both in his poems and in his
prose writings, with the deterritorialization inflicted both on a national
consciousness by the effects of colonialization, and on the individual subject

* Reprinted from *Anomalous States: Irish Writing and the Post-colonial Moment* (Dublin: The Lilliput Press,
1993), 20–37.

by acculturation. But in Heaney's writing such perceptions initiate no firm
holding to and exploration of the quality of dispossession; rather, his work
relocates an individual and racial identity through the reterritorialization of
language and culture. Heaney's rhetoric of compensation—"You had to
come back / To learn how to lose yourself, / To be pilot and stray" (*Door
into the Dark*, p. 50)—uncritically replays the Romantic schema of a return
to origins which restores continuity through fuller self-possession, and accordingly rehearses the compensations conducted by Irish Romantic nationalism. But his poetic offers constantly a premature compensation, enacted
through linguistic and metaphorical usages which promise a healing of division simply by returning the subject to place, in an innocent yet possessive
relation to his objects. "Digging," an instance still cited sometimes with
the authority of an *ars poetica*, finds its satisfactions in a merely aesthetic
resolution, which, indeed, sets the pattern for most of the subsequent work:

> Between my finger and my thumb
> The squat pen rests; snug as a gun.
>
> Under my window, a clean rasping sound
> When the spade sinks into gravelly ground:
> My father, digging. I look down
>
> Till his straining rump along the flowerbeds
> Bends low, comes up twenty years away
> Stooping in rhythm through potato drills
> Where he was digging.

That which is posed as problematic, the irreducible difference between physical and cultural labour, and consequently the relation of the writer to his
subjective history, is neatly resolved merely by reducing physical labour to
a metaphor for cultural labour, while displacing the more intractable question
of subjective history beyond the frame of the poem as the project of that
labour. At the same time, the intimation of violence, of a will to power,
carried in the opening lines already with more fashionable swagger than
engagement—"snug as a gun"—is suppressed at the end by suppressing
the metaphorical vehicle: "Between my finger and my thumb / The squat
pen rests. / I'll dig with it." With that suppression the writer can forget or
annul the knowledge of writing's power both for dispossession and subjec-
tion—"I look down"—and represent it instead as the metaphorical continuation of a work which has already been taken as a metaphor for writing.
What assures that continuity, both across generations and across the twenty-
year span of the writer's own history, is the symbolic position of the father
in possession of and working the land. Standing initially as a figure for the
writer's exclusion from identity with land and past, the father, by way of
his own father, slides across into the position of a figure for continuity:

By God, the old man could handle a spade.
Just like his old man.
My grandfather cut more turf in a day
Than any other man on Toner's bog.
Once I carried him milk in a bottle
Corked sloppily with paper. He straightened up
To drink it, then fell to right away
Nicking and slicing neatly, heaving sods
Over his shoulder, going down and down
For the good turf. Digging.

The cold smell of potato mould, the squelch and slap
Of soggy peat, the curt cuts of an edge
Through living roots awaken in my head.
But I've no spade to follow men like them.

"Digging" holds out the prospect of a return to origins and the consolatory myth of a knowledge which is innocent and without disruptive effect.
The gesture is almost entirely formal, much as the ideology of nineteenth-
century nationalists—whose concerns Heaney largely shares—was formal or
aesthetic, composing the identity of the subject in the knowing of objects
the very knowing of which is an act of self-production. This description
holds for the writer's relation to the communal past as well as to his subjective
past: in the final analysis, the two are given as identical. Knowledge can
never truly be the knowledge of difference: instead, returned to that from
which the subject was separated by knowledge, the subject poses his objects
(perceived or produced) as synecdoches of continuity: "poetry as divination,
poetry as revelation of the self to the self, as restoration of the culture to
itself; poems as elements of continuity, with the aura and authenticity of
archaeological finds, where the buried shard has an importance that is not
diminished by the importance of the buried city; poetry as a dig, a dig for
finds that end up being plants."[3] Poetry as divination, poetry as dig: in
both these formulations Heaney resorts to metaphors which seek to bypass
on several fronts the problematic relation of writing to identity. Firstly, the
objectification of the subject that writing enacts is redeemed either through
the fiction of immediate self-presence, or in the form of the significant
moment as synecdoche for the whole temporal sequence, in which is composed the identity of the subject as a seamless continuum. Secondly, the
predicament of a literary culture as a specialized mode of labour is that it
is set over against non-cultural labour, yet Heaney's writing continually rests
in the untested assumption that a return is possible through writing back
to the "illiterate" culture from which it stems and with which, most importantly, it remains at all times continuous. The actual, persisting relation
between the literate and the non-literate, at times antagonistic, at times
symbiotic, disappears along with such attendant problems as class or ethnic

stratification in a temporal metaphor of unbroken development.[4] No irreparable break appears in the subject's relation to his history by accession to culture, nor is culture itself anything but a refined expression of an ideal community of which the writer is a part. Thirdly, given that the "touchstone" in this context is Wordsworth, the specific relation of an "Irish identity" to the English literary—and political—establishment provides not only the language, but the very terms within which the question of identity is posed and resolved, the terms for which it is *the* question to be posed and resolved. For it is not simply the verse form, the melody, or what not, that the poet takes over,[5] it is the aesthetic, and the ethical and political formulations it subsumes, that the Romantic and imperial tradition supplies.

To this cultural tradition, it is true, Heaney seeks to give an Irish "bend," grafting it on to roots which are identified as rural, Catholic, and, more remotely, Gaelic. That grafting is enabled by the return to place, a reterritorialization in a literal sense initially, which symbolically restores the interrupted continuity of identity and ground. An implicit theory of language operates here, for which the name is naturally integrated with place, the sign identified with the signified, the subject with the object. The putative sameness of place supplies an image of the continuity underlying the ruptures so apparent in the history of language usage in Ireland. If identity slips between belonging in and owning the land, between object and subject, between nature and culture, in unrelenting displacement, the land as "preoccupation" furnishes the purely formal ground, the matrix of continuity, in which identity ultimately reposes. The signs of difference that compose the language are underwritten by a language of containment and synthesis, that is, "the living speech of the landscape," which is in turn identified with the poem itself, the single, adequate vocable: a word "with reference to form rather than meaning."[6] In all its functions, language performs the rituals of synthesis and identity, from the mysterious identification of the guttural and the vowel with Irishness, the consonantal with Englishness, to the symbolic function of metaphor which produces those recurrent stylistic traits of Heaney's metaphors of identity born by the genitive, the copula or the compound: "the hammered shod of a bay"; "the tight vise of a stack"; "the challenger's intelligence / is a spur of light, / a blue prong"; "My body was braille"; "Earth-pantry, bone-vault, / sun-bank."

Place, identity and language mesh in Heaney, as in the tradition of cultural nationalism, since language is seen primarily as naming, and because naming performs a cultural reterritorialization by replacing the contingent continuities of an historical community with an ideal register of continuity in which the name (of place or of object) operates symbolically as the commonplace communicating between actual and ideal continua. The name always serves likeness, never difference. Hence poems on the names of places must of their nature be rendered as gifts, involving no labour on the part of the poet, who would, by enacting division, disrupt the immediacy of the relation of culture to pre-culture:"I had a great sense of release as they were being written, a joy and a devil-may-careness, and that convinced me that one could be faithful to the nature of the English language—for in some sense these poems are erotic mouth-music by and out of the anglo-saxon [*sic*] tongue—and, at the same time, be faithful to one's own non-English origin, for me that is County Derry." The formulation renovates the concerns, even the rhetoric, of early nationalist critics.

Thus the name "Anahorish" resides as a metonym for the ancient Gaelic culture that is to be tapped, leading "past the literary mists of a Celtic twilight into that civilization whose demise was effected by soldiers and administrators like Spenser and Davies" (*Preoccupations*, p. 36). "Anahorish," "place of clear water," is at once a place-name and the name of a place-name poem in *Wintering Out*. The name as title already assures both continuity between subject and predicate and the continuity of the poet's identity, since titular possession of this original place which is itself a source guarantees the continuity of the writing subject with his displaced former identity:

Anahorish

My "place of clear water,"
the first hill in the world
where springs washed into
the shiny grass . . .

The writer's subjective origin doubles the Edenic and absolute origin, the untroubled clarity of his medium allowing immediacy of access to the place and moment of original creation, which its own act of creation would seem to repeat and symbolize, knowledge cleansed and redeemed to graceful polish. The poem itself becomes the adequate vocable in which the rift between the Gaelic word and its English equivalent is sealed in smooth, unbroken ground, speech of the landscape: "*Anahorish*, soft gradient / of consonant, vowel-meadow." The rhetoric of identity is compacted not only in these metaphors, representative again of Heaney's metaphors of identity, but in the two sentences that compose the first and most substantial part of the poem, where no main verbs fracture the illusion of identity and presence. The name itself asserts the continuity of presence as an "afterimage of lamps," while in the last sentence, those lamps appear to illuminate genii of the place—"those mound dwellers"—a qualification which expels history, leaving only the timelessness of repeated, fundamental acts. Their movement unites the visible with the invisible, while the exceptional moment of fracturing is regained as a metaphor for access to the source and the prospect of renewed growth:

> With pails and barrows
>
> those mound-dwellers
> go waist-deep in mist
> to break the light ice
> at wells and dunghills.

What is dissembled in such writing is that the apparent innocence, the ahistoricity, of the subject's relation to place is in fact preceded by an act of appropriation or repossession. "Anahorish" provides an image of the transcendental unity of the subject, and correspondingly of history, exactly insofar as it is represented—far from innocently—as a property of the subject. The lush and somewhat indulgent sentiment of the poems of place in *Wintering Out* ("Anahorish," "Toome," "Broagh," and "A New Song") can be ascribed to that foreclosed surety of the subject's relation to place, mediated as it is by a language which seeks to naturalize its appropriative function.

"Erotic mouth-music": it is indeed the seduction of these poems to open what would in the terms of its aesthetic be a regressive path through orality beyond the institution of difference in history and in writing. Hence perception of difference, through the poet's sense of his own difference, which is in fact fundamental to their logic of identity, has finally to be suppressed. Difference is of course registered throughout Heaney's work, at all those points of division and dispossession previously observed. Those divisions are, furthermore, embraced within sexual difference, which comes to provide for political, national and cultural difference a matrix of the most elementary, dualistic kind: "I suppose the feminine element for me involves the matter of Ireland, and the masculine strain is drawn from the involvement with English literature" (*Preoccupations*, p. 34). This difference, however, is posed as the context for a resolution beyond conflict, in the poem as in relation to the land, which is at once preexistent and integrating:

> I have always listened for poems, they come sometimes like bodies come out of a bog, almost complete, seeming to have been laid down a long time ago, surfacing with a touch of mystery. They certainly involve craft and determination, but chance and instinct have a role in the thing too. I think the process is a kind of somnambulist encounter between masculine will and intelligence and feminine clusters of image and emotion (p. 34) . . . It is this feeling, assenting, equable marriage between the geographical country and the country of the mind, whether that country of the mind takes its tone unconsciously from a shared oral inherited culture, or from a consciously savoured literary culture, or from both, it is this marriage that constitutes the sense of place in its richest possible manifestation. (*Preoccupations*, p. 132)

For all their rigid, dualistic schematization, which is only the more rigid for its pretension to be instinctual and unsystematic, and for all the inanity of the content of that dualism—oral, feminine, unconscious image and emotion versus cultured, masculine, conscious will and intelligence—such formulations acutely register the form of integration which is projected. Non-differentiation lies in the matter which precedes all difference and is regained in the product which is the end of difference, the aesthetic object, the poem. Culture repeats primary cultivation, its savour is oral, racy of the soil. Masculine and feminine marry likewise in the moment the poem is forged out of their difference, reproducing a unity of word and flesh always assumed to pre-exist that difference. In the insistent formalization of this rigidly gendered representation of difference, Heaney elides the complex and often contradictory heterogeneity of Irish social formations and their histories, recapitulating his similar dualization of the oral and literate elsewhere.[7]

Only when special and explanatory status is pleaded for this consolatory myth do contradiction and difference return, to use a Heaneyish notion, with a vengeance, as in the series of bog poems which commences with "The Tollund Man" in *Wintering Out*, and is extended through *North*. The origin of these poems in P. V. Glob's *The Bog People* is doubtless familiar, but it is as well to reproduce Heaney's own account:

> It [Glob's book] was chiefly concerned with preserved bodies of men and women found in the bogs of Jutland, naked, strangled or with their throats cut, disposed under the peat since early Iron Age times. The author, P. V. Glob, argues convincingly that a number of these, and in particular the Tollund Man, whose head is now preserved near Aarhus in the museum at Silkeburg, were ritual sacrifices to the Mother Goddess, the goddess of the ground who needed new bridegrooms each winter to bed with her in her sacred place, in the bog, to ensure the renewal and fertility of the territory in the spring. Taken in relation to the tradition of Irish political martyrdom for that cause whose icon is Kathleen Ni Houlihan, this is more than an archaic barbarous rite: it is an archetypal pattern. And the unforgettable photographs of these victims blended in my mind with photographs of atrocities, past and present, in the long rites of Irish political and religious struggles. (*Preoccupations*, pp. 57–8)

Heaney here posits a psychic continuity between the sacrificial practices of an Iron Age people and the "psychology of the Irishmen and Ulstermen who do the killing" (*Preoccupations*, p. 57). This is effectively to reduce history to myth, furnishing an aesthetic resolution to conflicts constituted in quite specific historical junctures by rendering disparate events as symbolic moments expressive of an underlying continuity of identity. Not surprisingly, it is the aesthetic politics of nationalism which finds its most intense symbolism in martyrdom.

As with the question of identity, so the question as to whether archetypes and archetypal patterns exist is less significant than the formal role their invocation plays. Something of that role emerges in "The Tollund

Man" (*Wintering Out*), apparently the first of the bog poems to have been written:

> Some day I will go to Aarhus
> To see his pear-brown head,
> The mild pods of his eye-lids,
> His pointed skin cap.
>
> In the flat country nearby
> Where they dug him out,
> His last gruel of winter seeds
> Caked in his stomach,
>
> Naked except for
> The cap, noose and girdle,
> I will stand a long time.
> Bridegroom to the goddess,
> She tightened her torc on him
> And opened her fen,
> Those dark juices working
> Him to a saint's kept body . . .

The distance of the historical observer rapidly contracts in this first section into an imaginary immediate relation to the corpse, and ultimately to the putative goddess as, in a singularly deft piece of composition, the appositions "Naked except for / The cap, noose and girdle," and "Bridegroom to the goddess" slip between the poet and the victim. The immediacy of that relation, brought thus to the very brink of identification, facilitates the elimination of human agency, which is distilled to thematically equivalent operations of sacrifice (by which the corpse is worked "to a saint's kept body") and poetic rememoration which reverses, by analogy with exhumation, the direction of sacrifice without invalidating it. The subordination of human agency to aesthetic form is reinforced in the second section as the two atrocities there described are contained within the faintly redeeming notion of their possible germination, their flesh scattered like seed:

> I could risk blasphemy,
> Consecrate the cauldron bog
> Our holy ground and pray
> Him to make germinate
>
> The scattered, ambushed
> Flesh of labourers,
> Stockinged corpses
> Laid out in the farmyards,

> Tell-tale skin and teeth
> Flecking the sleepers
> Of four young brothers, trailed
> For miles along the lines.

The matter of the form in which they will germinate, as Cadmus's warriors, perhaps, or as "The Right Rose Tree," is carefully hedged.[8] In so purely aesthetic a performance, which evades the logic even of its own mythologies, the "risk" of "blasphemy" is easily carried. In the third section, the poet is confirmed as the stable centre of this tableau of identifications:

> Something of his sad freedom
> As he rode the tumbril
> Should come to me, driving,
> Saying the names

> Tollund, Grabaulle, Nebelgard,
> Watching the pointing hands
> Of country people,
> Not knowing their tongue.

> Out there in Jutland
> In the old man-killing parishes
> I will feel lost,
> Unhappy and at home.

What is the "sad freedom" that the poet as tourist or pilgrim in Jutland will take over from the Tollund man other than that derived from the aesthetic rehearsal of rites whose continuity with the present is preassured by the unquestioned metaphoric frame of the writing, a writing whose dangers have been defused into pathos by their subordination to that same metaphoric function? Thus the repetition of place-names ("Tollund, Grabaulle, Nebelgard"), abstracted from context and serving a cultural purpose as synecdoches of continuity, overrides the actual alienation of one "Not knowing their tongue," only to issue in the "at home-ness" always available to those whose culture is a question of reterritorialization. The bodies of Jutland are, one recalls, "disposed under the peat" for the poet-archaeologist's appropriation.

Metaphorical foreclosure of issues, by which the proposed matter of the poem acts simultaneously as the metaphor justifying the mode of its treatment, has been a constant feature of Heaney's writing since such early poems as "Digging," perfectly sustaining its drive towards cultural reterritorialization and the suturing of identity, because the concepts of culture and individuation thus appear as the formal repetition of the primary ground to which they are thereby returned. The racial and psychological archetype, like the reified human nature of bourgeois ideology from which it stems, subserves this circularity. The archetype allows the process of individuation and the specific forms taken on by any given culture to be envisaged as retaining a continuity with an homogeneous, undifferentiated ground, such as indeed the symbol is supposed to retain with that which it represents and, crucially, of which it partakes. The regressive nature of this model is significant less in the evident psychoanalytical sense, which doubles Heaney's own temporal schema, than in the neatness with which the location of that archetypal or indifferent ground can be pushed back as far as required—from oral culture and territory to the abstract form of the land, for example. This regression, nevertheless, does not affect the essential structure by which the immediacy of a primary relation to origins and ground can be replaced by a cultural medium, though in sublimated form and with the gain of pathos, as in Heaney's myth of Antaeus:

> a blue prong graiping him
> out of his element
> into a dream of loss
>
> and origins—the cradling dark,
> the river-veins, the secret gullies
> of his strength,
> the hatching grounds
>
> of cave and souterrain,
> he has bequeathed it all
> to elegists.
>
> (North)

That which is foregone is the most efficient myth of integration, supplying the lost object by which the work of mourning is transformed into the work of identification, specifically, here, identification with an inheritance.

Contradiction returns where the myth that has most effectively furthered the goal of integration by obviating the state's need for overt coercion clashes with those "civilized values" that it underwrites. For both unionists and nationalists in Ireland, in ways which agree in form but differ in specific content, concepts of racial identity asserted since the nineteenth century have performed such an integrative function in the service of domination, at the cost of institutionalizing certain differences. That the interests promoted by these myths should have come into conflict at various periods, of which the current "troubles" are only the latest instance, does not affect the correspondence that subsists between those ideologies. Even insurgent or anti-colonial violence, generally speaking directed against the state apparatus, can become in the strict sense "terrorist" where it seeks by symbolic rather than tactical acts to forge integration or identity within the discursive boundaries already established and maintained by dominant hegemony. A socialist or feminist critique of such tendencies has to be located not in a generalized criticism of "men of violence," but in the analysis of the totalizing effect of an identity thinking that discretely links terrorism to the state in whose name it is condemned. For what is at stake is not so much the practice of violence—which has long been institutionalized in the bourgeois state—as its aestheticization in the name of a freedom expressed in terms of national or racial integration. This aesthetic frame deflects attention from the interests of domination which the national state expresses both as idea and as entity.

The aestheticization of violence is underwritten in Heaney's recourse to racial archetypes as a means "to grant the religious intensity of the violence its deplorable authenticity and complexity" (*Preoccupations*, pp. 56–7). In locating the source of violence beyond even sectarian division, Heaney renders it symbolic of a fundamental identity of the Irish race, as "authentic." Interrogation of the nature and function of acts of violence in the specific context of the current "troubles" is thus foreclosed, and history foreshortened into the eternal resurgence of the same Celtic genius. The conflict of this thinking with "the perspectives of a humane reason" (*Preoccupations*, p. 56) is, within the poetry that results, only an apparent contradiction, insofar as the function of reason is given over to the establishment of myths. The unpleasantness of such poetry lies in the manner in which the contradictions between the ethical and aesthetic elements in the writing are easily resolved by the subjugation of the former to the latter in order to produce the "well-made poem." Contempt for "connivance in civilized outrage" is unexamined in the frequently cited "Punishment" (*North*) where the "artful voyeurism" of the poem is supposedly criticized as the safe stance of the remote and lustful "civilized" observer, yet is smuggled back in as the unspoken and unacknowledged condition for the understanding of the "exactness" of "tribal, intimate revenge":

> I can feel the tug
> of the halter at the nape
> of her neck, the wind
> on her naked front.
>
> It blows her nipples
> to amber beads,
> it shakes the frail rigging
> of her ribs.
>
> I can see her drowned
> body in the bog,
> the weighing stone,
> the floating rods and boughs.

> Under which at first
> she was a barked sapling
> that is dug up
> oak-bone, brain-firkin . . .
>
> My poor scapegoat,
>
> I almost love you
> but would have cast, I know,
> the stones of silence.
> I am the artful voyeur
>
> of your brain's exposed
> and darkened combs,
> your muscles' webbing
> and all your numbered bones:
>
> I who have stood dumb
> when your betraying sisters,
> cauled in tar,
> wept by the railings,
>
> who would connive
> in civilized outrage
> yet understand the exact
> and tribal, intimate revenge.

The epithet "tribal" cannot, in this context, be immanently questioned, since it at once is sustained by and reinforces the metaphor of tribal rites which organizes the whole poem, and which is at once its pretext and its subject-matter. Neither the justness of the identification of the metaphor— the execution of an adulteress by Glob's Iron Age people—with the actual violence which it supposedly illuminates—the tarring and feathering of two Catholic "betraying sisters"—nor the immediacy of the observer's access to knowledge of his object ("I can feel . . . I can see") is ever subjected to a scrutiny which would imperil the quasi-syllogistic structure of the poem. Voyeurism is criticized merely as a pose, never for its function in purveying the intimate knowledge of violence by which it is judged. As so often in Heaney's work, the sexual drive of knowing is challenged, acknowledged, and let pass without further interrogation, the stance condemned but the material it purveys nevertheless exploited. Thus a pose of ethical self-query allows the condemnation of enlightened response—reduced in any case to paralytic "civilized outrage," as if this were the only available alternative— while the supposedly irrational is endowed as if by default with the features of enlightenment—exactitude, intimacy of knowledge—in order to compact an understanding already presupposed in the selection and elaboration of the metaphor. The terms of the dilemma are entirely false, but the poem rehearses with striking fidelity the propensity of bourgeois thought to use "reason" to represent irrationality as the emotional substratum of identifications which, given as at once natural and logical, are in fact themselves thoroughly "irrational."[9]

2

> So much in Ireland still needs to be done . . . the definition of the culture, and the redefinition of it. If you could open students into trust in their own personality, into some kind of freedom and cultivation, you could do a hell of a lot.[10]

In its play with atavisms, with the irrational substrata of its identifications, aesthetic ideology effectively excludes both violence and difference from the ideal image of its own internal structure. The irrational—all which eludes the governing principle of identity—is reduced to the originating matter which is repeatedly to be cultivated into unity. While it supplies the ground for culture, it is debarred from either real agency or representation, and figures thenceforth when "active" as a "disruption" of the supposedly natural ordering of cultivation. Thus its return merely bolsters up the rationale of an essentially exclusive culture, supplying at once the pretext and the matter upon which that culture's work is performed. The discourse of culture itself originates in the moment that the division of intellectual and physical labour has become such that "culture" as a specialization is privileged yet entirely marginalized in relation to productive forces, and seeks to disguise, or convert, both privilege and marginalization in a sublimation which places it beyond division and into a position whence it can appear to perform the work of unification. Hence the importance not only of the image of the man of culture as a non-productive worker, but also the idea of a method which brings to an epistemology already analogous to industrial processes the privilege of unity retained even in transition, that of the "science of origins" which reconciles where it first dissolves and finds differences."[11] The discourse of culture consistently seeks, by representing itself as withdrawn from implication in social divisions, as indifferent, to forge a domain in which divisions are overcome or made whole. The realization of human freedom is deferred into this transcendent domain, with the consequence that an ethical invocation is superadded to the exhortations of culture.

It is a cultural resolution of this order that Heaney proposes in *Field Work*, a generally acclaimed volume.[12] The sonnets composed in the "hedge-school of Glanmore" pose as an apt centre-piece to the book, thematizing at once the notion of withdrawal and the agricultural root of that culture which is its goal: "Vowels ploughed into other, opened ground, / Each verse returning like the plough turned round" (Glanmore Sonnets, II). Though this withdrawal is envisaged as a return and a grounding, it is still a ground whose otherness is carefully contained as a metaphor for the locus and source of poetic activity, and as such is resolutely cultivable. Secure in its protected, pastoral domain, the writing is full of unrealized resolve, governed primarily by a conditional mood which mimes the celebration of conditions for writing, yet is in actuality reduced to the almost contentless formal reiteration of the paradigms which sustain its complacencies. The small reminders that might threaten the benediction of that "haven," the word with which Heaney obliquely encapsulates his relief at being harboured in a poetic which allows him the shelter of the English tradition and voice (Glanmore Sonnets, VII), are either framed carefully on the outside—"Outside the kitchen window a black rat / Sways on the briar like infected fruit" (Glanmore Sonnets, IX)—or smothered in a rhetoric so portentous that it merely accentuates the bathos of its referents:

> This morning when a magpie with jerky steps
> Inspected a horse asleep beside the wood
> I thought of dew on armour and carrion.
> What would I meet, blood-boltered, on the road?
> How deep into the woodpile sat the toad?
> What welters through this dark hush on the crops?
>
> (Glanmore Sonnets, VIII)

It is difficult to credit the solemnly voiced pursuit of an "apology for poetry" (Glanmore Sonnets, IX) in these sonnets with any real intellectual strenuousness, reduced as they are to such highly strung aestheticism. Whatever slight resonances they evoke are gained from political and ethical concerns which the knowledge of matters beyond their refined scope must supply.

The sonnets' implicit thesis that the preciousness of art—and the pathos of human being—may lie in the vulnerability of its fragile pieties to the "ungovernable and dangerous" ("Elegy") is elsewhere delivered over to the test of more exacting conditions. The elegy "Casualty"—which, of the three in the volume, most nearly confronts the supposed saving power of art with "danger"—labours uneasily with the realization of the remoteness of this art from the pathos of the everyday which it celebrates elsewhere, and, as if in abreaction, asserts the more strongly the difference of art as the image of freedom posed against conformity to putative "tribal" values. The assertion nevertheless regrounds itself through finding its paradigm in labour, in a labour, however, which is crucially predetermined as gratuitous, "natural" and free, that of "A dole-kept breadwinner / But a natural for work." This image of the fisherman's labour as essentially free underwrites the concluding lines, which render fishing as a paradigm for art in its transcendence:

> I tasted freedom with him.
> To get out early, haul
> Steadily off the bottom,
> Dispraise the catch, and smile
> As you find a rhythm
> Working you, slow mile by mile,
> Into your proper haunt
> Somewhere, well out, beyond . . .

At once natural and transcendent, freedom finds its image in gratuitous creative work, in a "taste" which is shared beyond the divisions established by the "incomprehensibility" of the poet's "other life." That such "condescension" is always one-sided is debarred from consideration, as is the wider context of unfreedom which sustains that aesthetic once the idea of constraint has been reduced to the myth of the tribe.

The cautious limits which Heaney's poetry sets round any potential for disruptive, immanent questioning may be the reason for the extraordinary inflation of his current reputation. If Heaney is held to be "the most trusted poet of our [*sic*] islands,"[13] by the same token he is the most institutionalized of recent poets. At the functional level of school and college teaching and examination, much of the prominence given to Heaney's writing may be attributed to its aptness for the still dominant discipline of practical criticism. Almost without exception, the poems respond compliantly to analysis based on assumptions about the nature of the well-made lyric poem: that it will crystallize specific emotions out of an experience, that the metaphorical structure in which the emotion is to be communicated will be internally coherent; that the sum of its ambiguities will be an integer, expressing eventually a unity of tone and feeling even where mediated by irony; that the unity will finally be the expression of a certain identity, a poetic "voice" (*Preoccupations*, pp. 43–4). On the side of the writer, writing is envisaged as at once constitutive and expressive of an identity liberated from the incoherent unity of its ground. That act of self-production gives the writer his representativeness as human despite the specialization of his labour. For the reader, the act of reading appears also as a liberating act. To read, to criticize, is to exercise the right of private judgment and thereby to develop one's best self. The illusion of a free-market economy, where taste pretends to be an expression of the consumer's uncoerced judgment, thrives in the pedagogical method that furnishes the core of those literary institutions which in fact arbitrate cultural values.

In this period where the illusion of a free-market economy is disintegrating in crisis, it is appropriate that, within the increasingly marginalized domain of high culture, a pedagogy locating the autonomy of the individual subject in the private arbitration of value should become increasingly retrenched and all the more earnestly defended. It is perhaps only a small irony that the product of this pedagogy turns out to be such an unprecedented homogeneity of "taste" that a reviewer can state, "Everyone knows by now that Heaney is a major poet," and be confirmed not only by the accord of his peers, but by the remarkably high sales of the volumes concerned.[14] But that small irony—scarcely to be attributed to the benevolent dissemination of the sweetness and light of culture—is nonetheless symptomatic of a contradiction implicit in cultural discourse, and in some sense even recognized there, as if the terms of the discourse already resolved it. The contradiction, formally congruent with that produced by bourgeois ideology's attempts to "reconcile individual liberty with association," lies in the fact that the cultivation of the individual's best self is to be conducted under the arbitration of an authority whose end is the constitution of a more integrated whole beyond divisions.[15] If that authority has tended to shift from the individual critic-teacher to institutions in which the existence of single tone-setting figures is much less apparent, this tendency belongs with a general shift from the concentration of power in the entrepreneur to its disposition through larger structures.[16] So much is implicit in common parlance when one speaks of one or other "critical industry."

The democratization of education that has stemmed in large part from nineteenth-century cultural discourse has followed the track of industrialization, and with similar effects in view. Where the net effect of increased technological efficiency has been to override the perception of difference with the homogenizing image of general prosperity, the end of literary education has been to override class and individual difference with the image of a common culture, both as something inherited and as something currently produced. The concept of a common culture can be seen to double that of the common land (whence, indeed, the concept of "culture" has always derived its specific etymological and metaphorical resonances), and this conveniently underwrites the nominal decentralization of literary production. Pre-programmed as this development is, the resulting notion of the revitalization of the centres of culture through the influence of less deracinated, less cultivated regional sensibilities, continues to subserve the linked fictions of indigenous and subjective identity. Just as rhetoric about enterprise and the free market exploits the image of individualism while masking the actual diffusion of power through larger heterogeneous structures, so the celebration of regionalism dulls perception of the institutional and homogenizing culture which has sustained its apparent efflorescence at the very moment when the concept of locality, enclosed and self-nurturing, has become effectively archaic, and, indeed, functions as such. The pathos which the defenders of high culture and regional identity win from a stance offering to protect the vulnerable and vanishing against imponderable forces of technology and progress is gained in spite of the contradiction that the higher integration, which culture was to maintain beyond the class society, coincides perfectly with that being produced by technological development. The thematizing and defusing of these elements within Heaney's poetry provides the basis of the trust with which it is currently accepted, at every point confirming—as only such poetry can—the aesthetic and cultural expectations whence it stemmed and to which it promises an apparently authentic renovation. The seeming coherence between this scenario of the elevation of a minor Irish poet to a touchstone of contemporary taste and a discourse whose most canonical proponent argued for the Celtic literature as a means to the integration of Ireland with Anglo-Saxon industrial civilization is appropriate and pre-programmed.[17] It is, for all that, profoundly symptomatic of the continuing meshing of Irish cultural nationalism with the imperial ideology which frames it.

*Notes*

1. Seamus Heaney, *Death of a Naturalist* (London 1966), pp. 13–14, and *Door into the Dark* (London 1969), pp. 25–6.

2. Harold Bloom, "The Voice of Kinship," *TLS*, 8 (February 1980), pp. 137–8.

3. Seamus Heaney, "Feeling into Words," *Preoccupations* (London 1980), p. 41.

4. On the continuing vital relation between literate and non-literate, high and low, see the last two essays in this volume.

5. Frank Kinahan, "Artists on Art: An Interview with Seamus Heaney," *Critical Inquiry*, 8.3 (Spring 1982), p. 406; see also Seamus Heaney's lines in "The Ministry of Fear," *North* (London 1975), p. 65: "Ulster was British, but with no rights on / The English Lyric."

6. See *Preoccupations*, pp. 36–7. I allude to the *COED* definition of "vocable."

7. For further discussion of gender issues in Heaney's writings that have appeared since this essay was first published, see Elizabeth Butler Cullingford, "Thinking of Her . . . as . . . Ireland: Yeats, Pearse and Heaney," *Textual Practice*, 4.1 (Spring 1990), pp. 1–21, and Patricia Coughlan, " 'Bog Queens': The Representation of Women in the Poetry of John Montague and Seamus Heaney" in Toni O'Brien Johnson and David Cairns (eds), *Gender in Irish Writing* (Milton Keynes 1991), pp. 88–111.

8. See Richard Kearney's comments on the intertwining of both aspects of this mythology in "The IRA's Strategy of Failure," *The Crane Bag*, 4, no. 2 (1980–1), p. 62.

9. See Theodor Adorno's remarks on this subject, specifically in relation to the mobilizing of "additional regressive memories of its archaic root" in the bourgeois nation state, in *Negative Dialectics*, p. 339.

10. See the interview with Seamus Heaney in John Haffenden, *Viewpoints* (London 1981), pp. 59–60.

11. See Coleridge, "Essays on Method," *The Friend*, Barbara Rooke (ed.) (Princeton 1969), p. 476; Matthew Arnold, "On the Study of Celtic Literature" in R. H. Super (ed.), *Lectures and Essays in Criticism*, vol. III of *The Complete Prose Works* (Ann Arbor: Michigan 1962), p. 330. Adorno comments on the duplication of the mechanical reproductive process in Kant's *Critique of Pure Reason*. See *Negative Dialectics*, p. 387.

12. Reviews acclaiming *Field Work* range from Harold Bloom's in the *TLS* to one by Gerard Smyth in *The Irish Times* ("Change of Idiom," *IT*, 20 October 1979, p. 11). Reviewers are almost unanimous in regarding the volume as a steady advance on the previous body of work.

13. Christopher Ricks, "The Mouth, the Meal, and the Book," review of *Field Work* in *The London Review of Books*, 8 November 1979, p. 4.

14.   Neither Faber and Faber nor Farrar, Straus and Giroux have been willing to divulge detailed figures concerning sales of Heaney's works. I am, however, obliged to Craig Raine of Faber and Faber for the following "approximate figures," whose "general lesson is sound and obvious enough": "We would probably have printed 2000–3000 copies of his first book, whereas now we would print somewhere in the region of 20,000 copies" (letter, 12 October 1983).

15.   See Matthew Arnold, "The Function of Criticism in the Present Time," *Lectures and Essays*, pp. 265–6: "*Force till right is ready*; and till right is ready force, the existing order of things, is justified, is the legitimate ruler" (original emphasis).

16.   John Kenneth Galbraith, *The New Industrial State*, 2nd ed. (Harmondsworth 1974), especially chapter 5, "Capital and Power." The analysis, if not the conclusion, of this study is valuable, and challenging to any materialist view of the current economy.

17.   Arnold, "On the Study of Celtic Literature," pp. 296–7.

# Queasy Proximity:
# Seamus Heaney's Mythical Method

NATHALIE F. ANDERSON*

Every discussion of contemporary mythopoesis might begin with T. S. Eliot's proclamations in " 'Ulysses,' Order, and Myth"[1]—that by "manipulating a continuous parallel between contemporaneity and antiquity" James Joyce had found "a way of controlling, of ordering, of giving a shape and a significance to the immense panorama of futility and anarchy which is contemporary history," that in *Ulysses* Joyce had taken "a step toward making the modern world possible for art." "Manipulating," "controlling," "ordering," ensuring "shape" and "significance," "making . . . possible"—Eliot's vocabulary insists on authorial mastery. Yet his concluding sentence, less frequently quoted, hints at a more private, even psychological, basis for the power of the mythical: "And only those who have won their own discipline in secret and without aid, in a world which offers very little assistance to that end, can be of any use in furthering this advance." "In secret and without aid," writers "[win] their own discipline," by trial, with luck, at risk. As Ted Hughes says of Eliot: "I can't believe that he took the disintegration of Western civilization as a theme which he then found imagery and a general plan for. His sickness told him the cause. Surely that was it. He cleansed his wounds and found all the shrapnel."[2] Seamus Heaney[3] came of age in a country where cleaning wounds of shrapnel was to be no idle metaphor. Although the "futility and anarchy" particular to Northern Ireland were not especially overt while he was a child, the divisions which exploded in the late 1960's were certainly implicit in the society, a "fundamental blueprint"[4] in Heaney's phrase. To the extent that Heaney shares and recognizes this blueprint, his mythic exploration of division in *North* traces societal ills, orders societal anarchy, finds significance in societal futility.

But Heaney's earlier volumes, only faintly political, bear the marks of more personal dis-ease. Many critics have commented, for example, on the repressive formality of the early love poems, the fascination and repulsion for what Dick Davis has called the "fecund, breeding darkness"[5] of lubricious earth. In winning his secret discipline, we might posit that Heaney has

* Reprinted from *Éire-Ireland* 23, no. 4 (Winter 1988): 103–13.

found the means to submerge private obsession in public concern, to turn it to political account, to manipulate, control, order, give shape and significance to both inner and outer chaos. More particularly, if Heaney's poems manifest a sexual ambivalence, in *North* he has provided a context in which the sexual serves metaphoric ends, in which ambivalence becomes responsibility.

To assess Heaney's "mythical method" in *North*, then, we must first examine the traces of ambivalence observable in the early work. In *Death of a Naturalist* we might concentrate on the pervasive references to watery ground, references underscored by the poet's characteristic use of vivid onomatopoeia. A survey of certain loaded instances of such words suggests a pattern of emphasis and of response: "squelch," "slap," "gargled," "slobber," "clotted," "plop," "farting," "clogging," "glutting," "slugged," "flabby," "coagulated," "plash," "gurgle," "pat," "sogged," "cudding," "grubbing," "pus," "slabber," "potters," "puddling," "muck," "sucking," "clabber," "mush," "blotch," "mulch." These are wet words, but not so liquid as for example the "glinting, sifting" waves of "Lovers on Aran" (DN 47)—they are thick, bodied. We can categorize their respective textures: the "slap" of an object on a wet surface, the "muck" of thick mud, the "slobber" of spit, the "clot" of coagulating cream. In each case the effect is disturbing, even nauseating, the more so because the fluid material at times seems quick with life: "the warm thick slobber / Of frogspawn that grew like clotted water." To this configuration we might add references to excrement, to putrefaction, to slime.

Of course these images color each other. The "clotted water" of "Death of a Naturalist" (DN 15–16), which solidifies into the excremental "slime kings" "Poised like mud grenades, their blunt heads farting," for example, influences our response to the "glossy purple clot" of the first ripe blackberry (DN 20). The image is different here—not murk but blood—but the earlier associations contribute to the undercurrent of revulsion implicit in the word and prepare for the metamorphosis of "clot" to "rot": "The juice was stinking too . . . the sweet flesh would turn sour." We might perceive "Churning Day" (DN 21–22) as redeeming this imagery—although the word "clot" does not appear, the "flabby milk" surely clots to "yellow curd," "coagulated sunlight," "gilded gravel." Yet the description of the churns—"their heavy lip / of cream, their white insides"—anticipates the potatoes of "At a Potato Digging" (DN 31–33): "Split / by the spade, they show white as cream," "the halved seed shot and clotted," "wet inside"—healthful images, but treacherous: "the new potato . . . / putrefied," "Hope rotted." "Putrefied" here mocks the "purified" churn of the earlier poem. Not every metamorphosis is vile, but slime is always treacherous. The speaker's distrust, born of revulsion, is evident in these poems, as is his attempt to master his revulsion by recasting the imagery.

Of course, the imagery is sexual as well: the frogs "cocked," the "sweet flesh" "sour," the potatoes "wet inside," "slime" "finger[ed]" (DN 57).

Davis sees such metaphors as evidence that Heaney perceives "the natural world . . . as feminine," "a fecund, pullulating maternal principle, an all-absorbing, threatening lover"[6]—but here sexuality remains implicit—displaced, deflected, denied, refused: controlled, that is, by metaphor or by negation.

The impulse to control is conspicuous again in Heaney's second volume, *Door Into the Dark*, where male labor is posed against fecundity and thus against female labor, capable male against capacious female. Male expertise is in evidence throughout the volume, in the blacksmith's effort "To beat real iron out" (DD 19), in the thatcher's skill at "pinning down his world" (DD 20), in the "Labourers" "white with . . . [the] powdery stain" of the clay they dig "All day in open pits" (DD 53). The poems that turn the concept of labor toward sexual management are thus surrounded by assertions of mastery achieved through physical effort, external evidence of potency. At first glance, "Rite of Spring" (DD 25) seems a continuation of this pattern: an unspecified "we" thaw a frozen pump by wrapping it in straw which they then burn. But the last two lines imply as well expert management of a frigid woman: "It cooled, we lifted her latch, / Her entrance was wet, and she came."

Heaney explores this metaphoric management more fully in the poem that follows, "Undine" (DD 26), described in his 1974 essay "Feelings into Words" as a portrayal of "the liberating, humanizing effect of sexual encounter" (P 53). We might expect words like "liberating" and "humanizing" to derive from one's own experience, but Heaney projects this "humanizing"—and the former deplorable inhumanity it implies—onto the female other: "Undine," he states, "was a cold girl who got what the dictionary calls a soul through the experience of physical love." In the poem, the distinguishing behaviors of male farmer and female water are apparent from the first stanza: "He slashed the briars, shovelled up grey silt / To give me right of way in my own drains / And I ran quick for him, cleaned out my rust."

The man labors purposefully; his purpose is management. The woman responds. True, the man's effort is a gift, and his goal apparently freedom and self-determination for the woman, but implicitly these privileges must be granted—she cannot achieve them on her own—and her subsequent running is "for him"—for his notice, in his debt.

The second stanza finds her "finally disrobed," but he seems unimpressed: "saw me . . . with apparent unconcern." Although the stanza closes with simple chronological statements—"Then he walked by me. I rippled and I churned"—the implied casuality makes this "rippl[ing]" a flirtation, an effort on the woman's part to shake male "unconcern." The third stanza brings consummation, but the imagery—perfectly suited to the agricultural conceit—makes us flinch at the violence of the implied subjugation:

> Until he dug a spade deep in my flank
> And took me to him. I swallowed his trench
>
> Gratefully, dispersing myself for love
> Down in his roots . . .

Having "swallowed his trench"—the implicit fellatio is unmistakable—the woman here is emphatically "[Grateful]," the position of the word at the start of an enjambed stanza stressing the projection of male fantasy onto the woman supposedly eager to submit. The poem's final words insist on the metamorphosis of that "cold girl"—"Human, warmed to him"—but we might well wonder whether the man's "unconcern," his masterful possession through penetration ("a spade deep in my flank") can be considered either warm or particularly human.

That Heaney is himself aware of the dangerous presumption implicit in such self-assured mastery is evident in the following poem, "The Wife's Tale" (DD 27–28), a realistic monologue that qualifies the gratitude and self-abnegation of "Undine" through a farm wife's dissatisfaction. The husband here labors not to manage his wife sexually but to harvest grain; nevertheless, his work becomes a display of his potency:

> Always this inspection has to be made
> Even when I don't know what to look for.
>
> But I ran my hands in the half-filled bags
> Hooked to the slots. It was hard as shot,
> Innumerable and cool.

"It" refers of course to the grain, but the conjunction of "half-filled bags," "hard as shot," and "cool" suggests testicles capable of "Innumerable" impregnations, and indeed the husband is "as proud as if he were the land itself." This woman, like "Undine," seems to center her life around service of her husband, she brings lunch to the fields, "spread it all on linen cloth," "buttered the thick slices that he likes," inspects the grain at his insistence. While he and his fellow workers "lay in the ring of their own crusts and dregs, / Smoking and saying nothing," we notice that she has not eaten, has not entered the "ring" of their wordless companionship. But this woman does not seem grateful; her detailed account of the ordinary event conveys quiet outrage, a consciously critical assessment of her husband's detachment: "And that was it. I'd come and he had shown me / So I belonged no further to the work." We might notice here Heaney's ambiguously pointed use of "come"—if she's come, metaphorically speaking, what more can she want? As the wife leaves, the laborers "still kept their ease," "Spread out, unbuttoned, grateful." The gratitude of the water-woman, we recall, led her to "[swallow] his trench," "[disperse] myself"; here the "grateful" men—it is hard not to read this cynically—lie in post-coital attitudes, ignoring the wife's departure.

In "Bann Clay" (DD 53–54), Heaney ratifies this implicit criticism of male labor in a more archetypal depiction of (male) digging toward a (female) core: "Under the humus and roots / This smooth weight. I labour / Towards it still. It holds and gluts."

There is little sense here that "labour" is mastery. Unlike the pump that "came" so readily, or the "disrobed, / running" water of "Undine," the "smooth weight" of the clay has a massive integrity beyond masculine ease; it demands "labour," "holds" the laborer. "Holds" of course refers explicitly to the clay itself, to its anchored hold, almost a suction, as it "gluts" with water, but it suggests as well a blind insatiable suckling, a sexual tenacity and fullness, a birth. "I labour" is thus significantly ambiguous: "I labour" for her sexual satisfaction; "I labour" to assist her delivery; "I labour" to give birth to her; "I labour" to birth and even nourish myself.

Heaney's first two volumes thus record attempts to redefine the sensual ground so as to deny the anxiety aroused by its lubriciousness and fecundity or attempts to assert a metaphoric control through the concept of husbandry; but submerged intimations of threat and explorations of female discontent weaken the credibility of these strategies. In *Wintering Out*, Heaney infuses landscape with sexual potency—"A swollen river / / a mating call of sound / rises to pleasure me" (WO 25)—so that poems of sexual disfunction or broken harmony like "Summer Home" reflect as well on the implicitly political landscape poems. The first section of "Summer Home" (WO 59) sets the tone:

> was it wind off the dumps
> or something in heat
>
> dogging us, the summer gone sour,
> a fouled nest incubating somewhere?

The source of the smell, the couple discovers, is the door mat, "larval, moving." How intensely Heaney's familiar revulsions communicate here— the pervasive odor, the live slime. "Whose fault," the speaker asks the "possessed air," but the larger answer, the "fouled nest," is clear: "O love, here is the blame," the speaker admits in the second section, announcing himself.

Heaney employs this discourse of "fault" and "blame" as well in the more explicitly political "Roots" (WO 39) where sexual tension merges with political tension, beloved land with cold wife. In the dark bedroom "Your body's moonstruck / To drifted barrow, sunk glacial rock"—a landscape dominated by the grave, the cold, given over to desolation, to the prehistoric. Once, presumably, "The touch of love, / Your warmth heaving to the first move" might humanize this landscape, but now love-making "Grows helpless" as "gunshot, siren and clucking gas" claim even the woman's dreams—"you keen / Far off'—and "the fault is opening." The "fault" is the division implicit in their country's politics; it is the inadequacy they feel in the face of extremity; it is the very earth opening, rending the wife's "moonstruck" body by association, severing lovers, shattering wholeness.

By the time of writing *North*, then, Heaney has moved from revulsion and attempted control to a conscious use of sexual tension in a political context. This method is muted in *Wintering Out*, where we may find it difficult to separate the political significance of frigidity and implied infidelity from a more seductive autobiographical significance. In *North*, though Heaney's use of sexual ambivalence is subtle, it clearly forms a coherent part of his larger, political design. Throughout the volume, the sectarian war between Catholic and Protestant, the civil dis-ease between Ireland and England, find analogues in structure and metaphor: introduced by two dedicatory poems; divided into two distinct sections, one mythic, one realistic; the first framed by poems that oppose Hercules and Antaeus, the second detailing the speaker's dual allegiances, *North*, is grounded in division. Yet examination proves these oppositions to be far less distinct than my overview suggests, and although the archaeological, archetypal emphasis of Part I finds no echo in the self-conscious ironies of Part II, and assessing pessimism underlies both sections, making the ambivalence toward "Our mother ground" an ambivalence toward the role of "Unacknowledged Legislator" as well. I will concentrate here on the overtly mythical first section, but we should recall that the power of Heaney's "mythical method" derives in large part from the juxtaposition of "contemporaneity and antiquity" afforded by the second section.

Part I enacts a gradual absorption of the speaker—whom we might characterize as an amateur archaeologist intent on revelation—into imaginative participation in the past; this absorption affirms as well an awareness of a female object so thoroughly associated with the earth as to seem its personification, and involvement gradually intensifies into an act of love. This intimacy becomes explicitly sexual in "Bone Dreams," first through its conceit of the skeleton—Old English *"ban-hus"*—as actual house:

> There was a small crock
> for the brain,
> and a cauldron

> of generation
> swung at the centre:
> love-den, blood-holt,
> dream-bower.
>
> (N 28–29)

The "swung" "cauldron" could signify either male or female sexual organs, but its rounded shape, its function as oven or stewpot, its associations in Celtic myth, suggest that Heaney perceives it as female, a warm den within the skeletal house where a small animal might burrow. The culmination of this necrophiliac conceit comes in section V, where

> I holy my lady's head
> like a crystal
> and ossify myself
> by gazing . . .

The intensity of this gaze recalls Marvell's projected excesses in "To His Coy Mistress," but here the "lady's" passivity renders that speaker's witty seduction superfluous. The held head might be Yorick's skull, might be the mineral it is compared with, might be a "crystal" to see the future in. This poem is more complex than I have indicated—it moves from literal bone to language to earth to nation—but contextually we lose sight of the equations; what strikes us most vividly is this intense absorption—the speaker's stony gaze, the lover's corpse-like passivity, her geological repose. At each stage, as the reader assents intellectually to association or conceit, that assent implies an emotional involvement as well, a concealed relation that makes the reader complicit in the speaker's fascination, in morbid or occult sexuality.

In "Bone-Dreams" it is possible to reassure ourselves that the speaker applies his metaphysical wit to a real woman, or merely personifies a landscape. "Come to the Bower" (N 31) offers no such reassurances. In one sense, of course, its speaker describes an archaeological recovery: "Foraging past the burst gizzards / Of coin hoards," "I unwrap skins and see / The pot of the skull . . ." Each detail proclaims the deadness of the woman. But the speaker's discovery is inescapably sexual—even the "sweet briar and tangled vetch" that impede his foraging bear a sensual charge, a suggestion of dishevelment, a hint of the genital, a reminder of the thorn hedge that shields Briar Rose. The "queen" "Is waiting," "dark-bowered"; "I unpin," "I unwrap"; as "spring water / Starts to rise around her,"

> I reach past
> The riverbed's washed

> Dream of gold to the bullion
> Of her Venus bone.

The details of anchoring willow rods and rising spring water will be familiar to readers of P. V. Glob's *The Bog People*[7]—the source for Heaney's archaeological iconography in a number of these poems—but Heaney turns their implications. The rising water suggests a sexual readiness, the speakers "reach" a sexual caress; "unpin" and "gently" convert wooden stakes to intimate fastenings; the "bullion / Of her Venus bone" is implicitly more valuable than "The riverbed's washed / Dream of gold." We read the poem with the double vision of the archaeologist's fascination and the lover's absorption in his partner's pleasure. Moreover, the "black maw / Of the peat" suggests the interior of a devouring beast whose teeth of "sharpened willow[,] / / Withdraw[n] gently," imply as well a protective nurturance, a crib that opens at the appropriate moment. The queen is thus both ingested by the peat and in gestation within it; the speaker's reaching is again, though secondarily, obstetric.

These associations recur in "Bog Queen" (N 32–34)—"the seeps of winter / digested me"; "The plait of my hair, / a slimy birth-cord"—where the first phrase, "I lay waiting," reverses the perspective of "Come to the Bower." Stylistic similarities tie "Bog Queen" to the characteristic voice of the other Part I poems, however, so that although the queen speaks, it is as if she speaks inside the archaeologist's consciousness, as if he shares her experiences. And while "Bone Dreams" and "Come to the Bower" sustain a distinct if queasy distance between speaker and object, the identification in "Bog Queen" forces the reader's comprehension of what in those poems remains implicit—a conscious dissolution, an animate putrefaction: "my brain darkening, / a jar of spawn / fermenting underground. . . ."

In "Come to the Bower," we infer that the "dark-bowered queen / . . . Is waiting" for the speaker: "whom I unpin" conveys a proprietary intimacy. In "Bog Queen," though the phrase "I lay waiting" is repeated twice, the poem emphasizes not what the queen waits for, but the process of waiting, a blending of woman and landscape in the most literal sense. We are aware of the woman's sex—"my breasts' / / soft moraines," "the nuzzle of fjords / at my thighs"—but even as "dawn suns groped over my head" and "My body was braille / for the creeping influences," we perceive that her lovers have scarcely been adept, their impersonal groping matched by her indifference to them. Though the man who found her "veiled me again," she is neither grateful nor sexually responsive; rather, her voices her outrage:

> My skull hibernated
> in the wet nest of my hair.

> Which they robbed.
> I was barbered
> and stripped
> by a turfcutter's spade. . . .

Certainly she did not lie "waiting" for this. Heaney has identified "robbing the nest" as "a sexual metaphor, an emblem of initiation" (P 42); here "wet nest" and "stripped" reinforce such an interpretation, but the contemptuous "Which they robbed" swings our sympathy from the initiate to the cold chatelaine for whom the initiation constitutes inexcusable intrusion. Though the consistent past tense of the poem mutes the effect, the last stanza recalls Sylvia Plath's "Lady Lazarus" in its suggestion of vengeful potency unchained:

> and I rose from the dark,
> hacked bone, skull-ware,
> frayed stitches, tufts,
> small gleams on the bank.

The image is at once macabre and delicately evanescent, the "tufts" and "gleams" indistinguishable from "the bank," the "gleams" like elf-lights one might follow. As the threat dissipates, it seems manageable, even appealing, but the glimpse of "hacked bone," the assertion of "I rose from the dark" shadow the appeal with insidious significance. The archaeologist's devotion, manifested with increasing clarity through the previous poems, seems inadequate to its object, myopically naive.

In context, of course, there is every reason to identify "Queen" and "Bog" with Ireland. The queen's location "between turf-face and demesne wall," however, makes this rising symbolic rather than allegorical: she is the creature of neither side. To use Lévi-Strauss's vocabulary, the queen schematically mediates the dichotomy between illiterate (Catholic) peasant and cultured (Protestant) colonial: she is neither living nor dead, at once human and mineral, both fecund womb and quickening embryo, mother and wife equally and equally indifferent. The Irish partisans are mediated by queen, by corpse, by vampire. Estranged from her people, ambivalent to their attention, the queen arouses ambivalence in return, first through her terrible aspect and intimate decay, then through her implicit rejection of the attention we have been led to believe she expects and desires. The culminating ratification of this ambivalence comes in Part IV of "Kinship" (N 45), an injunction to the ancient historian Tacitus to "report" how

> Our mother ground
> is sour with the blood
> of her faithful,

they lie gargling
in her sacred heart . . .

how we slaughter
for the common good . . .

how the goddess swallows
our love and terror.

Here, the suggestion of fellatio merges with the implicit *vagina dentata* to double the goddess's insatiable appetite.

In "Feeling into Words," Heaney defines Irish sectarian violence as

a struggle between the cults and devotees of a god and a goddess. There is an indigenous territorial numen, a tutelar of the whole island, call her Mother Ireland, Kathleen Ni Houlihan, the poor old woman, the Shan Van Vocht, whatever and her sovereignty has been temporarily usurped or infringed by a new male cult whose founding fathers were Cromwell, William of Orange and Edward Carson, and whose godhead is incarnate in a rex or caesar resident in a palace in London. What we have is the tail end of a struggle in a province between territorial piety and imperial power.

Now I realize that this idiom is remote from the agnostic world of economic interest whose iron hand operates in the velvet glove of "talks between elected representatives," and remote from the political manoeuvres of power-sharing; but it is not remote from the psychology of the Irishmen and Ulstermen who do the killing, and not remote from the bankrupt psychology and mythologies implicit in the terms Irish Catholic and Ulster Protestant. (P 57)

Here Heaney draws his oppositions more clearly than in "Bog Queen," but we notice that the sides are unequal, the goddess equivalent to the immutable territory, the god incarnate in a mere king, her "sovereignty" only "temporarily usurped." At the same time, the "psychology and mythologies" of both sides are "bankrupt." The assumptions of the male world, like those of the archaeologist, are ill-based; but even the devotee requires a new ritual to redeem "estrangement." The "emblems of adversity" Heaney finds in Glob thus figure not only the sectarian adversity external to the poet but the internal adversity of ambivalence. Heaney goes on in "Feeling into Words" to discuss the significance of the bog finds as "ritual sacrifices to the Mother Goddess, the goddess of the ground who needed new bridegrooms each winter to bed with her in her sacred place, in the bog, to ensure the renewal and fertility of the territory in the spring. Taken in relation to the tradition of Irish political martyrdom for that cause whose icon is Kathleen Ni Houlihan, this is more than an archaic barbarous rite: it is an archetypal pattern" (P 57). Edna Longley[8] has argued persuasively that in *North* Heaney "excludes the intersectarian issue, warfare *between* tribes, by concentrating on the Catholic psyche as bound to immolation, and within that immolation to savage tribal loyalties." We might recall in this context Heaney's comments in interviews with John Haffenden and Frank Kinahan[9] on the posture of supplication he finds typical of Catholics, the "something faintly amorous" in the Hail Mary, "the distrust of the world, if you like, the distrust of happiness, the deep pleasure there is in a mournful litany, the sense that there's some kind of feminine intercession that you turn to for comfort." In *North*, the queen's rejection of inappropriate attention suggests that the expectation of comfort is based in misunderstanding; the queen does not alleviate but rather confirms the essential distrust. Speaker—and thus reader—assents to devotion, then comprehends its inadequacy. The consciousness of Part I of *North* thus stands slightly to the side of "the Catholic psyche," conscious of the seductions of self-sacrifice and therefore implicitly critical of it.

By so arranging the poems in *North* that the association of earth, grave, womb, vagina, and corpse manifests itself gradually, by thus seducing the reader into sensual complicity, by displacing intimacy to Glob's preserved victims—not just any corpses, but archaeologically significant icons—Heaney shapes a context in which revulsion might understandably be shared, and convincingly links revulsion and fascinated devotion. Moreover, although "Bone Dreams" and "Come to the Bower" work mainly to establish the bond between speaker and personified earth, "Bog Queen"—like "The Wife's Tale" in *Door Into the Dark*—turns the relation from male certainty, allowing Heaney not only to cast doubt on his speaker's enthusiasms but also to endow his characteristic ambivalences with political significance. Heaney draws his archaeologist-persona into absorbed relation with the personified land—Ireland—in order to convey the profound ambivalences at the heart of that bond—a sexual ambivalence that figures itself in necrophilia, a self-consious ambivalence which recognizes its own devotion as intrusion, a punitive ambivalence which perceives an implicit insastiable violence in its hope to deflect blame.

*Notes*

1. T. S. Eliot, " 'Ulysses,' Order, and Myth," *The Dial*, Nov. 1923, rpt. in *Selected Prose of T. S. Eliot*, ed. Frank Kermode (New York: Harcourt and Farrar, Strauss, 1975), pp. 177–78.

2. Ekbert Faas, "Ted Hughes and *Crow* (1970): An Interview with Ekbert Faas," *London Magazine* 10, No. 10 (Jan. 1971), rpt. in *Ted Hughes: The Unaccommodated University* by Ekbett Faas (Santa Barbara: Black Sparrow, 1980), p. 204.

3. Volumes by Seamus Heaney to which I refer in this essay include, in order of publication: DN *Death of a Naturalist* (London: Faber, 1966); DD *Door into the Dark* (London: Faber, 1969); WO *Wintering Out* (London: Faber, 1972); N *North* (New York: Oxford, 1975);

and P *Preoccupations*: *Selected Prose 1968–1978* (New York: Farrar, 1980). They will be cited in the text by the capital letter(s) here preceding the title.

4.　Monie Begley, "North," in *Rambles in Ireland* (Old Greenwich, Conn.: Devin-Adair, 1977), p. 166.

5.　Dick Davis, *"Door into the Dark,"* in *The Art of Seamus Heaney*, ed. Tony Curtis (Bridgend, Mid Glamorgan: Poetry Wales Press, 1982), p. 30.

6.　Davis, p. 30.

7.　P. V. Glob, *The Bog People*: *Iron-Age Man Preserved*, trans. Rupert Bruce-Mitford (Ithaca: Cornell Univ. Press, 1969).

8.　Edna Longley, " 'North': 'Inner Emigre' or 'Artful Voyeur'?" in Curtis, p. 78.

9.　John Haffenden, "Meeting Seamus Heaney: An Interview," *London Magazine*, June 1979, rpt. in *Viewpoints*: *Poets in Conversation with John Haffenden* (London: Faber, 1981); Frank Kinahan, "An Interview With Seamus Heaney," *Critical Inquiry*, 8 (1982), pp. 405–14. The quotations appear respectively in Haffenden, p. 60, and Kinahan, p. 409.

# The Feminine Principle in Seamus Heaney's Poetry

CARLANDA GREEN*

When speaks of the feminine aspect of his poetry, Seamus Heaney is referring to both language and theme. Linguistically, the feminine element is evident in the richness of vowels, the masculine in the acerbity of consonants. In this essay, however, I am concerned with the feminine principle in Heaney's poetry as a thematic element. For Heaney the feminine is associated with the Irish and the Celtic, the masculine with the English and the Anglo-Saxon. The feminine is the emotional, the mysterious the inspirational; the masculine is the rational, the realistic, the intellectual.[1] The best poetry, he believes, is achieved by a wedding of the two characteristics. In an essay for *The Guardian*, Heaney says: "I have always listened for poems, they come sometimes like bodies come out of a bog, almost complete, seeming to have been laid down a long time ago, surfacing with a touch of mystery. They certainly involve craft and determination, but chance and instinct have a role in the thing too. I think the process is a kind of somnambulist encounter between masculine will and intelligence and feminine clusters of image and emotion."[2]

My use of the term "wedded" and Heaney's reference to the bog images are particularly appropriate in discussing the feminine principle. As a young child Heaney and a friend stripped naked and bathed in a mossy bog. The event was a seminal experience in Heaney's life, so central that he says that he still feels "betrothed" to "watery ground."[3] His descent into the bog became the abiding metaphor of his poetry, and the female principle is inseparable from that metaphor whether he is delving into the depths of the earth, the bog, the womb, or the Celtic unconscious of the Irish people. Ultimately, the feminine principle is that which pulls man toward the sustaining earth and encourages his participation in the domestic and religious rituals which give life continuity.

Long before Heaney read P. V. Glob's *The Bog People* and discovered the specific "feminine cluster of images" which became his mythology, he felt an innate kinship with the boggy earth of his native land.[4] The bogland

*Reprinted from *Ariel* 14, no. 3 (1983): 3–13.

held "the memory of the landscape" for him.[5] He felt an intense need to incorporate his sense of place with his sense of the poetic, to translate the present by viewing it from the perspective of the past. In speaking of John Montague's poetry, Heaney has said that "the ancient feminine religion of Northern Europe is the lens through which [Montague] looks and the land-scape becomes a memory, a piety, a loved mother. The present is suffused with the past."[6] Heaney could well be describing his own work. Glob led him specifically to the cult of Nerthus, the fertility goddess of the bogs who was worshipped by the Germanic people of the Bronze and Iron Ages. Evidence of human sacrifice to the "loved mother" Earth has been found in Northern Europe and in Ireland, hence the actual physical connection be-tween the two areas. For Heaney, however, the connection is less geographical than mystical. The cult of the Earth Mother is the "cultural matrix" out of which Heaney derives order and harmony sufficient to regenerate the blighted land of modern Ireland.[7]

The female principle derives, then, from the Earth Mother herself and from man's pull toward the land and toward woman. It is a principle estab-lishing certain basic qualities associated with the female, whether human or animal, animate or inanimate. For Heaney, the feminine essence may be embodied in a woman, an otter, a cow, or a water pump. Wherever it is found, the feminine principle indicates an otherness about the female, an instinctive difference in the way she perceives life and reacts to it. Her actions are often intuitive; she senses, feels things to a greater degree than man so that the felt experience is a commonplace with her. Because he often cannot understand how she knows what she knows, man, chiefly rational, finds her mysterious and often mistrusts her. Without her, however, he is fragmented and disoriented. In Heaney's poetry, man must learn to trust woman and to rely on her superior understanding of life's creative urge. Through union with woman, man finds rejuvenation, increased sensitivity to life's mysteries and self-completion. Because of the potential fulfilment in such a union, life may become a productive continuum rather than a linear frustration. Consequently, the ring or the circle is associated with both the Earth Mother and the feminine principle.

Throughout Heaney's work, the potential for regeneration and rebirth is associated with the ring, whether it be the golden ring of marriage or the cyclical round of the seasons, the harvest, or birth and death. Significantly, the ring, or more specifically the torc, was the single distinguishing character-istic of the earliest representations of Nerthus. Many of her victims wore neckrings or nooses, suggesting that they were consecrated to the goddess to insure fertility of crops, animals, and man as well.[8] Man's sexual union with or marriage to the goddess is a central aspect of the cult of Nerthus. Out of that nexus come regeneration and creativity. I should emphasize again, however, that the ring image, as well as the images of marriage, sexual union, and the bog appear in Heaney's earliest work, prior to his

1969 reading of Glob. The discovery of Nerthus merely gave order and coherence to his perception of the female principle.

In many of the poems in *Death of a Naturalist*, his first book, Heaney pays homage to that principle. He is, in these poems, the questing, newly indoctrinated initiate into the mysteries of life. In "Poem for Marie," he is the child-man whom union with his wife perfects.[9] She expands the finite limits of his narrow, clumsy world to the "new limits" of the inclusive world of "the golden ring." Thus, he matures into completion. The potentially productive power of such a union is suggested in "Honeymoon Flight" in which the new couple are thrust out of "the sure green world" of youth and innocence into a roiling, chaotic world where the elements are unsettled. The couple are frightened of their voyage into a new life. They must trust their ability to achieve the perfection symbolized by "the golden ring" which binds them.

*Door Into the Dark* establishes the feminine principle as the matrix, the dark fertile womb which brings increase to the earth. "The Rite of Spring" describes the process by which a frozen plunger is freed by fire from a pump: "Cooled, we lifted her hatch, / Her entrance was wet, and she came." The consummation of fire and water, of the masculine plunger and the feminine pump, brings forth the life-renewing spring waters. Similar images are evident in "Mother," a poem about a pregnant woman pumping water for her husband's cows. She is weary of her task and her burden, the baby which she describes as the plunger within her. She is also discouraged over the state of her intimate life with her husband. Looking at a "bedhead" which her husband has used as part of the pasture fence, she notes that "it does not jingle for joy any more." Yet she is the Earth Mother, and she finds joy in the winds that blow her skirts about her thighs and "stuff air down [her] throat."

For the first time, the real Earth Mother appears in the last poem of *Door Into the Dark*. By the end of that volume, Heaney had read *The Bog People*, and Nerthus makes her appearance in "Bogland" as the womb of earth, her "wet center . . . bottomless." Her womb gives forth increase of grain and life, but it also sucks into itself great beasts, trees, and men who feel compelled as Heaney does, to dig "inwards and downwards" to learn its secrets.

The impact of Heaney's discovery of the myth of the bog goddess is increasingly evident in his third volume, *Wintering Out*, which has numerous poems concerned with her. "Nerthus" is a brief poem depicting the simple wooden images of the goddess discovered in the bogs. Glob describes a slender branch having a natural fork in it with no markings except the sign of its sex gashed into the wood where the fork begins.[10] The image is headless and armless. Heaney's Nerthus is "an ash fork staked in peat, / Its long grains gathering to the gouged split; / A seasoned, unsleeved taker of the weather."

Further images of the bog goddess appear in "The Tollund Man." The best of Heaney's bog poems, it is about the most famous of Nerthus' victims.[11] The Tollund Man was exhumed in 1950, two thousand years after his consignment to the bogs. He was found in extraordinarily well-preserved form, his face peaceful, his last meal still in his stomach, his throat encircled with the goddess' torc, the sign of his consecration to her. The head of the Tollund Man, all that was preserved of the body, is on display in Aarhus, as Heaney says in his poem. He also describes the cap and girdle worn by the victim as he was cast naked into the bog to join Nerthus, "bridegroom to the goddess." In his emphasis on marriage and rebirth, Heaney captures the sexual and sacred implications of the ritual:

> She tightened her torc on him
> And opened her fen,
> Those dark juices working
> Him to a saint's kept body.

The Tollund Man is a good example of Heaney's treatment of the myth. He is not content with exploiting the myth for its sake alone, but must relate it to the Irish land which shares topographical and cultural characteristics with the home of the goddess. Thus, the Tollund Man is not an isolated figure from the Iron Age, but a saint who might be implored, though he were pagan, to restore the ritual significance of death in contemporary Ireland. In his essay, "Feeling Into Words," Heaney talks about what the Tollund Man and his sacrifice to Nerthus mean to him. He says that there is "an indigenous territorial numen" in Ireland, a feminine numen referred to as Kathleen Ni Houlihan or the poor old woman. Her authority has been usurped by a violent male cult which he identifies with modern violence and historical English violation of Ireland. The sacrificial victims of Nerthus become, for Heaney, "an archetypal pattern" inspiring awe and fear.[12] The fertility ritual of death and consequent rebirth becomes the symbol of a people guided by a feminine sense of place which Heaney believes must be renewed if the present is to be tolerated.

The difference between the present and the past is suggested in "The Last Mummer." Modern man is threatened by physical violence, but in that, he is not unlike ancient man. He is unlike ancient man, however, in that he lacks the sustaining rituals, like that of the mummer, which give life richness and death significance. In contrast to the mummer's celebration of the return of summer, Heaney's modern family celebrates the television set. The "charmed . . . ring" of their gazing faces is a denial of the regenerative cycle symbolized by the mummer at their backs and the mystical significance of "the moon's host elevated in a monstrance of holly trees." The images of the moon, the monstrance and the holly suggest the joyous, fertile principle of the old rites. It is a sacred, female principle which Heaney fears is becoming less intrinsic to the lifestyles of his contemporaries.

Though much of the sectarian violence of Ireland fills *Wintering Out*, Heaney perseveres in his faith in the Earth Mother. To establish a new sense of relevance and spiritual coherence in his life, man must return to the ancient mother. He must again join himself to the land, a "woman of old wet leaves," "her breasts an open-work of new straw and harvest bows" ("Land"). In "her loop of silence," he will find his senses awakened and sensitive to the sustaining "soundings" of the past. For modern man, the common earth becomes a bulwark against chaos.

"A Northern Hoard," the longest poem of *Wintering Out*, clearly establishes Heaney's view of the crisis of modern times. Man is uprooted. Having lost his connection with the earth, he is isolated from woman. "The touch of love" is helpless in the encroaching, terrifying war just beyond the "curtained terrace / Where the fault is opening." Faced with losing a sense of the past and the coherence of ancient rituals, the poet searches for the tinder that will "strike a blaze from our dead igneous days."[13] For Heaney, the tinder is that which reaffirms life and hope in the face of the yawning chasm of violence. The strife common to Irish life threatens death and obliteration. Man must turn from violence so that the creative spark may be kindled. Only then will the "moonstruck" body of the Earth Mother thaw and the warmth of "the touch of love" return.

Heaney's concern over rekindling the vital spark in the twentieth-century female counterparts of Nerthus takes particularly modern expression in Part II of *Wintering Out*. Colin Falck has said that Heaney's later writings lack significant emotion and that he seems unable to deal with "modern areas of the modern world."[14] To the contrary, Heaney is poignantly aware of the difficulty of cultivating faith in marriage and in other rituals in the face of today's anarchic confusion. Beset with so much that is negative, men and women find difficulty in holding on to each other and to the faith that their union is, in fact, the only means to fulfilment. He does not take a simplistic, idealistic view of the modern dilemma whether personal or political.

Heaney returns to the bridal theme in "Wedding Day," a poem which establishes man's dependency on woman because she has the strength to see the ritual of the wedding through to its end in spite of his doubts and her own fears. In this poem, the intrusion of reality into the idealized love of the newlyweds is poignantly depicted in a bit of graffiti on a toilet wall: "a skewered heart / And a legend of love." Man's union with woman is necessary and rewarding, but it is not an easy coexistence. The groom's independence and freedom chafe under female supervision, but eventually, he acknowledges his need for her sustenance. Thus, the new husband seeks comfort at his wife's breast as they leave for the airport.

"Summer Home" is a painful exposé of the couple's ensuing difficulties. The air is fouled by the odour of an insect-infested mat, which can be easily taken out and scalded. The marriage itself cannot be so easily rid of the unpleasant smell of "something in heat / Dogging us, the summer gone sour." The husband blames himself and makes an offering of summer flowers; he is the suppliant to his lady. The flowers and the sex act are the "chrism" to heal and annoint the couple's wounds. Their union, like the ripeness of the summer, is blessed with increase. But children are no magical cure for the difficulties of two people living together. Wounds leave scars and arguments are inevitable. Heaney suggests that only in the fecundity of the "old, dripping dark" of the womb / cave is there hope to find solutions to the difference between them. The cave, like the womb and the wife's breasts, which the poet describes as "stoups" holding the living waters, are images associated with the Earth Mother's regenerative potential.

The bog goddess is explicitly recalled in *North*, Heaney's fourth volume, one in which his concern grows over the contrast between the ritual and ceremony associated with bog worship and the violence and anarchy of his times. In poems such as "Kinship," Heaney reaches downward and inward in order to find a context in which to view modern chaos. "Kinship" is a fine poem which establishes the racial kinship of the Irish with the "hiero-glyphic peat" and its secrets of the past. The bog is "the lovenest in the bracken" where Heaney finds the bog goddess, but she appears less attractive than in the earlier poems.[15] Once again, Heaney confronts the complexity of espousing a mythology which condones human sacrifice. As he gets more deeply mired in the politics of Northern Ireland, he sees the victims of the religious strife of his day in an increasingly personal light. He cannot, on one hand, preach the virtues of the bog goddess as the giver of life, without, on the other hand, acknowledging her as the taker of life. In "Kinship," she is "the insatiable bride," both beautiful and terrible. It is necessary to know both aspects of Nerthus if one is to know either. The poet accepts that responsibility, but he refuses to ignore the human, personal tragedy of her insatiable lust.

Because the old balance between life and death has been upset, the victims of the Earth Mother have lost their serenity. So much blood has been spilled on the "mother ground" of Ireland, that it is soured ("Kinship"). The poems of *North* which describe victims of Nerthus reflect a loss of consecration and peacefulness, a condition Heaney relates to the victims of the Irish strife. The face of the "Grauballe Man," for instance, has none of the Tollund Man's peacefulness; it is anguished and strained.[16] Many female sacrificial victims have been beheaded, their golden hair clipped short.[17] In these poems, the poet identifies with the victims; he refuses to become accustomed to the horror of death, for to do so would be to become less than human and no better than those who are untouched by the nameless dead of Ireland.[18]

Despite the grimness of death, Heaney does not give up his faith in the creative aspect of the Earth Mother. He rejects the violence associated with her worship, yet he continues to see potential only in man's union with her. Without woman, man is cut off from the earth; he is lost, as is Ge's son, Antaeus, when he dies at the hand of Hercules. "Hercules and Antaeus" concludes the first part of *North*, and it is significant that there are no poems governed by the female principle in Part II of that volume. The ring is evident only in such images as the stockade of "machine gun posts" or the Orange drums beating out the rhythms of violence ("Whatever You Say, Say Nothing"). The braided torc of the goddess is "the braid cord looped into the revolver butt" of a constable's gun holster ("Singing School"). Circles are evident in the "dark cyclones" of a violent Goya painting, but they imply destruction, not continuity ("Singing School"). These poems reflect Heaney's confrontation of the Irish problem from a political standpoint and less from a mythical one.

In *Field Work*, Heaney returns to the fields and bogs of the Earth Mother and to the significance of myth and ritual in modern times. In this volume, the poet's childhood and the cultural past of his people are the lens through which Heaney looks at the present. "Triptych" illustrates Heaney's quest for rejuvenation. He asks of a young "Sibyl," a youthful Nerthus laden with fruits of the earth, "What will become of us?" She advises him to turn from the worship of the helicoptering cycles of death and violence to the worship of the ancient mysteries. The poet must "go barefoot, foetal and penitential and pray at the water's edge" for the revitalization of his people. Heaney turns from the killing to the living waters which he has always associated with the Earth Mother. Earlier, in "Kinship," he referred to her as the "seedbed, a bag of waters, and a melting grave." Giver and taker of life, she is the source of understanding for the poet and the source of renewal for modern man. The edge of the bog, lake, or stream is holy ground for Heaney. To learn the mysteries of its ancient language, he must revert to a simpler, more innocent posture:

A similar turn back in time is evident in the "Glanmore Sonnets," which depict a ritualistic return to Heaney's youth. The way back is a journey through the darkness of the twilight and dusk. In the light of the risen moon, ancient symbol of the female, the potential restoration of the poet's skill and the quickening of the people are represented in the image of the flight of "a wild white goose / Heard after dark above the drifted house." Out of the "midnight and closedown" comes the possibility of light. The poet is joined with the woman, but she forces him to confront the dreaded rat, long a symbol for Heaney of untold horrors. Once he faces the grim reality of life and passes the ceremonial test of strength and maturity, he is ready for renewal with the moon-faced woman who lies down by his side in a dream reunion of ritualistic love. Thus, the cycle of life is renewed, and peace and hope are once again evident in the "dewy dreaming faces" of the couple.

The four volumes of Heaney's poetry are marked by a strong conscious-ness of the earthiness of life and the female principle which enunciates it. His discovery of the myth of Nerthus and her symbolic neck ring was a fortuitous event which gave form and substance to the concept of that principle as Heaney saw it in his earliest work. The continuous nature of the life cycle is evident in both the fruition and the death associated with the goddess' cult. For the poet, however, and the times in which he lives, the deathliness of the cycle has become predominant and the balance needs restoring. Important in overcoming the violence and fear of the Irish troubles is faith in the union of male and female. The male must ally himself with the female principle because it is the regenerative, spiritual principle of life. To lose touch with that principle is to lose the cohesion and order of the rituals which sustain life, and thus, to allow the nihilism of war to destroy its potential. Heaney is essentially an optimistic poet, and he draws much of his inspiration from his faith in such rituals and their timeless connection with the female principle.

*Notes*

1.  Seamus Heaney, "Belfast," in *Preoccupations: Selected Prose, 1968–1978* (New York: Farrar, Straus, Giroux, 1980), pp. 34–37.

2.  *Ibid.*, p. 34.

3.  *Ibid.*, "Mossbawn," p. 19.

4.  *Ibid.*, "Feeling Into Words," p. 54.

5.  *Ibid.*, p. 60.

6.  *Ibid.*, "The Sense of Place," p. 141.

7.  Arthur E. McGuinness, " 'Hoarder of Common Ground': Tradition and Ritual in Seamus Heaney's Poetry," *Eire*, 13, ii (Summer 1978), 71.

8.  P. V. Glob, *The Bog People: Iron-Age Man Preserved*, trans. Rupert Bruce-Mitford (Ithaca, N. Y.: Cornell Univ. Press, 1969), pp. 156–59.

9.  McGuinness, p. 77.

10.  Glob, p. 180.

11.  *Ibid.*, pp. 18–36.

12.  Heaney, pp. 57–60.

13.  See McGuinness, pp. 71–92.

14.  Colin Falck, review in *The New Review* (August 1975), p. 61.

15.  See Simon Curtis, "Seamus Heaney's *North*," *Critical Quarterly* (Spring 1976), pp. 81–88. See also Rita Zoutenbier, "The Matter of Ireland and the Poetry of Seamus Heaney," *Dutch Quarterly Review*, 9, i (1979), 4–23.

16.  See Glob, pp. 37–62.

17.  See Glob, pp. 91–100.

18.  See David Lloyd, "The Two Voices of Seamus Heaney's *North*," *Ariel*, 10, iv (October 1979), 5–13.

# POETIC CONTEXTS

◆

# Heaney and Dante

CARLA DE PETRIS*

> HUGH: Wordsworth? . . . no. I'm afraid we're not familiar with your litera-
> ture, Lieutenant. We feel closer to the warm Mediterranean. We tend to
> overlook your island.
>
> ——Brian Friel, *Translations*, 2. 1

The references to Dante and the *Commedia* in the most recent poetic work
of Seamus Heaney are emblematic of the salutary confrontation of Irish with
European culture anticipated by Joyce and ironically underlined by Brian
Friel in his most famous play.[1] In an interview in Rome in 1989, Heaney
elaborated on his attraction to Dante as a writer:

> It is the Joycean example, a way into free space, to dodge instead of allowing
> the English tradition—imperial politically—imposing culturally—to mar-
> ginalize the Irish poet. The strategy that Joyce viewed was to marginalize
> that Anglo-Saxon Protestant tradition by going to the Mediterranean, by
> going into Greece . . . but for me it is not just a tactic. It has to do with
> the psychic imprint of the Catholic faith. In Ireland we grew up as rural
> Catholics with little shrines at the crossroads, but deep down we realised that
> the whole official culture had no place for them. Then I read Dante and I
> found in a great work of world literature that that little shrine in a corner
> had this cosmic amplification.[2]

Thus Dante's mesmerizing presence in Heaney's work from the late
1970s onwards has been explained by the poet himself:

> What I first loved in the *Commedia* was the local intensity, the vehemence
> and fondness attaching to individual shades, the way personalities and values
> were emotionally soldered together, the strong strain of what has been called
> personal realism in the celebration of bonds of friendship and bonds of enmity.
> The way in which Dante could place himself in a historical world yet submit
> that world to scrutiny from a perspective beyond history, the way he could
> accommodate the political and the transcendent, this too encouraged my

*This essay was written specifically for this volume and appears here for the first time by permission of
the author.

161

attempt at a sequence of poems which would explore the typical strains which
the consciousness labours under in this country.[3]

The key words in this passage are: "local intensity," "personal realism," and
Dante's way of accommodating "the political and the transcendent." In what
follows, I will attempt to trace these elements in Heaney's "uses" of Dante.
Dante's influence on Heaney emerges in 1979 in *Field Work*, which is full
of direct and indirect quotations from the *Commedia*. The poem "The Strand
at Lough Beg" begins with a reference to the first canto of the *Purgatorio*,
to the act of purification that Virgil performs on Dante at the end of their
journey through Hell, binding him with a reed. The Irish poet kneels and
wipes with "handfuls of dew" the blood-fouled face of a cousin who fell in
an ambush and plaits a scapular of reed for the dead man. This is the first
of the emotional evocations of Dantean images introduced by Heaney:

> And gather up handfuls of dew
> To wash you, cousin. I dab you clean with moss
> Fine as the drizzle out of a low cloud.
> I lift you under the arms and lay you flat.
> With rushes that shoot green again, I plait
> Green scapulars to wear over your shroud.
> (*Field Work*, 18)

*Field Work* is centred on two poems, "September Song" and "An Afterwards,"
both of which sound an ironic Dantean note. The first poem begins with
an obvious echo of the *Commedia*'s opening line, "In the middle of the way,"
an autobiographical reference to Heaney's age (forty) at the time of the
poem's writing. "An Afterwards" contains another Dantean allusion, this
time to the Ninth Circle, the frozen lake of Cocytus where the traitors are.
Heaney's wife considers all poets a bunch of traitors and backbiters, but she
also dooms her husband to the same torment because, choosing not to leave
his study and spend more time with her and the family, he has *betrayed* life
in the name of art. Finally, at the end of *Field Work*, Ugolino's story (*Inferno*
32, lines 124–39 and 33, lines 1–90) is retold in its entirety *in translation*.
Because the translation of the Ugolino episode is central to Heaney's work
and marks a turning point in his poetic career, it is worth examining Heaney's
version closely. From the very first lines of Heaney's translation, the reader
is impressed by his ability to render into English the Dantesque "visible
speech," changing for example a substantive, *cap*, into a verb:

> Noi eravam partiti già da ello,
> ch'io vidi due ghiacciati in una buca,
> sì che l'un capo all'altro era cappello.
> (*Inf.* 32, 124–26)

We had already left him. I walked the ice
And saw two soldered in a frozen hole
On top of other, one's cap capping the other.
(*Field Work*, 61)

Further on, Dante's address to Ugolino becomes brutally modern, and the "bestial segno" (bestial sign) becomes *rut*, animal lust.

O tu che mostri per sì bestial segno
odio sovra colui che tu ti mangi,
dimmi 'l perché, diss'io, per tal convegno.
(*Inf*. 32, 133–35)

"You," I shouted, "You on top, what hate
Makes you so ravenous and insatiable?
What keeps you so monstrously at rut?
(*Field Work*, 61)

The exasperated physicality of the Heaneyan vocabulary reaches its peak in the famous lines:

Ma se le mie parole esser dien seme
che frutti infamia al traditor ch'ì rode,
parlar e lagrimar vedrai insieme.
(*Inf*. 32, 7–9)

Yet while I weep to say them, I would sow
My words like curses—that they might increase
And multiply upon this head I gnaw.
(*Field Work*, 61)

The Dantesque metamorphic image "Se le mie parole esser dien seme" becomes the much more direct and Heaneyesque "I would sow my words like curses."

In order to render the protraction of the suffering which torments Ugolino, trapped as he is between the conflicting drives of hope and despair, Heaney uses an obsessively repetitive language:

Breve pertugio dentro dalla muda
la qual per me ha il titol della fame,
e'n che convien ancor ch'altrui si chiuda,

m'avea mostrato per lo suo forame
più lume già, quand'io feci'l mal sonno
che del futuro mi squarciò'l velame
(*Inf*. 33, 22–27)

> Others will pine as I pine in that jail
> Which is called Hunger after me, and watch
> As I watched through a narrow hole
>
> Moon after moon, bright and sonambulant,
> Pass overhead, until that night I dreamt
> The bad dream and my future's veil was rent.
>
> (*Field Work*, 62)

The translator is often forced to privilege a single sense in a polysemous text. In the passage that follows, for example, the ambiguous words of Dante hold the reader in check, as De Sanctis rightly observes, with "a line thick with obscurity and hidden meanings, because of the swarm of sentiments and images it arouses, because of the many "perchances" it suggests, all intensely poetical. Perhaps he called on death. . . . Perhaps he did not cease calling his children. . . . Perhaps while nature drove his teeth into the 'wretched flesh,' that flesh became the flesh of his enemy in his imagination, in a last delirium of hunger and vindictiveness. . . . This would be a feeling of canine fury. . . . Each conjecture finds its basis in some word, in the possible interpretation of some idea."[4]

Heaney does not stress his complexity, even though it would so powerfully support his denunciation of the dehumanizing power of political vengeance:

> già cieco, a brancolar sovra ciascuno,
> e due dì li chiamai, poi che fur morti:
> poscia, più che 'l dolor, poté 'l digiuno.
>
> (*Inf.* 33, 73–75)

> Searching, blinded,
> For two days I groped over them and called them,
> Then hunger killed where grief had only wounded.
>
> (*Field Work*, 63)

The Florentine poet's vehement insult of Pisa offers the last superb example of the Irish poet's exceptional skill as translator. He transforms the complex metaphor of the pacific "Sì" threateningly inverted in the very name of the volatile Tuscan city into a powerful alliteration; the "s" hisses in these lines like a snake in the grass.

> Ahi, Pisa, vituperio delle gente
> del bel paese là dove 'l sì sona,
>
> (*Inf.* 33, 79–80)

Pisa! Pisa, your sounds are like a hiss
Sizzling in our country's grassy language.
(*Field Work*, 63)

After "Ugolino," Heaney will rely constantly upon Dante in two essential ways. The first is his growing interest in both the practice and concept of translation, which we shall consider in more detail later. The other involves what might be called Dantesque thematics, especially in the design of Heaney's next book, *Station Island*. There the poet narrates his pilgrimage to Lough Derg, known as St. Patrick's Purgatory, a traditional "rite of passage" for Irish Catholics. During his pilgrimage, Heaney meets private and public ghosts: friends, relatives, his first love and three masters, William Carleton, Patrick Kavanagh and James Joyce. Beyond its overall design, the book contains at least two explicit allusions to the *Commedia*: the poem "Sandstone Keepsake" borrows from the twelfth canto of the *Inferno* (118–20), and the third sonnet of Section 6 of the titular sequence makes use of the second canto (127–32). Once again the appropriation of Dante goes hand in hand with the theory and practice of translation.

a window facing the deep south of luck
Opened and I inhaled the land of kindness.
*As little flowers that were all bowed and shut*
*By the night chills rise on their stems and open*
*As soon as they have felt the touch of sunlight,*
*So I revived in my own wilting powers*
*And my heart flushed, like somebody set free.*
Translated, given, under the oak tree.
(*Station Island*, 76)

The italicized lines are translated from the *Commedia* and bequeathed to the Irish poet under the tree of the Druids, the ancient poet-priest of celtic culture. Heaney's conception of the role of the poet in contemporary Ireland at the time he was writing *North* and *Field Work* was in fact Druidical. The great poet was the one who could "accommodate the political and the transcendent." He challenged this conception in *Station Island*. Since then it has changed and has become more and more controversial, doubtful and painfully mature. "And after the commanded journey, What? / Nothing magnificent, nothing unknown. / A gazing out from far away, alone" (*Seeing Things*, 55). The purgatorial pilgrimage to and from Station Island has left him "like a convalescent" as the experience has given clear evidence of his incapacity to accept his people's ways and religious beliefs. In the last section he has left the island to stand "there on the tarmac among the cars," alone but for the "alien confort" of Joyce's "fish-cold and bony" hand. He seems to be ready to accept his betrayal of the tribe, the poet's unavoidable role of translator.

In fact, it is the question of language that makes Dante and the translation of Ugolino's story so significant for Heaney. One must keep firmly in mind the genetic given of anglophone Irish literature, its dichotomy, which causes a painful cultural alienation, a kind of interior exoticism. This literature is the marvelous fruit of a cultural grafting, always preserving the memory of the wound that has generated it. Heaney ironically explains his own relation to language: "I think of the personal and Irish pieties as vowels, and of the literary awareness nourished on English as consonants."

Dante's struggle with the inadequacies of medium to matter provides Heaney with a wider perspective on the complexities of his own search for poetic expression. Dante's "head-clearing similes" fulfill his desire for "simplicity and amplitude." "Trasumanar significar per verba / Non si poria" ("*Transhumanised*—the fact mocks human phrase," *Paradiso* 1, 70–71). In the contemporary Irish poet who confronts the political violence of Ulster with the inaccurate signs of English one can sense the same frustration and recklessness of the great Christian and Moslem mystics of the Middle Ages who are Dante's forefathers and who, as Furio Jesí writes in *Letteratura e Mito*, "have often despaired of successfully expressing in appropriate language the climax of their experiences. In their writings is the constant lament over the powerlessness of language, insufficient to embrace the reality of their illuminations; still, they have continued to speak and write, opening up unknown paths of language and paradoxically enriching the sphere of language with bold and marvellous formulations at the very moment they endure and announce its limits." This could be said of almost every Irish writer using English from the seventeenth to the twentieth century. Changing the religious into a secular perspective it could easily apply to Joyce and Beckett, who in different ways "opened up unknown paths" for English. An Irish writer—and even more so a poet—writing in English experiences a sort of mystical stupor at the marvelous potentialities of his medium, his hidden numen.

Heaney, like Dante, works upon language as though against the grain of its own nature. The critic Robert Buttel, referring to Heaney's first poetic attempts, has written that "the vividness of physical detail . . . , the energy of word and speech in But God, another was *nimbling* / Up the far bank or A rat *Slimed* out of the water'—with adjective and noun here metamorphosing into disturbing active verbs: these are typical qualities in the first volume."[5] Since his debut Heaney has shown a great ability to exploit the metamorphic potential of English. No matter that Sante is situated at the roots of Italian while the Irish poet is the product of late mutations of the English language—for both of them *"the natural object is always the adequate symbol."* Hence it becomes verb—and that means action. Life generates the name. The poet's linguistic act implies a particular kind of responsibility, involving reality as well as its shaping in words. Dante returns whenever Heaney is at odds with this idea of linguistic as well as ethical responsibility.

For Heaney, realism—he calls it "personal"—is not a literary device, rather it is "visible parlare" ("visible speech," *Purg.* 60, line 95). He probes this idea in his most recent collection *Seeing Things* (1991). In fact, the opening poem of Part 2, "The Journey Back," centered on a quotation from *Inferno* 2, lines 1–5, ends with the line "A nine-to-five man who has *seen poetry*" (italics mine). *Station Island* was the "journey into" the poet's past—the Land of the Dead; *Seeing Things* is his "journey back / into the heartland of the ordinary" after having "seen poetry." Its imagery is that of navigation: by air—"a ship appeared above them in the air"; by water—"One by one we were being handed down / Into a boat that dipped and shilly-shallied / Scaresomely every time"; often inland—"My lowlands of the mind. / Heaviness of being. And poetry / Sluggish in the doldrums of what happens."

The leitmotiv played for the first time in *Field Work*, echoing in *Station Island*, returns in this latest book in a new melody. The poet's responsibility to life consists in the absolute devotion to his craft; seeing things is saying things. And Dante still helps:

> Now I turn it upside down and it is a boat—
> A paper boat, or the one that wafts into
> The first lines of the *Purgatorio*
> As poetry lifts its eyes and clears its throat.
> (*Seeing Things*, 29)

The priest's triangular biretta—meaningless leftover from Heaney's religious upbringing—recovers a meaning through poetry and becomes a metaphor of "la navicella del mio ingegno" ("My ship of genius," *Purg.* 1, line 2).[6]

Dante has always been at the centre of Heaney's reflection on what we might call "linguistic loyalty." Already in 1980, in an essay entitled "A Sense of Place," he writes: "I like to remember that Dante was very much a man of a particular place, that his great poem is full of intimate placings and place-names, and that as he moves round the murky circles of hell, often heard rather than seen by his damned friends and enemies, he is *recognized by his local speech* or so recognizes them" (italics mine).[7] It should not surprise us that in the 1985 essay entitled "Envies and Identifications: Dante and the Modern Poet," after having mentioned W. B. Yeats, Geoffrey Hill, Wilfred Owen, and Thomas Kinsella, Heaney concentrates on T. S. Eliot's use of the *Commedia* in *The Waste Land* and later in *Little Gidding*. "When he [Eliot] makes Dante's confident and classically ratified language bear an almost allegorical force, he does less than justice to the untamed and thoroughly parochial elements which it possesses."[8]

On yet another occasion Heaney reaffirms his unconditional faith in the "familiar lexicon" of the tribe, the poet's "local speech," interwoven of vital juices, physicality, hate and love. He considers the rejection of standard language, the language of authority and power, to be Dante's greatest teaching, a teaching which was confirmed by Heaney's reading of Osip Mandel-stam's *Conversations with Dante*.

> What Mandelstam does . . . is to bring him (Dante) from the pantheon back to the palate . . . So in order to breathe freely, to allow his lips to move again with poems which were his breath of life, he had to come clean, spur his pegasus out of the socialist realist morass, and thereby confront the danger of death and the immediate penalty of exile. And his essay on Dante was written in the aftermath of this tragic choice. . . . Dante is not perceived as a mouthpiece of orthodoxy but as the apotheosis of free, natural biological process, a process of crystallization, a focus for all impulsive, instinctive, non-utilitarian elements in the creative life.

In a sort of literary triangulation, Heaney focuses on Mandelstam to find his own way to Dante. In a passionate comment on the poetic work of Mandelstam dating from 1980, Heaney says that "language is the poet's faith. . . . He has to bring that faith to the point of arrogance and trium-phalism. . . . Mandelstam served the people by serving their language."[9] These words are a challenging poetical / political manifesto to which Heaney is all too willing to subscribe, since the language of poetry is considered the shaping force of human history. For a long time, at least from *North* to *Station Island*, Heaney was tormented by the conflict between embracing his responsibility as a poet or accomplishing his tribal duty of political commitment. Both choices implied a different kind of treason. Dante pro-vided him with a "head-clearing simile." In the *Commedia* and especially in the story of Count Ugolino he found a perfect emblem of betrayal and of the inadequacy of human justice.

In a review of *Station Island* Seamus Deane has polemically maintained that Heaney's "internal debate is a fruitful one. The subject of the debate is betrayal." Betrayal as the utmost consequence of hate is a germinal force of human life, like its opposite, love. Therefore both Dante and Heaney exploit the image of food—"il fiero pasto" ("the savage repast")—so that the physical directly echoes the metaphysical. As the critic Blake Morrison said, "History . . . unloads its foul lumber, blundering in on the pleasures of the meal and the text."[10] Count Ugolino and his sons and nephews were imprisoned in the Pisan tower named "della fame" ("of the hunger") after their death by starvation. Their imprisonment was the result of Ugolino's betrayal of his countrymen. No one ever knew if, blinded by hunger, Ugolino had killed and eaten his own children. But Dante suggests that possibility. In the *Inferno* Ugolino is gnawing the head of his executioner, Archbishop Roger. They both are trapped in the Ninth Circle and they both are traitors. Dante sees them: "I walked the ice / And saw two soldered in a frozen hole / On top of other, one's skull capping the other" (*Field Work*, 61). But why is Ugolino "on top of the other"? Because his enemy, the winner of

their political struggle, had doomed Ugolino to a torment which could—
and most probably had—annihilitated in him all bonds of human love.
Archbishop Roger had betrayed the most sacred icon, that of Man. Therefore
in moral terms, he is more culpable than the count. Dante, himself a victim
of political unrest, maintains that only God can find an equilibrium between
betrayal and its punishment. The moral and political significance of the
episode has been summarized by Natalino Sapegno: "From every page of
these two cantos XXXII and XXXIII there should spring forth the firm
condemnation, no longer of this or that political party, but of the methods
and the forms of the entire political life of the age of the communes, viewed
and judged in its totality."[11] Thus Ugolino's story gives Heaney a true
*exemplum*, in the medieval sense, of the present situation in Northern Ireland.
Endless betrayal, as a result of prevarication, is at the root of that endless,
mortal ritual of violence, that banquet of Death.

But Heaney is either a political leader nor an ideologue. One might
say of him—using his own favorite method of triangulation—what Joyce
said of Bloom, striking a Dantean note: "At the critical turning point of
human existence he [Bloom] desires to amend many social conditions, the
product of inequality and avarice and international animosity."[12] One may
also apply to Heaney Gramsci's stricture on Dante's political views: "After
the defeat of his party, Dante's doctrine is relevant only as a feature of his
personal development. In fact his is not so much a political doctrine as a
political utopia . . . and, above all, it is an attempt to organize in a doctrinal
system what in fact was only the agitating stuff of poetry in the making"
(translation mine).[13] Therefore, centuries before Heaney, Dante was serving
his people by serving their language, by becoming their poet.

The language question reemerges constantly and threateningly, but at
the end of *Station Island* Heaney has no doubts about it, and the shade of
Dante looms at the back of the scene "on the tarmac among the cars." In a
uniquely Dantean and Joycean moment Heaney will *betray* "for the millionth
time" and re-create in English those works of art that are at the root of "the
conscience of his race." At the end of his pilgrimage Heaney has Joyce's
ghost to scold him ironically:

> "Who cares,"
> He jeered, "any more? The English language
> belongs to us. You are raking at dead fires,
>
> a waste of time for somebody your age."
> (*Station Island*, 93)

Here Heaney is using Dante's forceful image and metre. In fact section 12
is an experiment in terza rima. Heaney's voice has definitely become the
voice of Dante, the poet, who indefatigably and inexorably holds a mirror

to human history, to its tragedies as well as to its farces like that of the restoration of Irish as a spoken language in the Republic.

Moreover, Joyce's words movingly echo Cacciaguida's. Cacciaguida, one of Dante's ancestors, whom the poet meets in Heaven, foresees Dante's political ruin and future exile and advises him to betray (i.e., to abandon) his companions—"la compagnia malvagia e scempia"—once in exile and be faithful only to his poetic craft:

> che tutta ingrata, tutta matta e empia
> si farà contra te; ma, poco appresso,
> ella, non tu, n'avrà rossa la tempia.

> Di sua bestialità il suo processo
> farà la prova; sì che a te fia bello
> avertii fatta parte per te stesso.
> (*Paradiso*, 17, lines 68–69)

> (For with a savage fury shall they play
> The ingrate, and defame thee; yet anon
> Not thou shall feel thy forehead burn, but they—

> Fools all, and proved so by their goings-on;
> Well shall it be for thee to have preferred
> Making a party of thyself alone.)

Stressing a similar opposition between "they" and "you," Joyce warns Heaney in his poem: "When they make the circle wide, it's time to swim / / Out on your own and fill the element / With signatures on your own frequency" (*Station Island*, 93). After having been in the hell of Northern Ireland, stuck in ice as Ugolino, around the purgatory of sharp public rebuke and personal reticence, and under the paternal eye of Joyce / Cacciaguida, Heaney seems to be reaching now the Empireal sky of Form, animated by the same joy of the stupefied sailor on his journey back into the ordinary in poem 8 of "Lightenings": "the freed ship sailed, and the man climbed back / Out of the marvellous as he had known it" (*Seeing Things*, 92).

*Notes*

1. An earlier and abbreviated version of this article with the title "Poesia e politica nell'Irlanda contemporanea. Influenze dantesche nell'opera di Seamus Heaney" has been published in Italian in *Il Veltro: Rivista della civiltà italiana* 31, no. 3–4, (May–August 1987): 366–76.

2. The interview has been published only in Italian: C. de Petris, "La Pausa per la riflessione: Incontro con Seamus Heaney," *Linea d'ombra*, no. 42, (October 1989): 69–73.

3. "Envies and Identifications: Dante and the Modern Poet," *Irish University Review*, ed. M. Harmon, 15: 1 (Spring 1985): 18.

4. *De Sanctis on Dante*, ed. and trans. J. Ross and A. Galpin (Madison: University of Wisconsin Press, 1957), 126–27.

5. Robert Buttel, *Seamus Heaney* (Lewisburg: Bucknell University Press, 1975), 23.

6. The more navigation has become a paradigm of poetry for Heaney, the more we feel entitled to apply the nautical metaphor of triangulation to express and explain Heaney's use of literary influences, his habit of focusing on a writer who quotes or refers to another. Heaney's most recent work gives us many examples of this. Let us cite the two examples from *Seeing Things* that still strike the Dantean note: the opening of "The Journey Back," where we have the triad Heaney-Larkin-Dante: "Larkin's shade surprised me. He quoted Dante" (7); and "The Schoolbag—*in memoriam John Hewitt*," where Dante's Italian establishes a bond between the two Northern Irish poets from different generations and backgrounds: "My handsewn leather schoolbag. Forty years. / Poet, you were *nel mezzo del cammin* / When I shouldered it" (30).

7. *Preoccupations* (London: Faber and Faber, 1980), 136.

8. "Envies and Identifications: Dante and the Modern Poet," 12.

9. *Preoccupations*, 223.

10. *Seamus Heaney* (London: Methuen, 1982), 75.

11. N. Sapegno, ed., *La Divina Commedia*, 2nd ed. (Florence: La Nuova Italian, 1968), 356.

12. J. Joyce, *Ulysses* (London: Bodley Head, 1961), 681: 16.

13. A. Gramsci, *Quaderni dal carcere*, ed. V. Gerratana (Turin: G. Einaudi, 1975), 759–60.

# The Poet as Archaeologist:
# W. B. Yeats and Seamus Heaney

## Jon Stallworthy*

When Yeats called upon the holy martyrs of San Apollinarc Nuovo to be the singing-masters of his soul, he implied a contrast with the earlier singing-masters of the body that now seemed to him "a dying animal." The concept of a singing school, unfamiliar to many readers of "Sailing to Byzantium," had for the poet a precise and important meaning. He was aware, from his reading in John O'Leary's fine library of Irish books, from his research into oral traditions with Lady Gregory, that the arch-poets of ancient Ireland, the *filis*, were graduates of singing schools whose formal training in language, prosody, and historical lore could last as long as twelve years. So the young poet, who aspired to a place in the tradition that included Oisin and Seanchan, set himself "to study / In a learned school." His singing-masters included Blake, whom he liked to think was of Irish extraction,[1] and Spenser, who went to Ireland as secretary to the lord deputy and, in 1586, became one of the "undertakers" for the settlement of Munster. In due course, Yeats edited *The Works of William Blake* and published a selection from the poems of Spenser. His introduction to this selection declared that "When Spenser wrote of Ireland he wrote as an official, and out of thoughts and emotions that had been organized by the State. He was the first of many Englishmen to see nothing but what he was desired to see. Could he have gone there as a poet merely, he might have found among its poets more wonderful imaginations than even those islands of Phaedria and Acrasia."[2] Yeats omitted to mention that in Spenser's *View of the Present State of Ireland* he singled out the Irish "Bardes and rythmers" for special condemnation as liars and rabble-rousers; and there's a painful irony in the fact that, when the guerrillas finally burnt his castle, what the English poet no doubt regarded as a rabble was almost certainly roused by his Irish counterparts.

Yeats has no illusions about Spenser, the agent of the British crown: "Like an hysterical patient he drew a complicated web of inhuman logic out of the bowels of an insufficient premise—there was no right, no law, but that of Elizabeth, and all that opposed her opposed themselves to God, to

*Reprinted from the *Review of English Studies* 33, no. 130 (1982): 158–74.

civilization, and to all inherited wisdom and courtesy and should be put to death."[3] Yeats, however, praised the "poet of the delighted senses"[4] and can be seen, in retrospect, to owe more to his singing-mastery than to that of the Irish poets who drove him from Kilcolman; poets whose traditions Yeats venerated, but whose language he never thought to learn.

If there's a sense in which Yeats is of the lineage of Spenser, Seamus Heaney claims descent from those who burnt Spenser's castle. He depicts himself as

> a wood-kerne
>
> Escaped from the massacre,
> Taking protective colouring
> From bole and bark, feeling
> Every wind that blows. . . .[5]

In an earlier poem, "Bog Oak," his meditation on a gnarled roof-beam leads him back through the centuries, until he seems to

> make out
> Edmund Spenser,
> dreaming sunlight,
> encroached upon by
>
> geniuses who creep
> "out of every corner
> of the woodes and glennes"
> towards watercress and carrion.[6]

In that last stanza, Heaney is quoting—as before him, Yeats in his Introduction, had quoted—from a grim passage in Spenser's *View of the Present State of Ireland*: "Out of every corner of the woodes and glynnes they came creeping forth upon theyr hands, for theyr legges could not beare them; they looked like anatomyes of death, they spake like ghostes crying out of theyr graves; they did eate of the dead carrions, happy were they if they could finde them, yea, and one another soone after, insoemuch as the very carcasses they spared not to scrape out of theyr graves; and if they found a plot of watercresses or shamrokes, there they flocked as to a feast. . . ."[7]

And what of Heaney's own singing school? Boldly appropriating Yeats's phrase as the title for a poem of his own, he calls attention to its source in selecting as his second epigraph—the first being a quotation from Wordsworth's *Prelude*—a passage from the opening page of Yeats's *Autobiographies*: "He [the stable boy] had a book of Orange rhymes, and the days when we read them together in the hayloft gave me the pleasure of rhyme for the first time. Later on I can remember being told, when there was a rumor of a Fenian rising, that rifles were being handed out to the Orangemen; and presently, when I began to dream of my future life, I thought I would like to die fighting the Fenians." This is a cunning choice of epigraph, in that it undercuts the act of homage implicit in the title "Singing School" by defining the great gulf fixed between the young, still Protestant Yeats, nourished on dreams of conflict with the Fenians, and Heaney the Roman Catholic. Yeats was not one of his first singing-masters,[8] but Heaney's attitude to his great forerunner today has something in common with Yeats's complicated admiration for Spenser.

He pays eloquent tribute to the fruits of Yeats's imperial, imperious imagination in an essay to whose title—taken from an essay of Auden's— he adds a significant question-mark: "Yeats as Example?"[9] In another essay, "The Making of a Music," written in the same year, Wordsworth's ability to listen and respond to the voice of Nature, his "wise passiveness," is clearly preferred to Yeats's more active "music of energy reined down."[10] The true nature of Heaney's engagement (in both the peaceable and hostile senses) with Yeats, however, is to be seen less in the explicit civilities of his prose than in the unobtrusive way in which he engages and subverts the Yeatsian phrase.

"Singing-School" is also the title given to an autobiographical essay prefacing a selection of Heaney's poems in an anthology.[11] This, written in the same year as the poem with the Yeatsian epigraph, would seem to have those "Orange rhymes" in mind when it recollects rhymes of a different colour. Heaney's essay begins: "A few months ago I remembered a rhyme that we used to chant on the way to school. I know now that it is about initiation but as I trailed along the Lagan's Road on my way to Anahorish School it was something that was good for a laugh:

> 'Are your praties dry
> And are they fit for digging?'
> 'Put in your spade and try,'
> Says Dirty-Faced McGuigan.

. . . And there were other chants, scurrilous and sectarian, that we used to fling at one another: 'Up the long ladder and down the short rope / To hell with King Billy and God bless the Pope.' " Once again Heaney undercuts the Yeatsian title, "Singing School," this time mocking its romantic resonance with schoolboy jingles, but his *lèse-majesté* has a serious purpose: to define his own attitude to what, echoing Yeats, he calls his "art and sedentary trade."[12] He recalls that when, at the age of twelve, he went to a boarding-school in Derry, old neighbours nodded wisely and said: "The pen's lighter than the spade." That proverb and the jingle "Are your praties dry . . .?" reappear in a lecture, introducing in both contexts what Heaney describes as "the first poem I wrote where I thought my feelings had got into words, or to put it more accurately, where I thought my *feel* had got into words."[13] The poem, "Digging," was written in 1964 and, placed appropriately as the first poem of his first book, it begins: "Between my finger and my thumb / The squat pen rests; snug as a gun." Having given us a glimpse of himself "at his sedentary trade," his pen goes expertly to work redirecting our attention:

> Under my window, a clean rasping sound
> When the spade sinks into gravelly ground:
> My father, digging. I look down
>
> Till his straining rump among the flowerbeds
> Bends low, comes up twenty years away
> Stooping in rhythm through potato drills
> Where he was digging.

The pen digs back into the poet's memory, uncovering first his father and then; cutting deeper into time past, his grandfather, who "cut more turf in a day / Than any other man on Toner's bog." His digging done, the poet straightens up—like his grandfather—to take stock, and concludes with an admission and a resolution already brilliantly fulfilled:

> But I've no spade to follow men like them.
>
> Between my finger and my thumb
> The squat pen rests
> I'll dig with it.

Heaney has said in criticism of this poem that "there are a couple of lines in it that have the theatricality of the gunslinger rather than the self-absorption of the digger."[14] Clearly he refers to the gun image at beginning and end, but we should not be distracted by the American associations of "gunslinger" into overlooking the significance of such an image in such a poem by a young Irishman. Nor is it an isolated image. It is a curious fact that the poems of *Death of a Naturalist*, so justly praised for their loving evocations of the natural world, none the less abound in images of man-made violence. In the title-poem, the "gross-bellied frogs were cocked. . . . Some sat / Poised like mud grenades." Safety-catch and grenade have their place in the poem "In Small Townlands." In "The Barn," "The musty dark hoarded an armoury / of farmyard implements," and in "Churning Day," the four crocks "stood, large pottery bombs." Perhaps the most obvious example: "Trout"

> Hangs a fat gun-barrel. . . .
>
> His muzzle gets bull's eye;
> picks off grass seed and moths
> that vanish torpedoed.

> Where water unravels
> over gravel-beds he
> is fired from the shallows
> white belly reporting
>
> flat; darts like a tracer-
> bullet back between stones
> and is never burnt out.
> A volley of cold blood
>
> ramrodding the current.

Time and again the poet's pen / gun / spade holds up a living creature, or some object with only peaceable associations, to define it in terms of man-made violence. Heaney has said that

> Denis Donoghue probably got to the heart of the matter when he suggested, in a review, that I had seen too many war films when I was a youngster. But two other explanations occur to me (for I was not conscious of planting mines at the time). First, that Ted Hughes's poetry was a strong influence in releasing me, and the habit of explosive diction may have been caught from him. And second—a more tentative, perhaps mystifying thought—when I set about a poem in those days, I was tensed and triggered within myself. I usually wrote at a sitting and generated a charge within me: the actual writing was an intense activity, battened down. So maybe that state reflected itself in the diction and imagery.[15]

Whatever the true reason—and probably all three are true—*Death of a Naturalist* proclaimed that Heaney had inherited with his Irish blood not only a spade but a gun.

He has written eloquently of poetry "as divination, poetry as a revelation of the self to the self, as restoration of the culture to itself; poems as elements of continuity, with the aura and authenticity of archaeological finds, where the buried shard has an importance that is not obliterated by the buried city; poetry as a dig for finds that end up being plants.[16] The spade—whether it be the spade of the archaeologist, farmer, or turf-cutter—descends into darkness to bring what is buried to the light. His *Preoccupations* opens with "the music of somebody pumping water at the pump outside our back door," and proceeds to a childhood recollection of "men coming to sink the shaft of the pump and digging through that seam of sand down into the bronze riches of the gravel, that soon began to puddle with the spring water."[17] There is a good deal of spade work in *Death of a Naturalist*, and another related image for the poet, this poet, at work—that of "The Diviner," "Circling the terrain, hunting the pluck / Of water, nervous, but professionally / / Unfussed." The diviner's forked rod puts him in touch with what is hidden and the spade must bring to light. Heaney's pen re-enacts that divination as skilfully as it mimed the spade in "Digging." For him, as for Yeats, water has feminine and inspirational associations, and the book which began with the poem ends with "Personal Helicon." As later with "Singing School," the romantic and traditional expectations aroused by Heaney's title are at once disappointed and challenged by the homely nature of his subject:

> As a child, they could not keep me from wells
> And old pumps with buckets and windlasses.
> I loved the dark drop, the trapped sky, the smells
> Of waterweed, fungus and dank moss.

Having "let down a shaft into real life"—Heaney's description of what his poem "Digging" achieved—he again returns from past to present, from wet darkness to the light of self-revelation:

> Now, to pry into roots, to finger slime,
> To stare big-eyed Narcissus, into some spring
> Is beneath all adult dignity. I rhyme
> To see myself, to set the darkness echoing.

The resonance of that concluding sentence—so beautifully consonant with the opening sentence of *Death of a Naturalist*—should not blind us, or deafen us, to the ironic ambiguity of what led up to it. Prying, fingering, and staring are said to be "beneath all adult dignity" and, at a first reading, we take "beneath" to mean "incompatible with." On closer acquaintance, however, we perceive a secondary meaning that calls in question the adult dignity that would pretend it has outgrown them.

The wet darkness explored by Heaney's poems takes another—but closely related—metaphorical shape in his second book, *Door into the Dark*. Its title, he wrote, "comes from the first line of 'The Forge,' a poem that uses the dark, active centre of the blacksmith's shed as an emblem for the instinctive, blurred stirring and shaping of some kinds of art. And I was happy to discover after I had chosen the title that it follows directly from the last line in my first book."[18] The dark, still water of the well is the same element as the "strumming water" of the poem, "The Salmon-Fisher to the Salmon." The angler poet here searches for hidden enlightenment not with spade or divining rod, but rather with rod and line. The violence present in the imagery of the earlier poem "Trout" now recurs more directly:

> I go, like you, by gleam and drag

> And will strike when you strike, to kill.
> We're both annihilated on the fly.

> You can't resist a gullet full of steel.
> I will return home fish-smelling, scaly.

Fish and fisherman are "*both* annihilated." As the young poet had rhymed "to see [himself], to set the darkness echoing," there is a sense in which he is fishing for himself in a number of later poems. The clearest example is "A Lough Neagh Sequence," part 4 of which begins: "A line goes out of sight and out of mind / Down to the soft bottom of silt and sand / Past the indifferent skill of the hunting hand." Fisherman's hand and poet's hand together lift the hooked eels in part 5, and in part 6 Heaney follows one that escapes:

> a wick that is
> its own taper and light
> through the weltering dark.
> Where she's lost once she lays
> ten thousand feet down in
> her origins. The current
> carries slicks of orphaned spawn.

That original dark is plumbed again in somewhat similar terms in the poem that closes *Door into the Dark*, "Bogland":

> The ground itself is kind, black butter
>
> Melting and opening underfoot. . . .
>
> The bogholes might be Atlantic seepage.
> The wet centre is bottomless.

In 1967, the year that poem was published, his growing interest in the possible poetic resources of the bog led Heaney to read *The Bog People* by P. V. Glob. What he found there confirmed the truth of his intuitions and opened his eyes—as Jessie L. Weston's *From Ritual to Romance* opened Eliot's—to deeper levels of mythic and historical congruence. He writes of *The Bog People*:

> It was chiefly concerned with preserved bodies of men and women found in the bogs of Jutland, naked, strangled or with their throats cut, disposed under the peat since early Iron Age times. The author . . . argues convincingly that a number of these, and in particular, the Tollund Man, whose head is now preserved near Aarhus in the museum at Silkeburg, were ritual sacrifices to the Mother Goddess, the goddess of the ground who needed new bridegrooms each winter to bed with her in her sacred place, in the spring. Taken in relation to the tradition of Irish political martyrdom for the cause whose icon

is Kathleen Ni Houlihan, this is more than an archaic barbarous rite: it is an archetypal pattern. And the unforgettable photographs of these victims blended in my mind with photographs of atrocities, past and present, in the long rites of Irish political and religious struggles.[19]

The first poem to be generated by Heaney's reading of *The Bog People* was "The Tollund Man," published in his third book, *Wintering Out* (1972). In this "vow to go on pilgrimage," the poet's rhetorical suspension momentarily seems to identify him with the victim, "Bridegroom to the goddess": and the lucky near-pun on Aarhus *our house*, enables him to superimpose Ireland on Jutland: "Now his stained face / Reposes at Aarhus." He foresees himself trying to enter and inhabit that head:

> Something of his sad freedom
> As he rode the tumbril
> Should come to me, driving,
> Saying the names
>
> Tollund, Grauballe, Nebelgard,
> Watching the pointing hands
> Of country people,
> Not knowing their tongue.

"Not knowing their tongue," he knows he cannot hope to enter the head of the Tollund Man, but believes a liturgical naming of places familiar in the victim's mouth will admit him to *something* of his sad freedom. Elsewhere in *Wintering Out* the naming of places gives Heaney magical access to his own country through the mirror of its language:

> *Anahorish*, soft gradient
> of consonant, vowel meadow. . . .[20]
>
> The tawny guttural water
> spells itself: Moyola
> its own score and consort. . . .[21]
>
> My mouth holds round
> the soft blastings,
> *Toome, Toome*
> as under the dislodged
>
> slab of the tongue
> I push into the souterrain. . . .[22]

In this book, Heaney excavates not only the bog but language, the poet's native element, and his implement is the tongue, which is mentioned seven times.

Spade and tongue, working in unison, reappear in "Belderg," and other poems at the beginning of *North* (1975), but it would seem as if, under the pressure of the sectarian violence that dominates the central poems of the book, the tongue's gentler excavations had to be abandoned; its function now is simply to report the findings of the spade. Heaney's perception that "the bog bank is a memory bank"[23] provided him with an inexhaustible metaphor for the unforgiving memory that in Ireland, perhaps more than in any other country, has been each generation's legacy to the next. Having made his pilgrimage to "the holy blisful martyr" at Aarhus, he comes home equipped to feel more than "something of the sad freedom" of the ancient victims. He becomes the "Bog Queen" of his poem: "I was barbered / and stripped / by a turfcutter's spade. . . ." His lyrical description of "The Grauballe Man" in terms of natural imagery is brutally interrupted when he perceives that "The chin is a visor / raised above the vent / of his slashed throat. . . ." The wound is said to be "cured" but, in denial, as the poet's memory weighs "beauty with atrocity," we are made to feel the atrocity scale drop under "the actual weight / of each hooded victim / slashed and dumped." The repeated "slashed" and its companion past participles from the daily news bulletin, "hooded" and "dumped," jerk us out of antiquity into contemporary Belfast. The spade has passed from the archaeologist to the grave-digger but, significantly, we are left gazing at a hooded victim, of unspecified religion. Heaney is a Roman Catholic and he writes from a Roman Catholic perspective, but his vision and his compassion are consistently larger than those of the contending politicians.

"The Grauballe Man" in *North* lies beside the "Little adultress" of the poem "Punishment," and in this the poet orders the pronouns of his opening sentence to identify himself momentarily with her: "I can feel the tug / of the halter at the nape / of her neck. . . ." When he addresses her as "My poor scapegoat," adding "I almost love you," the reason for his earlier empathy begins to emerge as guilt. Once again, ancient and modern come into sudden conjunction:

> I who have stood dumb
> when your betraying sisters,
> cauled in tar,
> wept by the railings,
>
> who would connive
> in civilized outrage
> yet understand the exact
> and tribal, intimate revenge.

Heaney stands horrified but dumb—until now, dumb—before her "betraying sisters," shaved, stripped, tarred, and handcuffed by the IRA to the railings of Belfast in punishment for keeping company with British soldiers.[24] The poet who has appeared for the plaintiff now appears to take his place with the prosecution, but his indictment is directed less against the betraying sister(s) than against the onlooker—himself—who would connive with those who inflict this punishment, whilst admitting to contradictory feelings of *civilized* outrage and *tribal* satisfaction.

Heaney's "Bog Queen," "little adultress," and the girl's head of the poem "Strange Fruit" are at once victims, children, and priestesses of the maternal bog, the Mother Goddess that is his version of Kathleen Ni Houlihan. She bears little resemblance to Yeats's and, indeed, it's clear that she is not meant to. A reading of Heaney's poems supports his statement that "it was not really until 1970–75 that I confronted [Yeats] in any way."[25] The younger poet "confronts" the older for the first time in *North* and in the way of such confrontations, appropriates and subverts his terms. In the prefatory poem to *Responsibilities* (1914), Yeats had asked

> Pardon, old fathers, . . .
> Merchant and scholar who have left me blood . . .
> Pardon that for a barren passion's sake,
> Although I have come close on forty-nine,
> I have no child, I have nothing but a book,
> Nothing but that to prove your blood and mine.

When, in "Viking Dublin: Trial Pieces," Heaney says: "Old fathers, be with us . . ." *his* old fathers are "Old cunning assessors / of feuds and of sites / for ambush or town." Heaney's "fathers" are older than Yeats's; "scoretaking killers," whose legacy of blood is blood shed as much as blood transmitted, a legacy of violent death as much as a legacy of life.

In the poem "Kinship," Heaney twice echoes Yeats, apparently to contradict him. His speaker, having broached the bog with a turfspade, once again—at the end of section III—confronts the devouring goddess. Section IV opens:

> This centre holds
> and spreads,
> sump and seedbed,
> a bag of waters
>
> and a melting grave.

The centre that "cannot hold" in "The Second Coming" is a principle of order, engulfed by the "blood-dimmed tide." Though the "centre" of Heaney's poem is more like a principle of *dis*order, each poet offers a vision

of a watery and devouring grave. In the closing section of "Kinship," Heaney
declares that he is addressing himself to Tacitus:

> Come back to this
> "island of the ocean"
> where nothing will suffice.
> Read the inhumed faces
>
> of casualty and victim. . . .

He might also have declared that he was addressing himself to Yeats who,
meditating on blood-sacrifice in the closing section of "Easter 1916," had
asked himself: "O when may it suffice?" Heaney gives him his answer:

> nothing will suffice.
> Read the inhumed faces
> of casualty and victim:
> report us fairly,
> how we slaughter
> for the common good
>
> and shave the heads
> of the notorious,
> how the goddess swallows
> our love and terror.

Whereas Yeats looking back at the slaughter of Easter 1916, concluded: "A
terrible beauty is born," Heaney sees not birth but death, endlessly repeated:
"the goddess swallows / our love and terror." After these covert confrontations
with the master in part I of *North*, he confronts him squarely in part II, the
sequence "Singing School." I spoke earlier of the second, Yeatsian, epigraph
to this sequence. The first is a quotation from Wordsworth's *Prelude*, beginning: "Fair seedtime had my soul, and I grew up / Fostered alike by beauty
and by fear. . . ." The first five sections of "Singing School" have more to
do with fear than beauty; the fear of the potential victim threatened by a
policeman's sten-gun, by another constable's polished holster and baton case,
threatened by Orange drums. In the sixth and final section, from which I
have already quoted, the graduate of the "Singing School" questions his role:
"How did I end up like this?" He speaks of his friends' "Beautiful prismatic
counselling," but seems to derive more pleasure and better advice from the
"low conducive voices" of the rain falling through the alders.

We know now that Heaney answered the call of that rain—whose
"each drop recalls / The diamond absolutes"—when he left Belfast in 1972,
crossing the border to live with his family in Glanmore, Co. Wicklow. For
a Roman Catholic poet of his stature and reputation to make such a move

at such a time required a degree of moral courage far in excess of any physical courage he might have been thought to demonstrate by remaining in the north. In an interview with Seamus Deane, he explained *why* he moved: "I felt and still do feel a tension within myself between the given part of whatever talent I have and the work it might be put to do. I don't think my intelligence is naturally analytic or political. But I felt that the gift for surrender—which I liked in my own work—of listening and of rejoicing in language was rebuked and challenged by another part of myself that recognized the world around me was demanding something more."[26] Heaney's intelligence may not be naturally analytic, but he knows how to analyse his feelings and has the courage to follow them. If anyone doubted the wisdom of his move to Glanmore in 1972, their doubts must have been removed by *Field Work* (1979), the first fruits of those "four years in the hedge-school."[27] The book opens with the poet "surrendering"—to use his own word—to the objects of his contemplation, "Oysters." We listen to him "listening and rejoicing in language":

> Our shells clacked on the plates.
> My tongue was a filling estuary,
> My palate hung with starlight. . . .
>
> . . . I ate the day
> Deliberately, that its tang
> Might quicken me all into verb, pure verb.

As we share those oysters, we realize that we've been listening to something between an invocation and a rededication. The spade that went digging for potatoes, and found instead "The Tollund Man" and "the girls head," has been set aside. Now it is the turn of the tongue—quickened by the tang of the oysters, lifted from their dark seabeds—to return to its proper "field work."

> Vowels ploughed into other: opened ground.
> The mildest February for twenty years
> Is mist bands over furrows, a deep no sound
> Vulnerable to distant gargling tractors.

So begins the first of ten "Glanmore Sonnets" that stand at the centre of the book, and the second ends with a movement that beautifully enacts its theme: "Vowels ploughed into other, opened ground, / Each verse returning like the plough turned round." From that opened ground came "Sensings, mountings from the hiding places / Words entering almost the sense of touch. . . ." Undistracted in his hedge-school by political rhetoric and political violence, the poet listens to, rejoices in—and enables us to listen to, rejoice in—the turned-up acres breathing, cuckoo and corncrake, the bright names of fishing trawlers, *"L'Etoile, Le Guillemot, La Belle Hélène"* and the dark names of the radio gale-warning, "Dogger, Rockall, Malin, Irish Sea." Heaney's "field work" is so transparently a labour of love that it comes as no surprise that the last of the Glanmore Sonnets should celebrate the opened ground of human love. In a dream he sees himself and his wife, asleep out of doors, looking like

> Lorenzo and Jessica in a cold climate.
> Diarmuid and Grainne waiting to be found.
> Darkly asperged and censed, we were laid out
> Like breathing effigies on a raised ground.

The funeral imagery, relieved by the word "breathing" is succeeded by the happier "death" of "Our first night years ago." And sonnet and sequence end with a beautiful conflation of the indoor dream enfolded in the outdoor dream: "The respite in our dewy dreaming faces."

In an important sense *Field Work* celebrates a respite, but it would be wrong to characterize it as a piece of pastoral escapism. If the murderous themes of *North* are not at the heart of the new book, they are painfully present in five of the poems that follow "Oysters." Three of these are elegies for friends killed in the recent Troubles; and two have subtitles, "In Memory of Colum McCartney" and "In Memory of Sean Armstrong," that call to mind "In Memory of Major Robert Gregory" and "In Memory of Eva Gore-Booth and Con Markiewicz." It should be said at once that there is no confrontation with Yeats in *Field Work*, but a comparison of their elegies reveals the different focus of their visions.

The romantic archaeologist of *The Countess Kathleen and Various Legends and Lyrics* had exhumed the heroic figures of Fergus and Cuchulain from the turf-dark depths of the folk-memory, and many of his later elegies elevate their subjects into statues cast in a heroic mould. Yeats's strategy is to equate his subject with some larger figure from antiquity, so that the lustre of the old is transmitted to the new. Robert Gregory becomes "Our Sidney and our perfect man," and the "Sixteen Dead Men" of the Easter Rising "have an ear alone / For those new comrades they have found / Lord Edward and Wolfe Tone. . . ." Those martyrs of earlier risings against the British stand with the shade of Cuchulain in the background of Yeats's great elegy, "Easter 1916":

> I write it out in a verse—
> MacDonagh and MacBride
> And Connolly and Pearse
> Now and in time to be,
> Wherever green is worn,
> Are changed, changed utterly:
> A terrible beauty is born.

Their change is from men into martyrs, a transformation that the poet endorses and, by his endorsement, helps to effect. He meditates searchingly on their deaths, but concludes that "A terrible beauty is *born.*" The paradoxical yoking of birth and death is characteristic of the heroic vision that looked for, and found, victory in defeat, gaiety in tragedy. That is not Heaney's vision. His concern is not with victors in defeat, but with the victims: not with the heroes of 1916 but with the "croppies" of 1798,[28] "The Tollund Man," the little adulteress, and with his cousin, Colum McCartney, "victim" of a random sectarian shooting[29] and the subject of his elegy, "The Strand at Lough Beg." In this the poet does not, like Yeats, raise his voice that it may be heard in "time to be," but speaks quietly, as man to man:

> I turn because the sweeping of your feet
> Has stopped behind me, to find you on your knees
> With blood and roadside muck in your hair and eyes,
> Then kneel in front of you in brimming grass
> And gather up cold handfuls of the dew
> To wash you, cousin. I dab you clean with moss
> Fine as the drizzle out of a low cloud.
> I lift you under the arms and lay you flat.
> With rushes that shoot green again, I plait
> Green scapulars to wear over your shroud.

After the shooting of "the cold-nosed gun," it is the turn of the rushes to shoot green again under the plaiting hands of the poet. Heaney, like Yeats, acknowledges the ancient magic of his calling. But the religious connotations of those scapulars suggest that he is decking the shroud of Colum McCartney with green of a shade subtly different from that invoked at the close of "Easter 1916." Heaney's green is primarily the green of the vegetable kingdom and only secondarily that of the Irish flag. He is, like Keats, with whom he has much in common, a deeply compassionate poet. Where the later Yeats rejoiced in conflict, believing with Blake that "without contraries is no progression," Heaney's motto could be that of his harvest bow: *"The end of art is peace"*—Coventry Patmore's phrase, quoted by the early Yeats in a passage from *Explorations* with which Heaney prefaces his own *Preoccupations.* I quoted earlier his description of "poetry as a dig, a dig for finds that end up being plants." His "field work" has yielded a rich harvest. We must wish him many more.

*Notes*

1.  See *The Letters of W. B. Yeats,* ed. A. Wade (London: Macmillan, 1954), 125.
2.  'Edmund Spenser', *Essays and Introductions* (London: Macmillan, 1961) 372.
3.  Ibid, p 361.

4.  Ibid, p 370.
5.  "Exposure," *North* (London: Faber and Faber, 1975), 73.
6.  *Wintering Out* (London: Faber and Faber, 1972), 15.
7.  Quoted in Yeats, 'Edmund Spenser', 374.
8.  See James Randall, 'An Interview with Seamus Heaney', *Ploughshares*, v. iii, (1979) 13.
9.  Seamus Heaney, *Preoccupations: Selected Prose 1968–1978* (London: Faber and Faber 1980).
10.  Ibid., 73.
11.  *Worlds: Seven Modern Poets*, ed. Geoffrey Summerfield (London: Penguin 1974); reprinted in *Preoccupations*.
12.  'Whatever You Say Say Nothing', III, *North*, 59.
13.  'Feeling into Words', *Preoccupations*, 41.
14.  Ibid., 41.
15.  Letter to Jon Stallworthy, 6 March 1980.
16.  "Feeling into Words," *Preoccupations*, 41.
17.  "Mossbawn," *ibid.*, 20.
18.  *Poetry Book Society Bulletin*, No. 61: Summer 1969.
19.  "Feeling into Words," *Preoccupations*, 57–8.
20.  "Anahorish," *Wintering Out*, 16.
21.  "Gifts of Rain," *ibid.*, 25.
22.  "Toome," *ibid.*, 26. See also "Broagh," *ibid.*, 27
23.  *Poetry Book Society Bulletin*, No. 85: Summer 1975.
24.  See Arthur E. McGuinness's interesting discussion of the genesis of 'Punishment' in 'The Craft of Diction: Revision in Seamus Heaney's Poems', *Irish University Review*, IX. i (Spring 1979), 62–91. McGuinness, however, is surely wrong in seeing the 'betraying sisters' simply as 'modern young adultresses'.
25.  Quoted in James Randall, 'An Interview with Seamus Heaney', *Ploughshares*, v. iii, 1979 13.
26.  'Talk with Seamus Heaney', *New York Times Book Review*, 2 Dec. 1979, 47.
27.  'September Song', *Field Work* (London: Faber and Faber, 1979), 43.
28.  'Requiem for the Croppies', *Door into the Dark*, (London: Faber and Faber, 1969) 24.
29.  *Poetry Book Society Bulletin*, No. 102: Autumn 1979.

# Seamus Heaney and Wordsworth:
# A Correspondent Breeze

### Darcy O'Brien*

One evening Seamus Heaney said: "I've been getting a lot out of Words-worth lately."

"Really?" I replied, not wishing to appear imperceptive. I failed to see what possible connection there could be between the two poets. Personality defied the alliance: Wordsworth tediously earnest, slow, relentlessly profuse; Heaney spare, quick, sharp, clear, in his own phrase, as the bleb of an icicle. The two minds appeared to have as much in common as vinegar and treacle. Nor was any common ground of experience visible. True, Heaney had enjoyed a sentimental journey through France and Italy, but he had traveled with his wife and children, and it had been decades since the French Revolution. Philosophically, Heaney was and is a practicing Roman Catholic, and tran-substantiation has been known to incline toward pantheism, but that was pushing things. As for poetic form, Heaney had more in common with the Japanese than with the English Romantics.

It was in December 1973 that he made the remark, and seven years later I have begun to understand it. Then we were in my flat in Baggot Street, Dublin, going over the proofs of his "bog poems" which were to appear in the *James Joyce Quarterly* that coming spring.[1] The bog poems, with their themes of blood sacrifice, the continuum of human savagery, and the poet's complicity in atavistic tribal cruelties, were, to say the least, removed from Wordsworthian concerns and modes, or so it seemed. I asked him what in Wordsworth was intriguing him, and he said *The Prelude*. A child broke off our conversation, and I had forgotten it until now.

Heaney was living at the time in a country cottage that could be called Wordsworthian; not a lake in sight but rustic and bucolic the dwelling was, about the same size as Dove Cottage and well-filled by the poet, his wife, two young boys, and an infant girl. It nestled, that is the word, in a green, hilly spot in County Wicklow called Glanmore, was called Glanmore Cottage, and had once been part of the grand estate of the family of the playwright Synge. Wildflowers flourished there, and oaks, alders, birches.

*Reprinted from *The Nature of Identity* (Tulsa, Okla.: University of Tulsa Press, 1981), 37–45.

The Dublin road was close by and Dublin City only an hour's drive north, but gazing out through the wavy panes of the Cottage's windows, one could easily imagine oneself a hundred miles from anything and a hundred years ago, when the Cottage had been built. As if to assist the journey backward, the Heaneys had furnished the place with nineteenth-century pieces, and at night turf fire and candlelight warmed the room. At a certain point in the evening, the poet put nocturnes on the phonograph.

But had a domicilic analogy dawned on me then it would probably have been a bee-loud one, though Glanmore Cottage was made of brick and slate, not clay and wattles. What I did not know was that, even as Heaney was still fussing with the bog poems, fingering their spongy texture, deepening his kinship with their exhumed victims and conjured executioners, he was writing this

"Exposure"

It is December in Wicklow
Alders dripping, bushes
Inheriting the last light,
The ash tree cold to look at

A comet that was lost
Should be visible at sunset,
Those million tons of light
Lake a glummer of haws and rose hips

And I sometimes see a falling star
If I could come on meteorite
Instead I walk through damp leaves.
Husks, the spent flukes of autumn.

Imagining a hero
On some muddy compound.
His gift like a slingstone
Whirled for the desperate

How did I end up like this?
I often think of my friends'
Beautiful prismatic counselling
And the anvil brains of some who hate me

As I sit weighing and weighing
My responsible *tristia*.
For what? For the ear? For the people?
For what is said behind backs?

Rain comes down through the alders,
Its how conductive voices
Mutter about let downs and erosions
And yet each drop recalls

The diamond absolutes.
I am neither internee nor informer;
An inner émigré, grown long-haired
And thoughtful; a wood-kerne

Escaped from the massacre,
Taking protective colouring
From bole and bark, feeling
Every wind that blows;

Who, blowing up these sparks
For their meagre heat, have missed
The once-in-a-lifetime portent,
The comet's pulsing rose.[2]

The December of the opening line is that same December of 1973, when Heaney spoke of Wordsworth, and Wicklow evokes the setting of Glanmore Cottage. The comet that should have been visible at sunset but was not was Kohoutec, which as you may recall we sought in vain that winter. Two years later, "Exposure" would become the final poem in *North*, the volume that also contains the bog poems. And six years later Heaney would publish a distinctly Wordsworthian sequence called the "Glanmore Sonnets," all of them about life in the Cottage and what it had signified, for by 1976 he had moved house again, this time to Sandymount, Dublin, where he lives today. But more of the "Glanmore Sonnets" in a moment: they tell of what he meant by saying that he was getting a lot out of Wordsworth. First consider in some detail "Exposure," that primary evocation of Glanmore, because it prefigures later Wordsworthian themes and cadences.

"Exposure" here connotes self-revelation and confession, and in its directness it is atypical of Heaney's work up to 1975. He is a lyric poet who often leaves himself entirely out of his verse and usually refers to himself indirectly, appearing as a marginal figure in a word painting. But here one senses that he feels that he has come to the end of some personal and poetic rope and that like a condemned prisoner he must make a last statement, summing up. Recalling his somber and self-critical mood that year, somewhat alarming in a man normally jovial, I can see the poem as a frank disclosure of his state of mind. He had written the bog poems as a means of coming to terms with the sectarian violence in his native Northern Ireland. He knew the poems were good, but they had led him to the dead end of hopelessness. No end to the killings was in view, and he had concluded that the murderous impulse had some primordial root that defied rational analysis and, if it could be dug up at all, could not itself be killed and would continue to flourish, feeding on blood. Personally he felt guilty at having abandoned the North for the peaceful glades of Wicklow, even though the move had been a sensible and responsible one for his family. The move had made him, as he says, an exile, a wood kerne, that is a vagabond soldier hiding in a forest. Neither internee nor informer neither a prisoner of the British nor a traitor to the Nationalist cause, yet feeling vacuous and ineffectual from being neither this nor that, neither here nor there. "How did I end up like this?"

The poem confesses also a sense of artistic purposelessness. Having written well, he wonders why write at all, since "the people" remain unmoved. Is he merely making sounds? Does he care, really, for something so substanceless as reputation? He mulls over his responsibilities and his sadnesses, his *tristia*, evoking the title of Ovid's poems written in exile at the Black Sea.[3] Ovid had been banished by Augustus on the charge that the *Ars Amatoria* had corrupted the Emperor's daughters. Heaney's exile is the cometlike revelations he had expected as a poet have failed to materialize, and he is left with the small comfort of his verses, which he calls mere sparks, no meteorites.

Heaney's work is an unbroken voyage. You can see in his first book, *Death of a Naturalist* (1966), hints of the next book; his third volume, *Wintering Out* (1972), has *"The Tollund Man"* in it, his first bog poem, prefiguring the heart of *North*. Now in "Exposure," a song of despair, there is a glimmer of the way out for him, personally and artistically. Perhaps it is less a way out than a way of going on. In the terms of moral philosophy, what he will do will be to make a virtue of necessity. His exile will become the means of personal and poetic rebirth. Two poets will show him the way: Dante, another exile, and Wordsworth. This is not the place to explore the role Dante plays in Heaney's next book, *Field Work* (1979), but I would note that the volume ends with a translation of Cantos XXXII and XXXIII of the *Inferno* and that allusions to Dante appear throughout. In general Dante gave Heaney an image of a poet stranded in the middle of life, going ahead by means of the inspiration of another poet, Virgil, and a woman, Beatrice. Dante journeys to paradise. Heaney reaches a far less exalted place, but it is a place of at least momentary peace, and a good part of that tranquility and personal regeneration comes through a new sense of harmony with his wife, Marie, who happens like Beatrice to be fair—"birchwood in lightning" as Heaney describes her.[4]

The kinship with Wordsworth is more pervasive and complex. In "Exposure" Heaney speaks of himself as "feeling / Every wind that blows." There the image suggests the vulnerability of his exposed self, a banished child of Eve, naked and ashamed. But then, after a period of cowering in

Glanmore Cottage, he adjusts to his new home and begins to take nourishment from it and its surrounding landscape, in a way surprisingly akin to Wordsworth at Dove Cottage. The wind that had tormented his exposed self—here one remembers that exposure is something you die of—becomes a soothing friend and metaphorically resembles the romantic breeze that made melody on the strings of the Aeolian harp of romantic imagination. In the "Glanmore Sonnets" he celebrates the Cottage, an easy, rural way of life, the comforting beauties of the landscape and the companionship of his Friend, his wife, in a form and manner overly Wordsworthian. Consider "Glanmore Sonnet III":

> This evening the cuckoo and the corncrake
> (So much, too much) consorted at twilight.
> It was all crepuscular and iambic.
> Out on the field a baby rabbit
> Took his bearings, and I knew the deer
> (I've seen them too from the window of the house,
> Like connoisseurs, inquisitive of air)
> Were careful under larch and May-green spruce.
> I had said earlier, "I won't relapse
> From this strange loneliness I've brought us to.
> Dorothy and William—" She interrupts:
> "You're not going to compare us two . . .?"
> Outside a rustling and twig-combing breeze
> Refreshes and relents. Is cadences.[5]

The reference to Wordsworth and his sister is of course humorous, as Heaney's wife teases him for his dreamy comparison. But the humor does not sap the strength of the Wordsworthian themes and allusions, it only makes them more acceptable to a late twentieth-century sensibility. Here the wind has become a correspondent breeze, a manifestation of the link between man and nature. It soothes and it sounds of song, "is cadences." The poem echoes, and most deliberately, Wordsworth's "To My Sister":

> It is the first mild day of March
> Each minute sweeter than before
> The redbreast sings from the tall larch
> That stands beside our door
>
> There is a blessing in the air,
> Which seems a sense of joy to yield
> To the bare trees, and mountains bare,
> And grass in the green field
> . . . . . . . . . . . . . . . . . . . . . . . . . . . . .

> Then come, my Sister! come, I pray,
> With speed put on your woodland dress;
> And bring no book, for this one day
> We'll give to idleness.[6]

In his headnote to the poem Wordsworth takes note of the larch standing beside the door and says that when he visited the place forty three years later, the larch still stood. Heaney mentions larch trees too, just before invoking Wordsworth and his sister by name, and the spirit of this "Glanmore Sonnet" is in harmony with "To My Sister." His exile, here referred to as "this strange loneliness," has become a comfort, bringing him closer to his wife, allowing him to contemplate birds, beasts, trees, twilight, and the breeze, to be eased by them and to hear and see poetry in them. The cuckoo and the corncrake suggest phrases to him "(So much, too much)" as they sing.

The refreshing and relenting breeze also echoes the opening of "The Prelude":

> Oh there is blessing in this gentle breeze
> Whate'er its mission the soft breeze can come
> To none more grateful than to me, escaped
> From the vast city

Heaney, as he tells us in "Exposure," had "escaped from the massacre"; now he has found solace in a wooded vale. It could be said that, under the aegis of Wordsworth, Heaney's attitude to nature has done a complete about-face. *Death of a Naturalist* has as its major theme the poet's escape through art from his native rural background, and poem after poem in that volume presents images of dehumanizing country labors and a sense of nature as something impersonal, cruel and frightening. At the time Heaney reflected the influence of Ted Hughes, although the poems certainly conformed also to his own childhood experiences. But more than nature the "Glanmore Sonnets" celebrate the rejuvenating qualities of shared experience—the Cottage and its landscape conspire benignantly to bring husband and wife together, and the poet perhaps for the first time in his life feels not alone but happy, or relatively so, and at home.

A fascinating example of how Heaney has allowed Wordsworth to occupy his mind and to guide it and yet how he has also used Wordsworth for his own purposes can be gained from another look at *North*. The last section of that book consists of six poems that form a sort of abbreviated autobiography, because each brings to life a moment from the poet's past and the six poems are arranged in fairly chronological order, beginning with adolescent experience, passing through family memories, early political impressions, the year of his first book's publication, ending finally with

"Exposure." Heaney calls this section "Singing School," alluding to "Sailing to Byzantium," suggesting that the poems render formative incidents in his poetic growth; and he prefaces the section with two quotations, one from Wordsworth and one from Yeats. The Wordsworth is this familiar passage from *The Prelude*:

> Fair seedtime had my soul, and I grew up
> Fostered alike by beauty and by fear;
> Much favoured in my birthplace, and no less
> In that beloved Vale to which, erelong,
> I was transplanted . . .

Obviously Heaney expresses here both a debt to Wordsworth and his intention that the poems which follow be read as examples of the seedtime of his own poetic soul.

But a close look at the Wordsworth passage shows that Heaney used the 1805 edition and not the 1850, which has become the standard text. The last line as Wordsworth revised it reads not "I was transplanted" but "We were transplanted."[7] Wordsworth altered the line to include himself and his sister; Heaney, feeling isolated, exiled, so alone and "exposed" at the time, preferred the earlier version and in doing so suggested his state of mind. He also retained the punctuation of the earlier text, but this is less significant than his preference for the singular over the plural.[8] Now that we have the "Glanmore Sonnets" to consider, with their emphasis on the companionship and the shared experience of "that beloved Vale," we can see a considerable change in Heaney's outlook: how, at least for the moment, he has escaped from a sense of isolation.

"Singing School" is not his only effort at a "Prelude" or an overly Wordsworthian recapturing of youth. In 1975 he also published, in a small edition from Belfast, *Stations*. These are twenty-one prose poems, each a moment from childhood, each moment traumatic, formative. In his preface he again evokes Wordsworth:

> These pieces were begun in California in 1970/71 although the greater part of them came rapidly to a head in May and June last year. . . . those first pieces had been attempts to touch what Wordsworth called 'spots of time.' Moments at the very edge of consciousness which had lain for years in the unconscious as active lodes or modes.

He goes on to say that composition was interrupted by his return to Belfast. Political internment had been introduced; sirens filled the air. The pressures of the immediate stifled his reflections.

> So it was again at a remove in the "hedgeschool" of Glanmore, in Wicklow, that the sequence was returned to. I wrote each of them down with the

excitement of coming for the first time to a place I had always known completely.[9]

The most famous Wordsworthian phrase of all, "emotion recollected in
tranquility," must here impose itself. It is the best definition of *Stations*:
recalled moments of emotional jolt; the child lost and weeping; a challenge
from a Protestant schoolmate; the sound of Orange drums on the twelfth of
July. And the recollections came to a head in Glanmore Cottage.

One does not wish to strain the parallels in their careers, but it seems
worth noting that Wordsworth's lyrical ballads followed a period of political
involvement and then, after the bloody excesses of the French Revolution
affected him, political disillusion. It must be said that Heaney's political
poems exceed Wordsworth's in both art and wisdom, but like Wordsworth
he retreated from the contemplation of bloodshed into a reclusive period
marked by a communion with nature. The title *Field Work* has many connotations, among them the military sense of defenses, ramparts, trenches, bul-
warks. The poems in the book are Heaney's defenses against the onslaughts
which led to "Exposure," and they are the defenses of nature, companionship
and art itself—work in the fair field of poetry.

Since Seamus Heaney is a poet who is in the middle of the way, he will
doubtless find other poetic beacons than Wordsworth to guide him over the
next miles. It may be that he will travel on unaccompanied, alone once again.
One cannot say, because like Yeats he has that quality essential to artistic
longevity, the willingness to change mind, form, imagery, and language from
book to book. My guess is that he will leave behind Wordsworthian reflections
and Wordsworthian nature for a time, charting new territory, perhaps returning
some day to Wordsworthian matter and manner, perhaps not. In his earliest
writing days he called himself *"Incertus"*: "I went disguised in it, pronouncing
it with a soft church-latin c, tagging it under my efforts like a damp fuse.
Uncertain. A shy soul fretting and all that. Expert obeisance.

"Oh yes, I crept before I walked. The old pseudonym lies there like a
mouldering tegument."[10] But if that skin of uncertainty has been shed, the
questioning, doubting habit of mind has not. It will produce new frets and
torments, new resolutions, new poems. A new kind of physical or spiritual
dwelling will replace Glanmore Cottage. Perhaps it already has, but only
the next book will tell us of it. In the meantime if he happens to say that
he is getting a lot out of some poet or other, I will take the hint to heart.

*Notes*

1. *James Joyce Quarterly*, 11 (Spring 1974), 221–37. Of special interest here is this
first printing of the poem "Punishment." The last two stanzas of the poem are absent, because
Heaney had not written them yet. They add his sense of his complicity in the violence.

2. From *North* (London: Faber and Faber, 1975), pp. 72–73.

3. I am grateful to Joseph Kestner for pointing out this allusion to me.

4. In "Glanmore Sonnet VIII," *Field Work* (New York: Farrar, Straus & Giroux, 1979), p. 40.

5. *Field Work*, p. 35.

6. *English Romantic Poetry and Prose*, ed. Russell Noyes (New York: Oxford University Press, 1956), pp. 257–58.

7. See *North*, p. 62, and compare it with the Oxford text of *The Prelude*. The passage of course precedes the four dramatic epiphanies. The "Vale" referred to here is Esthwaite in Lancashire, Wordsworth's boyhood home; but I think Heaney was thinking not of his own boyhood home but of Glanmore.

8. "Seedtime" reads in the later text "seed-time"; "fear" is followed by a colon, not a semicolon; "erelong" is not set off by commas.

9. *Stations* (Belfast: Ulsterman Publications, 1975).

# Irish Poetry after Joyce
# (Heaney and Kavanagh)

DILLON JOHNSTON*

Seamus Heaney has already proven himself a more careful steward of a more copious talent than Kavanagh's. Like Kavanagh's verse, Heaney's poetry immediately attracts the reader: the images are vivid and precise; the speaking voice is reassuring; the lines seem, as Heaney said of Kavanagh, "lyrically opportunistic,"[1] incorporating radiant moments of ordinary rural life. For example, consider this description of Heaney's aunt from the first dedicatory poem of *North*:

> Now she dusts the board
> with a goose's wing,
> now sits, broad-lapped, with whitened nails
>
> and measling shins:
> here is a space
> again, the scone rising
> to the tick of two clocks.
>
> (*HP*, 161–62)

This depiction of time as gestation, which has already reappeared in major anthologies, probably has pleased more readers than Kavanagh's finest lyrics, which are seriously underread. Gauged by the number of major journals that have featured Heaney and the extraordinary sales of his recent volumes,[2] his success approaches that of novelists and the most celebrated American poets such as Ashbery and Warren.[3] Kavanagh's fantasies about fame and fortune, which he mocked in his own verse, could hardly have flared so high as to reach Heaney's actual success.

Nevertheless, an ingredient of Heaney's appeal, as revealed in this "Mossbawn" poem, is the observant eye, patient ear, and celebratory tone that he found in the poetry of Kavanagh. Kavanagh had already demonstrated that the subject they would share—vignettes from routines on the small farms

*Reprinted from *Irish Poetry after Joyce* (Notre Dame, Ind.: Notre Dame University Press, 1985), 138–50.

of Ulster—carried an extraordinary nostalgic appeal. Although Heaney's birthplace on the northern edge of the British Isles' largest lake, Loch Neagh, made fishing more important to Heaney than to Kavanagh, they both have written about cattle trading, thatching, churning, and other ancient trades and crafts studied in Estyn Evans' *Irish Folk Ways*.

Beyond this rich shared tradition, Heaney enjoyed two early advantages over Kavanagh. First, his aptitude for learning was encouraged by his parents as he advanced through secondary school in Derry and a course of literary study at Queens University toward a profounder and more balanced view of literature than Kavanagh ever attained. Secondly, from early in his career, Heaney could benefit from the example of Kavanagh's life and work, and from that of their intermediate, John Montague.

Kavanagh offered Heaney what MacNeice gave to Mahon, proof that out of inartistic settings poetry could arise or, in Heaney's words, "a confidence in the deprivations of our condition." To the younger poet Kavanagh conveyed "an insouciance and trust in the clarities and cunnings of our perceptions."[4] In his reaction to Yeats, Kavanagh demonstrated that poetry could be written independently of "a structure and a sustaining landscape" produced from elaborate mythologizing. Yet, Heaney remained free to synthesize Kavanagh's spontaneous realism and Yeats's ordering structure. In an interview with Heaney, Seamus Deane defined the kind of synthesis Heaney hopes to achieve: "a poetry that would be neither a matter of the day to day spontaneities alone, but a matter of making the day to day (*sic!* the myth?) become a form embedded in the day to day from which it arises.[5] In this *Crane Bag* interview with Deane, published midway between *North* and *Field Work*, Heaney confessed his frustrations in developing a sustaining formal myth, "a kind of singular universal": "The more one consciously tries to convey this imprint the more it seems to elude you. You see, the lift-off and push of the innocent creative moment can never be fully schematic."[6] Heaney's first four volumes progressively evolve a "myth," what may be seen as a synthesis between Kavanagh's "day to day spontaneities" and Yeats's "schematic mythologizing." *Field Work*, however, diverges sharply from lyrical myth to a dialogue about myth-making and the poet's role.

Heaney's poetry has never been as unfreighted as Kavanagh's best verse in which merely "naming these things is the love-act and its pledge; / For we must record love's mystery without claptrap . . ." ("The Hospital," *KCP*, 280). Even in the first volume, in which the most successful poems recount "the death of a naturalist," the youthful waking from nature into self-consciousness, Heaney suggests interesting psychological themes. After an overanthologized opening poem which associates poem-making with physical activities such as gun-toting and turf-digging, the poet recollects his adolescent fear of frogs and their spawn, toward which the child was ambivalent:

> There were dragon-flies, spotted butterflies,
> But best of all was the warm thick slobber
> Of frogspawn that grew like clotted water
> In the shade of the banks.

But, his fear surfaces when the masculine and martial bullfrogs invade the breeding ground: "The great slime kings / Were gathered there for vengeance and I knew / That if I dipped my hand the spawn would clutch it" (*HP*, 5–6). "Death of A Naturalist" suggests a temporary theme—a vivid but otherwise unexceptional record of an adolescent's anxiety about metamorphosis ("The fattening dots burst . . .") and excrescence—on which no poet could afford to fixate. However, two of Heaney's enduring themes are psychologically grafted to this adolescent anxiety.

First, the child's need to define the boundary between himself and encroaching nature has its correlation in the Romanticist interest in identifying the self in the perceived experience while attempting to make a more direct contact with nature. Heaney often achieves what the phenomenologists call a "noematic reflection," a recreation of perception in which we sense the reflected eye as well as the natural object in its fundamentally inhuman essence.[7] Through a rich vocabulary of Anglo-Saxon and Gaelic cognates, he conveys precise sensations of touch and smell and temperature that represent a dense and grainy nature. In his bogland poems, particularly, he is remarkably close to Theodore Roethke's green-house poems of 1948, in which that poet rediscovered his relation to primal forms of life, and, in his fidelity to the perceived natural object, Heaney parallels Ted Hughes's more single-minded attempts to capture the unique reality of various animals.

Secondly, and more importantly, the child's concern to distinguish himself from encroaching nature evolves into mature questions about the relation of poetic perception to the actual world, of poetry to experience, and of personal expression to communal and traditional patterns of thought and action. Questions to which Heaney returns in *Field Work* concerning the poem's relation to the world are raised in the final poem of his first volume, *Death of a Naturalist*:

> Now, to pry into roots, to finger slime,
> To stare big-eyed Narcissus, into some spring
> Is beneath all adult dignity. I rhyme
> To see myself, to set the darkness echoing.
>                                   ("Personal Helicon")

Heaney's next three volumes—*Door Into the Dark*, *Wintering Out*, and *North* (1969, 1972, and 1975)—pursue the phenomenological theme more urgently than the question of poetry. Although *Door Into the Dark* offers little evidence of poetic growth, it does deepen Heaney's concerns about our relation to the natural world. In the volume's weightiest poem, "A Lough Neagh Sequence," the threat of depersonalization becomes an overt theme. The seventh poem in the sequence, "Vision," recalls, with Freudian and animistic implications, a youthful association between eels crossing a flooded field and lice which elders had threatened would gather in his uncombed hair and drag him into the water. In a less explicit manner, many of Heaney's poems challenge the distinction, which psychologists call our ego-boundary, between ourselves and our excrescences, between our animated flesh and contiguous but alien life.

Of the volume's finest poems, "The Outlaw," "In Gallarus Oratory," "The Wife's Tale," and "Bogland," the latter summons Irish poetry from its typical bardic peregrinations to a vertical quest "into the cyclops' eye of a tarn." Anticipating the supporting evidence of P. V. Glob's *Bog People*, which Heaney read in 1969, he had represented the bog as a repository where the past is rendered contemporaneous with the present—"Butter sunk under / more than a hundred years / Was recovered salty and white"—a modernist assumption that snaps the catena of history. "Bogland" concludes:

> Our pioneers keep striking
> Inwards and downwards,
>
> Every layer they strip
> Seems camped on before.
> The bogholes might be Atlantic seepage.
> The wet centre is bottomless.

That *Wintering Out* (1972) extends this exploration is not at first apparent because the fallow setting and bleak tone suggest hibernation and because a number of poems are devoted to the theme of the poet's role through analogues such as a salmon fisher, a soul-smith, a mummer, and a thatcher. The seasonal mood pervades the volume. Like his surrogate "Servant Boy," Heaney is "wintering out / the back-end of a bad year," finding comfort in tactile and olfactory reminiscences ("Fodder") and, in the manner of Austin Clarke, regretting the loss of a more hospitable and humane age ("The Last Mummer").

However, of the five sections into which the book divides, two seem to reach new depths. The first section, through "Wool Trade," explores lost traditions, the individual's relation to the land, and religious, cultural, and linguistic differences between the two Ulster heritages. Yet, in "Anahorish," "Toome," "Broagh," "The Backward Look," "Traditions," and "A New Song," he rummages for some radical connection between the land and the language it nurtures. The tentative resolutions of these poems—that we can achieve "a soft gradient of consonant, vowel-meadow . . ." ("Anahorish") or that Irish vowels will irrigate consonantal English ("A New Song")—are less persuasive than his thickly textured language, the display of gutturals and vowels that seems as palpable as soil. Enriched by the revival of the Gaelic language and by Clarke's experiments with assonantal patterns in Gaelic poetry, Heaney can rival Hopkins in his ear for vowels and his etymological sense of diction.

While this first section of *Wintering Out* is pervaded by bad weather, the seasonal metaphor implies an eventual spring thaw. In the second section, however, from "Linen Town," to "Veteran's Dream," "the back end of a bad year" pervades various eras in Belfast's history. Although in "A Northern Hoard" Heaney promises to find in roots and loam surrogates for suffering humanity, elsewhere in this section he cannot maintain this detachment from the zone of conflict where he is bewildered and where his lines falter and lose faith. His best poems characteristically reside, in Muldoon's phrase, at "pain's edge where we take shelter." "First Calf," from the fourth section of *Wintering Out*, epitomizes Heaney's relation to life's painful center. His attention is drawn not to the suffering cow or her new calf but to "the afterbirth strung on the hedge," the mysterious margin of life, both mineral and carnal, where pain register: "The semaphores of hurt / Swaddle and flap on a bush" (*HP*, 152).

Heaney achieves a consummate poem in this section: "The Tollund Man." Drawing on Glob's account of a recovered Iron-Age man, sacrificed to an earth goddess and mummified in a Danish bog, he compares this sacrificial death to murder in Ulster. He succeeds because his attention is drawn to details of the Tollund Man, such as his undigested meal and "the mild pods of his eyelids" which perpetuate and make contemporaneous the mysterious suspension of life's process. The deity that demanded this sacrifice is also perpetuated as some life-denying feminine force in nature:

> Bridegroom to the goddess,
>
> She tightened her torc on him
> And opened her fen,
> Those dark juices working
> Him to a saint's kept body.
> (*HP*, 125)

The third section of *Wintering Out* represents the woman as an unwilling adversary and, thus, introduces the fourth and most complex section of the book. The seven poems from "A Winter's Tale" through "First Calf" transcend and tend to justify the early explanatory poems. They portray woman, moved by elemental forces of moon and tide, as antithetical to the pragmatic world of man. In "Shore Woman," as in several other poems, she establishes her margin, here between the sea of violent, sexual anarchy and the land she overshadows:

And I'm walking the firm margin. White pocks
Of cockle, blanched roofs of clam and oyster
Hoard of moonlight, woven and unwoven
Off the bay.

She concludes, "I have rights on this fallow avenue, / A membrane between moonlight and my shadow" (*HP*, 144–5).

The most successful poem in *Wintering Out* is "Maighdean Mara." Heaney explains the title is Irish for "mermaid," but the dedication, "For Sean Oh-Eocha," suggests some unidentified event on which the poem is based. The first and last of the three stanzas describe a drowned woman, while the second stanza recounts two seductions, the first by her husband who "charmed" her from the sea and "conjured / Patterns of home and drained / The tidesong from her voice." The second seduction by the thatcher, because it repeats the motifs of the first, breaks her spell and threatens her with land-locked recurrences: "the dead hold of bedrooms, / Dread of the night and morrow, / Her children's brush and combs." She prefers the endless rhythm of the sea's double swell, suggested by the even spacing of bacchics in the first line and of spondees in the seventh, and enacted by the two syllables of "dandled" and by the alliterative participles of the third line:

She sleeps now, her cold breasts
Dandled by undertow,
Her hair lifted and laid.
Undulant slow seawracks
Cast about shin and thigh,
Bangles of wort, drifting
Liens catch, dislodge gently.

This is the great first sleep
Of homecoming, eight
Land years between hearth and
Bed steeped and dishevelled.
Her magic garment al-
most ocean-tinctured still.
(*HP*, 146)

Sibilants and sonorants imitate the hiss and wash of the sea, whose movement is suggested through tempo and vowel change. The return at the conclusion of the third section of the poem's opening two lines stresses recurrence.

Although the form of the poem is elaborate, it creates the effect of a ballad or other basically oral form where artifice—rhyme and refrain—serves only to emphasize some undigested fact, whose mystery no abstraction can reduce. Heaney achieves this same oral quality in "A Winter's Tale," "Limbo," and "Bye-Child." The source of the mystery in "Maighdean Mara" may be sought in the allusion to *The Tempest* (2.2.68–69, 99) in the last two lines of the first section. The poem is about a counterspell, a ritual of immersion that breaks the conjuration of love and allows her to return to her natural, inhuman state. We wonder at, as we are threatened by, her beautiful form of nonbeing: she "doth suffer a sea-change / Into something rich and strange." The next two poems also represent the woman as governing dark domains, "a far briny zone" and "lunar distances . . . beyond love."

*North* attempts both to extend this myth and its application to the Troubles and to reestablish an ad-hoc, Kavanagh-like association with Heaney's audience. This calculated schizophrenia is reflected in a prefatory poem, the book's structure, and even the cover. The book's Part I (8 poems) and Part II (9 poems) are preceded by two dedicatory poems, one of which we have discussed. The second poem is significant, however, because it suggests the distinct modes of Parts I and II. It begins with the poet declaring self-consciously, "They seem hundreds of years away. Breughel, / You'll know them if I can get them true." and concludes: "O calendar customs! Under the broom / Yellowing over them, compose the frieze / With all of us there, our anonymities" ("The Seed Cutters," *HP*, 163). Does the imperative suggest that the poet has yielded the composition of his art to "calendar customs," ritual and tradition? The book's cover sustains the question by giving equal space to the poet's binary modes: the front cover is a "frieze" of stylized round-bottomed Vikings, sailing under the crane-bills of their swords: anonymities in the northern ritual of murder. The back cover presents a pop-portrait of Heaney "getting them true." The book's two parts develop these two modes. In Part I a bardic persona enlarges the Ulster violence to include the state of mind called *north*, the sinister side of man, inhabited by Norsemen, *Njal*'s Icelandic heroes, and Jutland Celts. Current inhumanity is displaced by ancient inhumations, the victims sacrificed to the Earth Mother, Nerthus. The invaders are Vikings or Elizabethans; the poet sings from the crannog, or meditates on history, or the bog, that

> casket, midden,
> floe of history.
>
> Ground that will strip
> its dark side,
> nesting ground,
> outback of my mind.
> ("Kinship," *HP*, 196–97)

In Part II the scop yields to the Ulster poet commenting on the carnage in Northern Ireland, which results in some uncharacteristically awkward poems. We may excuse section II as Heaney's dues paid to his compatriots and a response to prodding from Patrick Galvin, Padraic Fiacc, and other

Belfast writers.[8] In drawing close to the violence, Heaney's sensitive ear numbs, and he mocks the evasive clichés without renewing them:

> We tremble near the flames but want no truck
> With the actual firing. We're on the make
>
> As ever. Long sucking the hind tit
> Cold as a witch's and as hard to swallow
> Still leaves us fork-tongued on the border bit:
> ("Whatever You Say Say Nothing," *HP*, 213)

Part I offers pleasure as a lyric sequence that also contains some of Heaney's finest individual poems. Bound by two "Antaeus" poems, the sequence begins with "Belderg," where the poet engages in a neighborly chat about querns, ancient millstones recovered from the bog's trove. The poem concludes:

> I passed through the eye of the quern,
>
> Grist to an ancient mill,
> And in my mind's eye saw
> A world-tree of balanced stones,
> Querns piled like vertebrae,
> The marrow crushed to grounds.
> (*HP*, 169)

Read in light of this conclusion, the opening of the subsequent poem suggests the individual bearing the crushing burden of the north's funereal ritual— "I shouldered a kind of manhood / stepping in the lift the coffins / of dead relations." ("Funeral Rites," *HP*, 170)—in a poem that anticipates the macabre beauty of the bog mummies, the subjects of later bog poems. In describing a funeral session, the poet expands the scope of "neighborly murder" to a full northern and historical dimension which section I sustains.

> Quiet as a serpent
> in its boulevard
>
> the procession drags its tail
> out of the Gap of the North
> ass its head already enters
> the megalithic doorway.
> (*HP*, 172)

Heaney's standard quatrain is particularly flexible here, yielding some dramatic emphases while seeming spare and understated. We hear the voice of the bard for whom the Icelandic hero Gunnar is a proxy as the next poem, "North," confirms.

The succeeding poem, "Viking Dublin: Trial Pieces," ostensibly maintains the same archaeological approaches and northern theme in random musings on a Viking child's microscopic carvings on a bone. "These are trial pieces, / the craft's mystery / improvised on bone:" Joyce's city, but on different terms from Joyce's. Alluding to *Portrait*, Heaney invokes, not the mythological Dedalus, old artificer, but the murderous Vikings, "cunning assessors":

> Come fly with me,
> come sniff the wind
> with the expertise
> of the Vikings—
> . . . . . . . . . . . . . . .
> Old fathers be with us
> Old cunning assessors
> of feuds and sites
> for ambush or town.
> (*HP*, 178–9)

And so the carefully coordinated sequence continues. By contrast with Joyce's use of Dedalus's story, we can clarify the implications of what the jacket-blurb terms Heaney's "myth." Rather than a universal literary myth of man's creativity, Heaney constructs a hemispheric myth, inherent in the Viking foundations of Dublin, of man's homicidal nature, which is as inexplicable as nature's unconscious processes from which it is derived. Heaney associates war rites, ritual sacrifice, and sacrificial victims with the return of spring, sexuality, generation, and attachment to the mother, as they are associated in the ancient Celtic worship of Nerthus, to suggest that current Ulster killings are conditioned by preconscious forces.

The association of bog-burials—which were "northern" but not Irish—with mother-worship—a form of which preceded Christianity in Ireland—with the current atrocities in Ulster becomes too explicit to be historically accurate in certain poems, such as "Kinship":

> report us fairly,
> how we slaughter
> for the common good
>
> and shave the heads
> of the notorious,
> how the goddess swallows
> our love and terror.

Although the narrow, slean-like lines slice quickly and effectively toward this truth, efforts to extract from even a metaphorical bog a mythological and historical cause for "northern" behavior strain the authority of the speaker who must slide too quickly from *I* to *we*.

Assuming the collective point of view becomes more difficult for Heaney because his poetic voice has been nearly unvarying. In 1974 Heaney declared that in the opening poem of his first volume, he had found his voice: "Finding a voice means that you can get your own feeling into your own words and that your words have the feel of you about them; and I believe that it may not even be a metaphor, for a poetic voice is probably very intimately connected with the poet's natural voice. . . ."[9] So consistently had Heaney employed this voice—orchestrated assonance, consonantal textures, a plurality of words with Gaelic and Anglo-Saxon roots, Latinate words etymologically tuned, discrete specific detail—that he had acquired *timbre*. His *timbre*, a sound so familiar that it could border on self-parody, left little room for tone, the assumption of new voices or the adjustment of voice to audience.

My final point about the bog-poems concerns Calvin Bedient's accusation that "The Tollund Man" proves to be about Heaney's interest in the Tollund Man.[10] This charge could be made about other bog-poems as well, although finally it would be unfair. For example, consider "Strange Fruit," which begins,

> Here is the girl's head like an exhumed gourd.
> Oval-faced, prune-skinned, prune-stones for teeth.
> They unswaddled the wet fern of her hair
> And made an exhibition of its coil,
> Let the air at her leathery beauty.
> Pash of tallow, perishable treasure:
>
> (*HP*, 194)

This ironic title requires the startled reader to refocus, just as does the folksong with the same name which informs us chillingly that the strange fruit ripening under a Dixie sun is actually black humans lynched by a hysterical mob. Heaney's metaphors—gourd and prune—abet the bog in metamorphosing the girl from a human state. The metaphorically rich statement, "They unswaddled the wet fern of her hair," depicts the girl realistically as it also transforms her into artifact. *They* sounds ominously anonymous, and *exhibition* is tinged with the erotic, so the verb *let* becomes both the second action of *they* and the imperative of a complicit speaker. He too squanders her mysterious beauty as he exhibits it. As he says in the preceding poem, he is "the artful voyeur," as fascinated by his own embalming powers as by the mummified victim, who also provides a metaphor for his art.

What I am suggesting is that we are unfair to expect Heaney's vertical quest, striking inward and downward, to recover historical or mythological truths because his actual concern is the relation of his art to life. (No saffron tinges Heaney's theme: his concern is ontological and epistemological rather than aesthetic.) He can plumb himself, sounding to various levels, or establish a dialogue between private and public selves, between self and other, or between poet and community or tradition.

*Notes*

1. Seamus Deane, "Unhappy and at Home," 66.
2. Feature stories on Heaney have appeared in the *New York Times Magazine* (Francis X. Clines, "Poet of the Bogs," 13 March 1983); *New Yorker* (Helen Vendler, "The Music of What Happens," 18 September 1981, 146–52, 155–57, and Anthony Bailey, "A Reporter at Large: A Walk along the Boyne," 2 June 1980, 92, 95–122), and *Newsweek* (Peter Prescott, "Bard of the Irish Soul," 2 February 1981, 67–69).
3. Blake Morrison says that *North* sold 6,000 copies in England during its first month of publication. *Seamus Heaney*, Contemporary Writers Series (London: Methuen, 1982), 56.
4. Deane, "Unhappy and at Home," 66.
5. Ibid.
6. Ibid., 67.
7. For example, see M. Merleau-Ponty, *Phenomenology of Perception*, trans. Colin Smith (London: Routledge & Kegan Paul, 1962), x.
8. For example, see Padraic Fiacc, "Fiacc Answers Back," *Honest Ulsterman* 50 (Winter 1975): 134.
9. Heaney, *Preoccupations*, 43.
10. Calvin Bedient, "The Music of What Happens," *Parnassus* 8 (Fall / Winter 1979): 111.

# Orthodoxy, Independence, and Influence in Seamus Heaney's *Station Island*

$M$ore than that of any other contemporary Irish poet, Seamus Heaney's poetic *oeuvre* has been shaped and enriched by the need to address the problem of commitment. In making what Thomas Kinsella calls "the imaginative grasp at identity for himself" and in attempting to define himself as Ulsterman as well as poet, Heaney remains curiously ambivalent.[1] He is more inclined to voice contradictory claims and to mediate extremes of outlook or experience than he is to align himself with one side to the exclusion of the other. As Heaney's transcription and consideration of Czeslaw Milosz's "Native Realm" suggests, however, his sensibility is ostensibly one of balance and vacillation rather than of mere complacency:

> I was stretched between contemplation
> of a motionless point
> and the command to participate
> actively in history.[2]

Inasmuch as Heaney resists politicization and the active role it implies, the litany of violence and suffering rehearsed not only in Ulster's present-day sectarianism but in the equally unconscionable barbarities of ancient Ireland's bogland is something which merits sympathy yet also necessitates detachment. According to Dillon Johnston, Heaney's "honest ambivalence" resides in the "balancing" of these contradictory commands.[3] By Heaney's own estimation, the distinction between public pronouncement and personal sentiment necessarily helps to distinguish the propagandist or political mouthpiece from the legitimate poet of political conscience. Heaney observes in his Introduction to *North* (1975), "during the last few years there has been considerable expectation that poets from Northern Ireland should 'say' something about the 'situation,' but in the end they will only be worth listening to if they are saying something about and to themselves."[4] Insofar as Heaney

* Reprinted from *Agenda* 27, no. 1 (Spring 1989): 48–61.

is caught between his private and public selves, between the sense of his own political responsibility and "the tribe's" insatiable need for the expression and encodification of its own beliefs, he is equally at a loss to know, as Denis Donoghue explains, "which voice" among the many fractured voices "is to be trusted."[5]

The vacillation which governs Heaney's political sense and which underscores his deep political unease is equally vital to the growth of his literary identity and poetic imagination.[6] For Heaney, the task of poetic composition, much like the undertaking of political commitment, involves not so much an active pursuit as a passive yet sensitive response. On the question of poetic method, Heaney remarks, "what we are presented with is a version of composition as listening, as a wise passiveness, a surrender to energies that spring within the centre of the mind, not composition as an active pursuit by the mind's circumference of something already at the centre.[7] Much of Heaney's poetry, as Dillon Johnston claims, features "a vacillation between his own and other's language," between the voice he forges for himself and that which is bequeathed to him by the community or by tradition.[8] Heaney, especially as he emerges as the poet-pilgrim in the middle section of *Station Island* (1984), is caught up in the dilemma of conformity and attribution where he remains uncertain whether he is "to guide or to be guided," whether he is "to strike his own note" or adhere to the orthodoxies and probities of Irish Catholic culture as well as to the literary models which ultimately perpetuate them.[9]

That major poets of the modern era necessarily embrace the works of their "guides," the great masters, yet ultimately reshape those models according to their own purposes is not only an idea which Heaney addresses and espouses in his essay "Envies and Identifications" but one to which he gives full assent and articulation in the Dantean middle section of *Station Island*. In this regard, Heaney observes, "when poets turn to the great masters of the past, they turn to an image of their own creation, one which is likely to be a reflection of their own imaginative needs, their own artistic inclinations and procedures."[10] By appropriating the structure of Dante's *Purgatorio*, what Heaney regards as a "comforting" work, and by reworking it according to an Irish context rife with violence and discontent, he to some degree distances himself from the otherwise unmitigated horrors of sectarianism that he finds it necessary to confront.[11] At the same time, by locating his purgatory in Lough Derg's island, a site that is not only by history and tradition a place of Irish pilgrimage and penitence but also the subject of countless literary treatments, Heaney comments implicitly on the way in which a particular place, as much as a particular literary masterpiece, is subject to reinterpretation by successive generations. Since *Station Island* has served as a meeting place for Irish-society from pre-history to the present day, it functions naturally as a microcosm where the "religious, historical, and cultural affiliations" of "the tribe" are brought to the forefront and where the issue of commitment becomes all the more crucial.

In "Envies and Identifications: Dante and the Modern Poet," Heaney explains the essential dichotomy which not only informs his attempt at a Dantean sequence of poems but also operates within the collected consciousness of his country: "the main tension is between two often contradictory commands: to be faithful to the collective historical experience and to be true to the recognitions of the emerging self. I had hoped (in "Station Island") that I could dramatize these strains by meeting shades from my own dream life who had also been inhabitants of the actual Irish world. They could perhaps voice the claims of orthodoxy and the necessity to recognize / refuse those claims. They could probe the validity of one's commitment."[12] "Station Island," as well as the opening and closing sections which frame it, accommodates a veritable multitude of polarities which is only resolved, if at all, at the collection's conclusion where all roads eventually become one and where the artist's quest for inspiration and knowledge ultimately leads him back to an image of the tribe.[13] In *Station Island*, Heaney is invariably caught between the antithetical and often incompatible claims of religious or political orthodoxy and artistic independence, between the desire to "do the decent thing" (IV, XII) and the need to move out "on his own" (II, XII), between the exigencies of bondage and the privileges of emancipation, between ascetic denial and sensual pleasure, between the authority of the community and the rights of the individual. The language used to express such polarities is often correspondingly paradoxical if not altogether oxymoronic.[14] An inherent duplicity is suggested not only by the simultaneously "fortified and bewildered" lobster destined for the dinner table in "Away from it All" but also by the "inviolable and affronting" glass of cognac that momentarily wards off the prison darkness in "Chekhov at Sakhalin." While the fragmented sequential structure of "Station Island" that Heaney borrows from Dante's pilgrimage affords only a limited degree of unity, an alternative and perhaps more viable source of cohesiveness resides in the ubiquity of these oppositions and vacillations and in the continual attempt to negotiate, though not necessarily resolve, their disparity.[15]

The claims of orthodoxy Heaney finds it necessary to acknowledge are not only expressed through the dialogues with, among other shades, the young priest (IV) and the monk (XI) but also substantiated by the collection's subtext, Christ's advice to the rich young man in Matthew 19, by the doxology of Saint John of the Cross (XI), and by the structure appropriated from Dante as well as from the earlier Irish work, *St. Patrick's Purgatory*.[16] While assimilating a structure traditional to devotional life and devotional works, however, Heaney is none the less critical of the way in which those outward forms and rituals and the corresponding pressures of conformity preserve and perpetuate an attitude of complacency that Heaney believes is symptomatic of the Irish Catholic middle class.[17] As Alasdair Macrae remarks, "because the ground plan of "Station Island" is founded on a religious ritual, the terms of the investigation are religious, yet the poem is not narrowly or even primarily religious."[18] While Dante's pilgrimage in the *Commedia* incorporates a movement from profane to sacred love, the course on which Heaney embarks in "Station Island" constitutes an ironic reversal of this pattern since the pleasures of sexual love are not only celebrated in the fourth section but also intimated in James Joyce's affirmation of a creative as well as procreative "work-lust" at the end of the poem.[19] Chekhov similarly finds "holier joy" in a glass of cognac than any cantor might "in full throat by the iconostasis."[20] What Heaney abjures and challenges is not so much the route to salvation encapsulated in Christ's injunction "sell all you have and give to the poor and follow me" (Matthew 19:21) but the sensibility of "drugged" obedience and hollow conformity to which it lends itself. In "Envies and Identifications," Heaney explains, "the choice of Lough Derg as a locus for the poem did, in fact, represent a solidarity with orthodox ways and obedient attitudes, and that very solidarity and obedience were what had to be challenged.[21] Of the three recalcitrant ghosts who frame the journey to and from Station Island, Simon Sweeney warns the most vehemently against the dangers of pursuing the "drugged path" of the pilgrims' procession and the attitude of submission it implies. The procession of drunken Ribbonmen alluded to in II reinforces Sweeney's allegation that religion is a mere opiate of the masses that necessarily excludes all notions of choice or conscious commitment. Although Heaney, as pilgrim, compromises according to Sweeney's standards and joins the procession to the island, he is otherwise "dissociated from the other pilgrims by the physical positions" in which he finds himself.[22] Whenever we see him, he is invariably going against the crowd, clearing the way for other pilgrims (IV), facing the wrong way (V), or descending sets of steps while others ascend them (VI).

That poetry can become one with a religious sense is suggested in the monk's contention that poems should be read as prayers as well as in the collection's final poem where all roads, whether those leading to spiritual salvation or to artistic achievement, ultimately become one.[23] For the most part, however, the religious path retraced by the pilgrims and the aesthetic path pursued by Joyce and Carleton are not easily reconciled. Most often, the values which bind the group into an homogeneous unit necessarily conflict with and restrict the growth of the individual consciousness and the literary identity. For the alternative mentors of cantos I, II, and XII, whose unsolicited remarks point to the folly of Heaney's pilgrimage, religion, and expressly Roman Catholicism, can be apprehended only in terms of constraint or limitation.

James Joyce's early literary career was, in itself, directed towards the "spiritual liberation" of his country, towards the evasion of the "nets" within Ireland that impeded his own progress towards lasting aesthetic achievement.[24] Almost a century earlier, William Carleton, Heaney's "old fork-tongued turncoat," undertook his own alleged spiritual liberation by re-nouncing Roman Catholicism and by writing *The Lough Derg Pilgrim*, an unalleviated denunciation of the barbarities of the penitential custom.[25] Like his fellow recalcitrants, the "old Sabbath-breaker" Simon Sweeney, who haunts Heaney's childhood dreams and who returns to haunt him as an adult, is also an artist-figure, albeit one of a more local variety. While Sweeney holds his bow-saw "stiffly up like a lyre," his name also carries for Heaney the connotation of the historio-legendary poet-king Sweeney who ran afoul of St. Ronan and lived under the "bondage" of his curse.[26] Heaney writes in the Introduction to his translation *Sweeney Astray*, "Sweeney is also a figure of the artist, displaced, guilty, assuaging himself by his utterance. It is possible to read the work as an aspect of the quarrel between free creative imagination and the constraints of religious, political and domestic obligations." Like his legendary counterpart whom Lynchseachan can trace only by the trail of broken branches he leaves in his wake, Heaney's equally elusive "mystery man" can be sensed out instinctually where "cut or broken limbs of trees went yellow." [27] For the unregenerate Simon Sweeney, as for Joyce and Carleton, there exists the need to break through these manifold constraints to "damn all you know," to "swim out on your own," to seek freedom from the community and its obligations and values through estrange-ment, exile or isolation or, as Joyce would have it, through "silence, exile, and cunning."[28]

Throughout the three sections of *Station Island*, instances of bondage, imprisonment, and incarceration as well as images of flight or migration abound. By tradition, pilgrims to Station Island's cave, St. Patrick's Purga-tory, were customarily "shut up in it for hours in order to suffer some of the torments of Purgatory." According to Alwyn and Brinley Rees, this cave, allegedly the entrance to the Underworld, was "later closed and the purgatory housed in a chapel." By more recent accounts, the chapel in itself has earned the reputation of a virtual "prison house."[29] In this regard, Heaney's circuit of the obligatory stations is not merely an act of penitential pilgrimage, a movement towards the spiritual "centre," but, more signifi-cantly, yet another of his vertical quests, a movement downwards through the underworld of sectarianism and backwards through his own past as it interacts with the collective past of his country.[30] Heaney's imaginative re-working of his actual journeys to the "prison house" on Station Island is prefigured and paralleled in the collection by Anton Chekhov's cross-conti-nental journey to the prison island of Sakhalin. Like Dante, who alone among the multitudes in Purgatory retains his shadow, Chekhov moves through Sakhalin while "shadowing his convict guide." While Heaney is often the somewhat unwitting and unwilling party to his encounters with the shades, Chekhov, as Heaney explains in a note, went to Sakhalin expressly to inter-view the political prisoners and criminals who haunted that place.[31] The ringing of bells that calls Heaney to his devotional duty is consistent with the ringing of shattered glass and the disconcertingly similar ringing of convicts' chains, the sound of which not only continues to haunt Chekhov, but reminds him of the almost insupportable "burden of his freedom."[32] Chekhov's downward as well as lateral quest to the underworld of Sakhalin is coincidental with his corresponding attempt to plumb the depths of his own identity: "he looked down from the rail / Of his thirty years and saw a mile / Into himself as if he were clear water." For Chekhov "who thought to squeeze his slave's blood out and waken the free man," the purgatorial journey ends in other than its intended outcome, yet allows him, as it does for Heaney, to probe and analyze his own responsibility and commitment. In "Sandstone Keepsake," a poem which comments implicity on the other two, Heaney observes an internment camp "from my free state of image and allusion" with the knowledge that he, too, is being observed. Standing near an estuary and near the border as well, he not only occupies a liminal place in the landscape, but becomes a correspondingly ambivalent and non-committal figure, "a silhouette not about to set times wrong or right."

While Simon Sweeney, William Carleton, and James Joyce are similarly marginal figures, they are by no means uncertain or unforthcoming in their commitments. Although Heaney originally intended William Carleton to be "a sort of Tyrone Virgil," he makes him, in conjunction with the two others, not so much an impartial guide as an intransigent commentator.[33] From the comparatively secular mainland, these three voices of dissent attack the orthodoxies represented and perpetuated by the island. Having achieved the "migrant solitude" sought in "The King of the Ditchbacks", each is in his own right a wanderer, a gypsy like Sweeney, an impetuous wayfarer like Carleton, who "heads up the road" and disappears, or like Joyce, who "moves off quickly" once his appointed task has been completed. As well, the three are encountered in places of isolation: Sweeney by the side of a field; Carleton on the crown of the high road; Joyce on a remote jetty.[34] Of the three, Joyce, with "his fish-cold bony hand" and with his voice that eddies "with the vowels of all rivers" is associated with the sea in its abundance.[35] As the "old father," the old artificer to Heaney's Stephen Dedalus, Joyce offers not only artistic fosterage but also the potential healing and renewal.[36] In reaching out "like a convalescent" for Joyce's hand, Heaney finds an "alien comfort." Since both Sweeney, who comes "streaming from the shower," and Carleton, who is angered "by a shower of rain," are also associated with water at its most life-enhancing, they represent the possibility for renewed growth and inspiration and, as such, stand in stark contrast to Heaney the pilgrim who, at one point, feels "like the bottom of a dried up lake" (VIII) as well as to Heaney the wanderer who in "On the Road" pursues a path to "a dried up source." The "hardness" which governs Carleton's artistic as well as political philosophy and the "straightness" which characterizes Joyce's correspondingly uncompromising outlook are set in opposition to the ambivalence and uncertainty of Heaney, for whom even tentative repentance, much less indignation, requires considerable effort on the part of the shades.[37]

Through the pilgrim persona of "Station Island," Heaney is able to dramatize his own very real struggle, as a poet, to achieve and assert his independent voice and artistic integrity. Like the rich young man who is told by Christ that he must give up everything he owns to be saved, Heaney finds himself at a similar crossroads in terms of his poetic career.[38] That Heaney himself refers to *Station Island* as his "book of changes" suggests that the collection is in fact a transitional one, a point of departure from what Neil Corcoran calls "the modes and manners which have created his reputation, to the genuinely new and unexpected things."[39] For Alasdair Macrae, *Station Island* embodies Heaney's determination to see "where he has come to in the middle of his life and to sift through the emotional and spiritual and artistic accretions to ascertain what should be jettisoned."[40] James Joyce's contention that "you've listened long enough, now strike your own note" seems to suggest that Heaney, at least by his own estimation, has mastered what he calls poetic "craft," "what you can learn from other verse," and now must move on towards the development of "poetic technique," a task which involves, a definition of the poet's stance towards life, a definition of his own reality and the watermarking of his own essential patterns of perception, voice and thought.[41] The task which Heaney identifies as "finding a voice" or, as may be the case in "Station Island," of finding a new one is not only facilitated but in fact dramatized by the dispersed narrative authority and polyphony of that section.[42] More than this, however, *Station Island* represents a departure in another respect. The vertical quest downwards and inwards which assumes vital importance in Heaney's previous work and which continues to operate throughout *Station Island*, most notably in its opening and closing poems, gives way in part to a countervailing movement upwards and outwards.[43] Through figures such as William Carleton, who is compared to "a diver surfacing," and James Joyce, who advises "swim out on your own," Heaney not only advances the idea of an inevitable surfacing, but also promotes the concept of a lateral, as opposed to vertical, quest. What Heaney moves towards in *Station Island* is not so much a commitment to his political responsibilities as a renewed and revitalized commitment to his poetic art.

Inasmuch as Heaney makes use of the Dantean tradition and adapts it according to his own "imaginative needs," he is equally aware of the way in which other poets of this century have re-invented Dante to reflect their own artistic affinities, procedures and inclinations. The fundamental opposition between orthodoxy and artistic freedom that operates throughout "Station Island" also informs Heaney's essay "Envies and Identifications: Dante and the Modern Poet," an examination of T. S. Eliot's debt to Dante for

"Little Gidding" and Osip Mandelstam's radically dissimilar assimilation of the same poet and tradition. Eliot, with his Anglican, monarchist, and hence, thoroughly orthodox leanings, naturally rejects the local intensity that originally attracted Heaney to the *Commedia* and offers in its place "a transcendence through language, a purity beyond dialect and tribe," that conveys little sense of the vernacular Dante originally championed.[44] Since for Eliot Dante's poem "was written on official paper," his own "stern and didactic" rendering of the tradition amounts to a virtual canonization of Dante "as the aquiline patron of international modernism."[45] Osip Mandelstam, who like Dante writes under the threat of political persecution, identifies the Tuscan master not with the inheritance of culture but with the processes of nature. Heaney explains, "Mandelstam's Dante is not distinguished by his cultural representativeness, his conservative majesty or his intellectual orthodoxy. Rather he is fastened upon as an exemplar of the purely creative, intimate and experiental act of writing itself. Dante is not perceived as a mouthpiece of orthodoxy but as the apotheosis of free, natural biological process, a process of crystallization, a focus for all impulsive, instinctive, non-utilitarian elements in the creative life . . . a guide who wears no official badge, enforces no party line . . . a woodcutter singing at his work in the dark wood of the larynx."[46] Heaney's William Carleton and James Joyce echo Mandelstam's perception of Dante in their own understanding of the role and nature of poets in general. That the artist and his function are associated with the natural cycle is suggested by William Carleton's assertion,

> "All this is like a trout kept in a spring
> or maggots sown in wounds—
> another life that cleans our element.
>
> We are earthworms of the earth and all that
> has gone through us is what will be our trace."[47]

For both Joyce and Carleton, as Dillon Johnston claims, "writing is a natural functioning, not self-expression so much as self-maintenance."[48] Joyce dismisses the Feast of the Holy Tundish and the constraints of dialect it implies, yet he also promotes, through his espousal of a "work-lust," the idea of the writer as an "exemplar of the purely creative."[49] For Heaney, "Joyce speaks to the pilgrim as he leaves the island in an encounter reminiscent of "Little Gidding" but with advice that Mandelstam might have given, yet the obvious influence is the *Commedia*."[50] In writing "Station Island," Heaney absorbs not only Dante but the full scope of his tradition, yet somehow manages to maintain a middle ground between extremes of interpretation.

*Notes*

1. Thomas Kinsella, "The Divided Mind," in *Irish Poets in English*, ed. Sean Lucy (Dublin: The Mercier Press, 1972). p. 216. See Dillon Johnston, *Irish Poetry After Joyce* (Notre Dame: Univ. of Notre Dame Press, 1985). p. 162.

2. Seamus Heaney, "Away from it All." in *Station Island* (London: Faber, 1984), p. 16.

3. Johnston, p. 162.

4. Heaney quoted by Alasdair Macrae, "Seamus Heaney's *New Voice in Station Island*," in *Irish Writers and Society at Large* (Genrards Cross, Bucks: Colin Smythe, 1985). p. 123. According to Robert F. Garratt. "Joyce advises the younger poet to liberate himself from the responsibility of public poetry." See Garratt, *Modern Irish Poetry: Tradition and Continuity from Yeats to Heaney* (Berkeley: Univ. of California Press, 1986), p. 250.

5. Denis Donoghue quoted by Dillon Johnston. p. 250.

6. Barbara Hardy speaks of Heaney's political unease. "Meeting the Myth: *Station Island*," in *The Art of Seamus Heaney*, ed. Tony Curtis (Bridgend: Poetry Wales Press, 1985). p. 153.

7. Seamus Heaney: "The Makings of a Music," in *Preoccupations: Selected Prose, 1968–1978* (London: Faber, 1986). p. 63.

8. Johnston, p. 162.

9. Heaney, *Station Island*, pp. 92–93.

10. Seamus Heaney, "Envies and Identifications: Dante and the Modern Poet," *Irish University Review*, 15. No. 1 (Spring 1985). p. 5.

11. John Haffenden, "Seamus Heaney," in *Viewpoints: Poets in Conversation* (London: Faber, 1981), p. 68.

12. Heaney, "Envies and Identifications," p. 18. The discrepancy arises from Neil Corcoran's reading of the text. *See Seamus Heaney* (London: Faber, 1986). p. 160.

13. The image of the deer, particularly of the deer drinking at a pool, recurs throughout *Station Island*. It can be found in "A Migration," "An Aisling in the Burren," canto IX of "Station Island," and "On the Road." As the object of the hunt, the deer brings about the unification of the tribe.

14. See Dillon Johnston, p. 162.

15. Barbara Hardy, p. 155. Heaney's variations on *terza rima* also underscore his debt to Dante.

16. See Dillon Johnston, p. 160.

17. Haffenden, p. 60.

18. Alasdair Macrae, p. 135.

19. Heaney, *Station Island*, 93.

20. Heaney, *Station Island*, 18.

21. Heaney, "Envies and Identifications," 19.

22. Corcoran, 165.

23. See Heaney, *Station Island*, 89, 119.

24. James Joyce quoted by Robert F. Garratt, 88.

25. Corcoran, 159.

26. Heaney, *Sweeney Astray* (London: Faber, 1983). 28.

27. Heaney, *Sweeney Astray*, 21.

28. James Joyce quoted by Robert F. Garratt, 88.

29. Alwyn and Brinley Rees, *Celtic Heritage: Ancient Tradition in Ireland and Wales* (London: Thames and Hudson, 1961). 304.

30. Heaney's poetry, from his earliest collections onwards, attempts to embrace and recover historical or mythological truths by means of digging or tunneling. This is turn may encompass anything from crop cultivation to archaeological excavation.

31.  Heaney, *Station Island*, 122.
32.  As Macrae remarks, Chekhov is "confused between images of bondage and images of freedom" (p. 128).
33.  Heaney, "Envies and Identifications," 11.
34.  Joyce's advice to the younger poet to "keep at a tangent" (p. 93) seems to reflect his more general policy of isolation and solitude.
35.  Corcoran. p. 169.
36.  In *North*'s "Viking Dublin: Trial Pieces," Heaney ascribes a similar relationship to the founders of Viking Dublin:
Old fathers, be with us.
Old cunning assessors
of feuds and sites
for ambush or town.
37.  See Corcoran, 167.
38.  The image of motif of the rich young man which runs throughout *Station Island* and which perhaps constitutes one of the collection's thematic centerpieces is seen specifically in "The King of the Ditch-backs" and "On the Road," Incorporating part of the same biblical text. "The Railway Children" attunes to the "eye of the needle" (Matthew 19:24).
39.  See Heaney, *Station Island*, 121
40.  Macrae, p. 131.
41.  Heaney, "Feeling into Words," in *Preoccupations*, p. 45.
42.  Heaney, "Feeling into Words," p. 43.
43.  A journey through the subterranean corridors of the London Underground or to the "deepest chamber of a cave is part of both "The Underground" and "On the Road."
44.  Heaney, "Envies and Identifications", 9, 12.
45.  Heaney, "Envies and Identifications" 16. Heaney claims that Eliot was recreating Dante in his own image (p. 12).
46.  Heaney, "Envies and Identifications," 14, 16.
47.  Heaney, *Station Island*, 66.
48.  Johnston, 165.
49.  Heaney, "Envies and Identifications," 16.
50.  Heaney, "Envies and Identifications," 19.

# Selected Bibliography

♦

## PRIMARY WORKS

*Death of a Naturalist*. London: Faber and Faber, 1966.

*Door into the Dark*. London: Faber and Faber, 1969.

*Wintering Out*, London: Faber and Faber, 1972.

*North*. London: Faber and Faber, 1975; New York: Oxford University Press, 1976.

*Field Work*. London, Faber and Faber, 1979; New York: Farrar, Straus & Giroux, 1979.

*Preoccupations: Selected Prose, 1968–78*. London: Faber and Faber, 1980; New York, Farrar, Straus & Giroux, 1980.

*Selected Poems, 1965–1975*. London: Faber and Faber, 1980; New York: Farrar, Straus & Giroux, 1980.

*Sweeney Astray*. London: Faber and Faber, 1984; New York: Farrar, Straus & Giroux, 1984.

*Station Island*. London: Faber and Faber, 1984; New York: Farrar, Straus & Giroux, 1984.

*The Haw Lantern*. London, Faber and Faber, 1987; New York, Farrar, Straus & Giroux, 1987.

*The Government of the Tongue*. London, Faber and Faber, 1988; New York, Farrar, Straus & Giroux, 1988.

*The Place of Writing*. Atlanta: Scholars Press, 1989.

*New Selected Poems*. London: Faber and Faber, 1990; New York: Farrar, Straus & Giroux, 1990

*The Cure at Troy*. London: Faber and Faber, 1990; New York: Farrar, Straus & Giroux, 1990.

*Seeing Things*. London: Faber and Faber, 1991; New York: Farrar, Straus & Giroux, 1991.

## SECONDARY WORKS

In addition to those works cited in the Introduction, the following books provide commentary on Heaney's writing.

Andrews, Elmer. *The Poetry of Seamus Heaney: All the Realms of Whisper*. New York: St. Martins Press, 1988.

Bloom, Harold, ed. *Seamus Heaney*. New Haven, New York, Philadelphia: Chelsea House Publishers, Modern Critical Views Series, 1986.

Brown, Terence. *Northern Voices: Poets from Ulster*. Dublin: Gill and Macmillan, 1975.

Burris, Sidney. *The Poetry of Resistance: Seamus Heaney and the Pastoral Tradition*. Athens: Ohio University Press, 1990.

Buttel, Robert. *Seamus Heaney*. Lewisburg: Bucknell University Press, 1975

Corcoran, Neil. *Seamus Heaney*. London: Faber and Faber, 1986.

Curtis, Tony, ed. *The Art of Seamus Heaney*. Brigend: Poetry Wales Press, 1982.

Deane, Seamus. *Celtic Revivals*. London: Faber and Faber, 1985, 174–186.

Foster, Thomas C. *Seamus Heaney*. Boston: Twayne Publishers, 1989.

Longley, Edna. *Poetry in the Wars*. Newcastle-upon-Tyne: Bloodaxe, 1986.

Morrison, Blake. *Seamus Heaney*. London: Methuen, 1982.

# Index

♦

Abrams, M. H., 85
Adams, Hazard, 8
Anderson, Nathalie, 8
Armstrong, Sean, 41, 184
Ashbery, John, 1, 196
Auden, W. H., 84, 91, 111, 174;
    "Schoolchildren," 111

Bakhtin, Mikhail, 101, 102
Barthes, Roland, 83–84
Baudelaire, Charles, 39, 57
Bedient, Clavin, 205
Belfast, 36, 40, 45, 180, 181, 182, 193,
    203
Bishop, Elizabeth, 6
Blackmur, R. P., 84
Blake, William, 90, 172
Bloom, Harold, 121
Boland, Evan, 112, 118; "An Irish
    Childhood in England: 1951," 112;
    "Fond Memory," 112; *The Journey,* 112
Bradley, Anthony, 7
*Buile Suibhne,* 58, 64, 97
Buttel, Robert, 7, 166

Carleton, William, 2, 52, 64–65, 165,
    210–13, 214
Carson, Ciaran, 4, 100, 106
Cather, Willa, 53
Catholicism, 30, 31, 36, 45, 52–53,
    71–73, 75, 76, 88, 98, 115, 124,
    132, 144, 147, 149, 161, 174, 180,
    182, 187, 210–11
Chekhov, Anton, 51, 61, 211–12
Clare, John, 27

Clarke, Austin, 199–200
Coleridge, Samuel Taylor, 67, 76
Corcoran, Neil, 101, 213
*The Crane Bag,* 197

Dante Alighieri, 2, 3, 5, 6, 42, 45, 49,
    52, 53, 57, 62, 79, 98, 107,
    161–71, 190, 207, 208, 209, 210,
    211, 213–14; *Divine Comedy,* 49, 52,
    53, 161, 162, 165, 210; *Inferno,* 5,
    62, 190; *Paradiso,* 162, 167, 207;
    *Purgatorio,* 162, 167, 207; terza rima,
    79, 169; *Vita Nuova,* 53
Davis, Dick, 139, 141
Deane, Seamus, 88, 89, 92, 97, 98, 100,
    115, 116, 118, 183, 197; *Celtic
    Revivals,* 89
de Petris, Carla, 8
Derrida, Jacques, 83; *Glas,* 83
Derry, 26, 34, 57, 125, 174, 197
Di Piero, W. S., 23
Donegal, 73
Donne, John, 27
Donoghue, Denis, 208
Dostoevsky, Fyodor, 101, 102
Dublin, 187, 188, 189

Eliot, T. S., 2, 6, 56, 57, 82, 139, 167,
    178, 213–14; "Liddle Gidding," 167,
    213; "Ulysses, Order and Myth,"
    139; "The Waste Land," 167
Ellmann, Richard, 84
Emory University, 84
Evans, E. Estyn, 26, 30, 197; *Irish Folk
    Ways,* 26, 197; *Irish Heritage,* 26

219